A Culinary History
of Taipei

Big City Food Biographies Series

Series Editor

Ken Albala, University of the Pacific, kalbala@pacific.edu

Food helps define the cultural identity of cities in much the same way as the distinctive architecture and famous personalities. Great cities have one-of-a-kind food cultures, offering the essence of the multitudes who have immigrated there and shaped foodways through time. The **Big City Food Biographies** series focuses on those metropolises celebrated as culinary destinations, with their iconic dishes, ethnic neighborhoods, markets, restaurants, and chefs. Guidebooks to cities abound, but these are real biographies that will satisfy readers' desire to know the full food culture of a city. Each narrative volume, devoted to a different city, explains the history, the natural resources, and the people that make that city's food culture unique. Each biography also looks at the markets, historic restaurants, signature dishes, and great cookbooks that are part of the city's gastronomic make-up.

Books in the Series

New Orleans: A Food Biography, by Elizabeth M. Williams

San Francisco: A Food Biography, by Erica J. Peters

New York City: A Food Biography, by Andrew F. Smith

Portland: A Food Biography, by Heather Arndt Anderson

Chicago: A Food Biography, by Daniel R. Block and Howard B. Rosing

Kansas City: A Food Biography, by Andrea L. Broomfield

Rio de Janeiro: A Food Biography, by Marcia Zoladz

Madrid: A Culinary History, by Maria Paz Moreno

The Food and Drink of Sydney: A History, by Heather Hunwick

A History of the Food of Paris: From Roast Mammoth to Steak Frites, by Jim Chevallier

The Food and Drink of Seattle: From Wild Salmon to Craft Beer, by Judith Dern, with Deborah Ashin

A Culinary History of Taipei: Beyond Pork and Ponlai, by Steven Crook and Katy Hui-wen Hung

A Culinary History of Taipei

Beyond Pork and Ponlai

Steven Crook and Katy Hui-wen Hung

ROWMAN & LITTLEFIELD
Lanham • Boulder • New York • London

Published by Rowman & Littlefield
An imprint of The Rowman & Littlefield Publishing Group, Inc.
4501 Forbes Boulevard, Suite 200, Lanham, Maryland 20706
www.rowman.com

Unit A, Whitacre Mews, 26-34 Stannary Street, London SE11 4AB

British Library Cataloguing in Publication Information Available

Library of Congress Cataloging-in-Publication Data
Names: Crook, Steven, author. | Hung, Katy Hui-wen, 1958– author.
Title: A culinary history of Taipei : beyond pork and ponlai / Steven Crook
   and Katy Hui-wen Hung.
Description: Lanham : Rowman & Littlefield, [2018] | Series: Big city food
   biographies series | Includes bibliographical references and index.
Identifiers: LCCN 2018016730 (print) | LCCN 2018017910 (ebook) |
   ISBN 9781538101384 (electronic) | ISBN 9781538101377 (cloth : alk. paper)
Subjects: LCSH: Food—Taiwan—Taipei. | Food industry and trade—
   Taiwan—Taipei—History. | Food habits—Taiwan—Taipei—History. |
   Grocers—Taiwan—Taipei—History. | Restaurants—Taiwan—Taipei. |
   Cooking, Chinese—Taiwan style.
Classification: LCC TX360.C63 (ebook) | LCC TX360.C63 T354 2018 (print) |
   DDC 641.300951249—dc23
LC record available at https://lccn.loc.gov/2018016730

Printed in the United States of America

Contents

Big City Food Biographies—Series Foreword   vii

Foreword by the Authors   ix

Acknowledgments   xi

Introduction   1

Chapter 1   Nature's Larder   7

Chapter 2   The Kitchen   23

Chapter 3   Iconic and Emerging Foodways   37

Chapter 4   Offerings, Festivals, and Special Foods throughout the Year   71

Chapter 5   The Farms That Feed Taipei   97

Chapter 6   Supplying the Consumer: Taipei's Markets   119

Chapter 7   Landmark Restaurants   135

Chapter 8   Tipples and Teas   149

Chapter 9   Teaching, Sharing, and Learning Taiwanese Cuisine   165

Chapter 10   Signature Dishes and Recipes   179

Notes   195

Bibliography   213

Index   235

About the Authors   241

Big City Food Biographies— Series Foreword

Cities are rather like living organisms. There are nerve centers, circulatory systems, structures that hold them together, and of course conduits through which food enters and waste leaves the city. Each city also has its own unique personality, based mostly on the people who live there but also on the physical layout, the habits of interaction, and the places where people meet to eat and drink. More than any other factor, it seems that food is used to define the identity of so many cities. Simply say any of the following words and a particular place immediately leaps to mind: bagel, cheesesteak, muffuletta, "chowda," and cioppino. Natives, of course, have many more associations—their favorite restaurants and markets, bakeries and donut shops, pizza parlors, and hot dog stands. Even the restaurants seem to have their own unique vibe wherever you go. Some cities boast great steakhouses or barbecue pits; others, their ethnic enclaves and more elusive specialties like Frito pie in Santa Fe, Cincinnati chili, and the Chicago deep dish pizza. Tourists might find snippets of information about such hidden gems in guidebooks; the inveterate flaneur naturally seeks them out personally. For the rest of us, this is practically unchartered territory.

These urban food biographies are meant to be not guidebooks but rather real biographies, explaining the urban infrastructure, the natural resources that make each city unique, and most importantly the history, people, and neighborhoods. Each volume is meant to introduce you to the city or reacquaint you with an old friend in ways you may never have considered. Each biography also looks at the historic restaurants, signature dishes, and great cookbooks that reflect each city's unique gastronomic makeup.

These food biographies also come at a crucial juncture in our culinary history as a people. Not only do chain restaurants and fast food threaten the existence of our gastronomic heritage, but also we are increasingly mobile as a people, losing our deep connections to place and the cooking that happens in cities over the generations with a rooted population. Moreover, signature dishes associated with individual cities become popularized and bastardized and are often in danger of becoming caricatures of themselves. Ersatz versions of so many classics, catering to the lowest common denominator of taste, are now available throughout the country. Our gastronomic sensibilities are in danger of becoming entirely homogenized. The intent here is not, however, to simply stop the clock or make museum pieces of regional cuisines. Cooking must and will evolve, but understanding the history of each city's food will help us make better choices, will make us more discerning customers, and perhaps will make us more respectful of the wonderful variety that exists across our great nation.

Ken Albala
University of the Pacific
Series Editor

Foreword by the Authors

What is Taiwanese cuisine? Several of East Asia's culinary traditions are firmly established in Western minds. Japanese cuisine is delicate and subtle. Sichuanese food is bold, pungent, and spicy. The Cantonese have dim sum. But how many outsiders could begin to describe Taiwan's culinary personality?

The island's distinctiveness has been muffled by a history of occupation and exploitation that ended only recently. For decades after 1949, the regime in Taipei presented itself to the world as the true government of China, and society here was depicted as a repository of everything that was splendid about pre-Communist China. In food terms, this meant celebrating foodways carried to the island in the late 1940s by refugee chefs and families, while ignoring those developed locally over hundreds or even thousands of years.

It was during the earlier period of Japanese rule that the term "Taiwanese cuisine" first appeared. The earliest book about Taiwanese cuisine, a Japanese-language volume titled *Taiwan ryōri no shiori* (Taiwan culinary bookmarks), was published in 1912. When the Japanese spoke of *Taiwan ryōri*, they had in mind the delicate banquet dishes presented to visiting dignitaries. When Crown Prince Hirohito (the future Emperor Showa) toured the island in 1923, Taipei's leading *Taiwan ryōri* establishment prepared braised soft-shelled turtle and grilled eight-treasure crab, not boiled millet, sweet potatoes, or other examples of the plain fare that sustained ordinary folks.

Then as now, Taipei was where outside influences gained footholds and melded with homegrown traditions. For at least a century, Taiwan's capital has had the country's most innovative chefs and its most adventurous gourmands. It was here, particularly during the 1970s, that wealthy businesspeople entertained each other in a manner that propelled the development of local cuisine.

Taiwanese cooking is often said to feature lots of soups and a great deal of seafood. Dishes are usually steamed, stewed, or stir-fried. Thanks to the climate, fresh ingredients are easy to obtain. Beyond that, generalizations do little to enlighten.

We have no interest in forcing something as lively and mutable as Taiwanese cuisine into a straitjacket, believing that it should be delicately explained, not forcefully defined. For sure, it is a fertile conversation—certainly not an argument or contest—between Chinese, Japanese, Austronesian, and other culinary traditions. And because Taiwan's food history cannot be divorced from its political history, it is only natural that the cuisine's conventions and boundaries should be as fluid and blurry as the island's status.

Acknowledgments

In addition to expressing our gratitude to all of the people who gave their time to answer our questions, both authors would like to especially thank Marlena Spieler. Believing that Taiwan's amazing food resources and fascinating history deserve to be more widely known, Marlena planted the seed by introducing us to Ken Albala. We are indebted to Ken, together with the entire team at Rowman & Littlefield, for handling this project with patience, skill, and wisdom. H. M. Cheng not only shared several fascinating anecdotes but also provided countless valuable suggestions while reviewing the manuscript. Stanford Chiou has been a source of constant encouragement. Robyn Eckhardt generously shared her expertise and contacts, while Tom Rook lent his artistic skills.

Steven Crook also wishes to thank his wife, Irene Wang Yi-ju, for sharing recollections of her childhood in a farming village in Taiwan's south, and for cooking everything from healthy steamed tilapia to indulgent braised pork. He dedicates his half of this book to her.

Katy Hui-wen Hung would also like to thank her father for making introductions that contributed significantly to this book, Rachel Laudan for timely support, and Tobie Openshaw, who made an introduction that inspired an early collaborative article on mushroom farming and gave valuable support throughout the project. Katy dedicates her half of this book to her mother, who passed away as the book was being planned: "She gave me the strength and drive to challenge myself to learn more about Taiwan, the land and its people—to explore, study, and share. She has been a constant inspiration, and this book is my ultimate tribute to her."

Introduction

Most people have heard of Taiwan, in part because "Made in Taiwan" was once nearly as common as "Made in China" seems to be now. But beyond its troubled relationship with the People's Republic of China—which has never controlled the island but continues to claim Taiwan's territory as its own—and the fact that Taipei is its capital city, the average North American or European knows little about this corner of East Asia.

The country that calls itself the Republic of China (ROC) covers 13,976 square miles, a little less than Maryland and Delaware combined. The ROC's population is slightly more than twenty-three million, of whom a third live in or around Taipei. The capital is near the island's northern tip, at the same latitude as the Everglades; yet winter temperatures in the capital can sink below 45°F. In summer, the island's urban centers suffer 95°F temperatures and uncomfortable humidity. Most of the rain falls between June and September. From October to April, the south of Taiwan is noticeably drier and generally warmer than Taipei. The capital gets more than ninety-five inches of precipitation in an average year;[1] a few places in the hills nearby get double that amount. Greater Taipei's principal rivers are the Tamsui, Keelung, Dahan, and Xindian, but even these broad waterways sometimes burst their banks in the wake of typhoons.

Taiwan is so ruggedly mountainous that steep hills are visible from every Taipei neighborhood. A third of the island is three thousand feet or more above sea level, while a tenth is at an elevation of eight thousand feet or higher.[2] Seven mountains are taller than Japan's Mount Fuji, which is more than twelve thousand feet—a fact that vexed the Japanese after the island was ceded to Tokyo by China's Qing Dynasty following the First Sino-Japanese War (1894–1895).

1

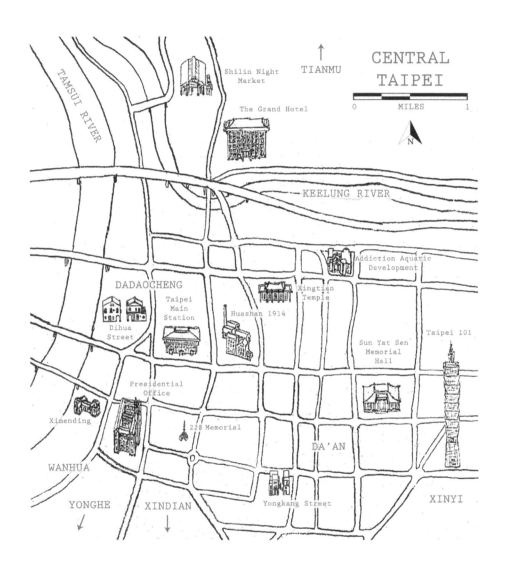

TAMSUI RIVER

Shilin Night Market

TIANMU

CENTRAL TAIPEI

0   MILES   1

N

The Grand Hotel

KEELUNG RIVER

Addiction Aquatic Development

DADAOCHENG

Taipei Main Station

Xingtian Temple

Huashan 1914

Dihua Street

Taipei 101

Sun Yat Sen Memorial Hall

Presidential Office

Ximending

228 Memorial

DA'AN

WANHUA

YONGHE

XINDIAN

Yongkang Street

XINYI

Central Taipei
Tom Rook

Taiwan (Republic of China)
Tom Rook

The 1895 takeover was neither the first nor the last time that Taiwan changed hands. Humans were living on the island at least twenty thousand years before the present, but it was not until five or six millennia ago that the ancestors of today's aboriginal Taiwanese—the sixteen Austronesian tribes that account for 2.4 percent of the current population—arrived from what is now southern China. According to studies of genetics, pottery, and languages, Austronesians from Taiwan began to populate the islands of Polynesia and Micronesia at least three thousand years ago.[3] As a consequence, approximately one-fifth of the modern world's languages (among them Hawaiian, Malagasy, and Māori) can be traced back to pre-Chinese Taiwan.[4]

For centuries, there was hardly any contact between Chinese people on the mainland—at its closest, a mere eighty-one miles from Taiwan—and the island's Austronesian peoples. This isolation began to end in 1624, when, having refused the Dutch East India Company (VOC) permission to establish a commercial base on the Chinese coast or on any islands near to it, the court of China's Ming Dynasty allowed the VOC to set up a trading colony on Taiwan's southwest coast,[5] at what is now Tainan, 165 miles down-island from Taipei. The Dutch called that location Tayouan, likely a corruption of an Austronesian toponym. This word evolved into "Taiwan" and came to be applied to the entire island, although until the second half of the twentieth century most Western sources referred to it as Formosa. This latter name is said to have been conferred by Portuguese sailors en route to Japan in 1542, who (the story goes) shouted "*Ilha formosa*," meaning "beautiful island," when they first glimpsed Taiwan's forest-covered slopes.

In 1642, the VOC seized the small Spanish bases in what are now Tamsui and Keelung,[6] extending its influence to the north. Over the next few decades, most of Taiwan remained thoroughly Austronesian, although Han Chinese were beginning to establish themselves in a few places on the west coast. The Ming Empire had no settlement strategy for Taiwan. Some early migrants came with the encouragement of the VOC. Others were fugitives, pirates, or those fleeing poverty.

The Manchu conquest of China saw the Ming court forced out of Beijing in 1644 and changed the course of Taiwan's history. By the 1650s, the new Qing Dynasty had forced a dwindling band of Ming loyalists deep into southern China. Under the leadership of Zheng Chenggong (known to seventeenth-century Europeans as "Koxinga"), the Ming counterattacked, were beaten back to the coastal province of Fujian, and plotted a retreat to Taiwan. Zheng's forces landed there on April 2, 1661, and laid siege to the VOC fortress in what is now Anping, Tainan. Nine months later, after a great many deaths on both sides, the Dutch surrendered.[7]

Koxinga established the Kingdom of Dongning in Tainan and introduced elements of classical Chinese culture to Taiwan. But this pro-Ming state collapsed in 1683, and Taiwan became part of the Qing Empire. Tainan remained the most important city until the late nineteenth century; it is still regarded as a bastion of traditional Han culture and a place famous for street snacks.

Settling the island was never a priority for the emperor in Beijing; yet population pressure in China ensured that there was no shortage of Chinese men willing to take their chances in Taiwan, even during the periods when migration across the Taiwan Strait was prohibited. Because Chinese females were scarce, many early migrants married aboriginal women, a phenomenon that hastened the gradual marginalization of indigenous people.[8] Only in remote parts of the Central Mountain Range and the east have Austronesian languages and cultures survived. Many Taiwanese who do not regard themselves as aboriginal have some Austronesian ancestry, and certain indigenous foodways have been incorporated into the cuisines of Holo-speaking Taiwanese (those whose ancestors came from Fujian, and who now account for around three-quarters of the population) as well as the Hakka minority (members of a Han Chinese subgroup who speak their own languages and mostly trace their bloodlines to Guangdong).

In 1709, the imperial authorities approved a scheme to develop the Taipei Basin. Han migrants poured in, and within a century the culture of the local Austronesian Ketagalan tribe was fast disappearing owing to intermarriage, assimilation, and migration. All that remains of this ethnic group are toponyms of Ketagalan origin, such as Beitou.

The place name Taipei (literally "Taiwan north") did not appear on maps until 1875. By then, Wanhua—now part of the capital's southwest—was a dynamic Han settlement with well over a century of history. "Wanhua" is the Mandarin pronunciation of the place name "Manka," which itself is thought to be derived from an indigenous word for the type of canoe that Ketagalan people would use to paddle to Wanhua so they could barter forest resources for needles and cooking pots. Dadaocheng (also called Twatutia) was founded in 1853 by merchants who had been forced to leave Wanhua. When Taiwan's tea industry took off in the late nineteenth century—thanks largely to US demand for oolong—Dadaocheng quickly overtook Wanhua.[9]

The Qing's surrender of Taiwan to Tokyo had a dramatic impact on the lives and eating habits of the island's people. The Japanese brought with them not only their traditional foods but also a determination to abolish practices they regarded as backward while reshaping the island's agrarian economy for the benefit of the Japanese Empire. Taihoku (Taipei's Japanese name) soon went from a town of just forty-seven thousand in 1896[10] to the island's largest city. The capital's straight roads and imposing public buildings are legacies of the Japanese era.

By 1946—a year after Japan's defeat led to Taiwan coming under the control of Chiang Kai-shek's Chinese Nationalists (Kuomintang, or KMT)—the capital was home to 271,000 people,[11] and fewer than two thousand privately owned cars.

But it was about to get much more crowded. By late 1949, Chiang's forces were clearly losing the Chinese Civil War against Mao Zedong's Communists, and KMT soldiers, government officials, and civilians from every province were fleeing the mainland. One estimate of the influx is 2.2 million,[12] at a time when the local-born population of Taiwan was less than seven million.

Retreating mainlanders changed the character of every Taiwanese city, none more so than Taipei. Catering to exiles who had money, many of those who had none set up food stalls. Some of these entrepreneurs benefited from the US aid that flowed into Taiwan between 1950 and 1965 in the form of subsidized wheat, soy, and other commodities. At the same time, American assistance facilitated an ambitious program of land reform. For a generation, this aid helped boost agricultural output and farmers' incomes, but it is one reason why so many farms are now too small to be economically viable.[13]

Successful stalls upgraded themselves into proper restaurants. As Carolyn Phillips points out, among the refugees of 1949 were some of China's finest chefs, and when Taiwan's economy boomed in the 1970s, these culinary masters were able to open their own establishments. By the 1980s, Taipei had become a fabulous place to enjoy a wide range of Chinese cuisines.[14] But, in other respects, it was a difficult city to love. Chiang Kai-shek had regarded Taipei as a temporary headquarters from which he would eventually retake the Chinese mainland, and his regime saw little reason to invest in infrastructure or tackle environmental problems.

In the 1970s, the ROC lost its seat in the United Nations; then Washington severed formal diplomatic ties with Taipei in favor of Beijing. Responding to difficult internal and external conditions, Chiang's son made the historic decision in 1987 to lift martial law and allow opposition political parties. He died the following year and was succeeded by his Taiwan-born vice president, Lee Teng-hui. Democracy is now deeply embedded in Taiwanese society; the presidency smoothly changed hands in 2000, 2008, and 2016. Politicians compete to make their cities and counties not only prosperous but also more livable.

Unlike the authorities in some other Asian cities, Taipei's leaders—like the city's 2.68 million residents—seem to cherish the capital's street foods and hole-in-the-wall eateries. This is a key reason, no doubt, why Taipei has begun to appear on lists of the world's best food cities[15] and has even been called "the hottest food destination on Earth."[16]

1

❖ ❖

Nature's Larder

When *Homo sapiens* arrived and prepared their first meals, Taiwan was not an island. Glaciation during the Late Pleistocene lowered sea levels, allowing rhinos, elephants, and crocodiles—all long extinct—as well as people to cross what is now the Taiwan Strait.[1] Fragments of wooden rubbing sticks used for making fire have been retrieved from the Baxian Caves, a five-hour drive from Taipei on Taiwan's east coast, and carbon-dated to 20,000–25,000 years BP.[2] But what archaeologists call the Changpin Culture (after the present-day town nearest the caves) neither farmed nor made pottery.[3] Instead, they foraged along the shoreline, no doubt for shellfish and seaweed, and fished with harpoons fashioned from antlers and fish-bone hooks.[4]

Nothing found so far indicates that these Paleolithic people were the ancestors of Taiwan's Neolithic inhabitants. Around 11,700 years BP, the Late Pleistocene gave way to the warmer Holocene; some millennia later, Neolithic seafarers (who are presumed to be the forefathers of the modern indigenous minority) began to settle on marine and river terraces, where they deposited clues as to their foodways.[5]

From sites associated with the Tapenkeng culture—named for a hillside just outside Taipei—archaeologists have recovered sophisticated jars, pots, grinding stones, fishing-net sinkers, and farming implements such as stone adzes and axes.[6] The ability to cultivate millet reached Taiwan from south China between 4,500 and 5,000 years ago.[7] Thousands of grains of domesticated broomcorn and foxtail millet dating from that period were unearthed during a recent dig in Tainan, as were rice grains. No evidence of a particular cooking method was found;[8] these cereals were likely boiled into a gruel or porridge. The absence of field ridges or clayed soil at the site suggests the rice was grown dryland style, rather than in paddies. The same method was used by seventeenth-century Han pioneers who had to sustain themselves until their terracing and ditch-digging work was done, and wetland cultivation could begin.[9]

The discovery of wild yellow foxtail millet among the other grains is proof cereals were simultaneously foraged and cultivated.[10] Another wild grain probably consumed in prehistoric Taiwan is *Oryza perennis formosana*, an ancient rice akin to the brownbeard rice US authorities regard as an invasive species. *Oryza perennis formosana* was common in irrigation ponds and ditches in northwest Taiwan as recently as the 1930s but was confined to only three locations by 1957. Y. T. Kiang, J. Antonovics, and L. Wu, writing in the *Journal of Asian Ecology* in 1979, recall revisiting those sites in 1976 and finding just one small population. Fortunately, samples were taken, because by the following year the rice had disappeared from the wild. The scientists attributed the species' near extinction to hybridization with cultivated strains, human management of water, and widespread use of chemical fertilizers; yet they urged its preservation, saying its genetic variability could be valuable for crop improvement.

An indigenous couple in south Taiwan sort djulis.
Rich J. Matheson

Native red quinoa (*Chenopodium formosanum*) was surely part of the paleo diet, although some researchers think indigenous people preferred millet and taro. In 1918, when a combination of drought and unusual cold led to severe food shortages, aborigines in the south fared better than other groups because red quinoa— also known as *djulis*—can flourish even in arid conditions.[11]

Agriculture did not become the predominant subsistence strategy for Taiwan's population until the Han influx. Scientists who have studied bone collagen taken from animal and human remains left by the Neolithic Yuanshan culture, which flourished close to where Taipei's Grand Hotel now stands, think grain cultivation and raising pigs (from as early as 4,200 years BP) took a backseat to gathering food from the wild.[12] Kitchen middens at Yuanshan confirm the importance of fishing; collecting marine and river mollusks; and hunting deer and boar.[13] The Formosan wild boar (*Sus scrofa taivanus*; in Mandarin, *shān zhū*, "mountain pig") has a notably large head and a tapering snout with white stripes down both sides. These days, it is both raised by farmers and hunted, and its meat is very often served to tourists in aboriginal villages—sometimes in the form of sausages, but more often barbecued on slabs of slate, heavily salted, cut into thin strips, then dipped in rice vinegar and eaten with slivers of garlic.

By analyzing skeletal remains recovered from an Iron Age site near the coast in central Taiwan, researchers have reconstructed dietary patterns of 2,000–400 years BP. The major type of food was protein from terrestrial animals, a finding that accords with the presence of many bones from deer, pigs, muntjac, feral goats, Eurasian badgers, and rats at this and related sites. The contribution of marine shellfish was deemed significant, while marine fish, freshwater fish, and plants appear to have been less important. Twelve species of shellfish were identified in the site's middens; turtles and birds were also eaten. No meaningful dietary differences between males and females, or between adults and juveniles, were apparent.[14]

By the seventeenth century, Taiwan's indigenous peoples displayed fabulous cultural diversity. In some tribes, the women tattooed their faces; in others, they tattooed their hands. The Siraya around Tainan and the Amis in the east were matrilineal; yet most groups were patrilineal. The Bunun observed a taboo against eating millet and sweet potatoes at the same time.[15] To appease the supernatural, it was customary among the Atayal (a tribe living close to what is now Taipei) to sprinkle a few morsels on the ground whenever eating outdoors.[16] At a time when the island's total population was barely one hundred thousand,[17] more than twenty Austronesian languages were spoken. But none of them had a written form, so the only accounts that supplement oral history and archaeological evidence were written by visitors such as Chen Di.[18] On the cusp of the Dutch incursion, horticulture was well established, yet primitive, according to John Robert Shepherd:

The Formosan groups shared largely similar productive technologies: swidden cultivation of millet, rice, taro, yams, and sugarcane, using hoes and digging sticks; rearing of domesticated pigs, dogs and chickens; hunting of deer and wild boar with bow and arrow, snares, and iron-tipped spears; and fishing along rivers and coasts using basket traps, nets, and derris poison.[19]

At Nankuanli, the archaeological site where broomcorn millet (*Panicum miliaceum*) and foxtail millet (*Setaria italica*) were found, the weight of fish bones recovered was about double that of dog remains; yet the latter outweighed the faunal remains of deer, boar, muntjac, hares, and crabs combined.[20] Cutting marks on many of the canine bones suggest dogs were raised for food as well as for hunting and guard duty.[21]

Europeans working for the Dutch East India Company (VOC) recorded that the Siraya were also growing bananas, coconuts, lemons, persimmons, and a citrus fruit known as Buddha's hand.[22] The Dutch and the Chinese, coming from crowded countries, were astonished that so much fertile land was left untilled. Shepherd notes that the first ordained minister to join the VOC settlement in what is now called Tainan attributed the aborigines' lack of interest in farming to both its laboriousness (the natives had neither plows nor draft animals before the VOC arrived) and the plenitude of alternative food sources.[23]

Siraya men stood as much as "a head and a neck" above the Dutch,[24] according to European visitors to seventeenth-century Taiwan. The outsiders were also deeply impressed by the herds of wild sika deer (*Cervus nippon taiouanus*) that roamed the southwest. The natives drank deer blood,[25] and Chen Di noticed that the Siraya ate every part of each deer they caught, including (to his revulsion) the intestines and contents thereof. He evenhandedly noted that the natives found the Chinese habit of eating chickens and pheasants quite disgusting.[26]

Deer provided not just abundant protein[27] but also hides that the aborigines bartered to Han traders for cloth, iron, rice, and salt.[28] As in other parts of the world, salt was used to keep food from going bad. Indigenous people were seen salting raw fish, as well as fish complete with their scales and viscera. Those living along the coast had their own crude way of making salt from seawater, but inland communities were dependent on merchants. For flavoring but not preservation purposes, some made do with a creamy substance derived from the fruit of Roxburgh sumac (a small deciduous tree endemic to Taiwan that grows at low altitudes).[29] Chinese doing business in Taiwan prior to the arrival of the Dutch preferred to ship salt in from the mainland, rather than produce it locally using the efficient sun-drying methods popular in Fujian, because they did not want the natives to learn the process and break their cartel.[30] Nonetheless, seawater evaporation ponds like those on the other side of the Taiwan Strait were producing salt in and around Tainan by the 1660s.[31]

Two decades later, having defeated the Ming loyalists who had evicted the Dutch from Taiwan, Admiral Shi Lang of the Qing Empire urged the emperor in distant Beijing not to abandon the island. Officials who had never visited Taiwan dismissed it as an insignificant and uncivilized place that would drain the imperial coffers. But in the report he submitted to the court, Shi Lang painted a rosy picture, and he ended up winning the argument: "I have personally traveled through Taiwan and seen firsthand the fertility of its wildlands and the abundance of its natural resources. Both mulberry and field crops can be cultivated; fish and salt spout forth from the sea; the mountains are filled with dense forests of tall trees and thick bamboo; there are sulfur, rattan, sugarcane, deerskins, and all that is needed for daily living. Nothing is lacking. . . . This is truly a bountifully fertile piece of land and a strategic territory."[32]

HUNTING CULTURE

Hunting was governed by taboos and omens. Among the Puyuma people of southeast Taiwan, the community diviner consulted splinters of bamboo in order to designate an elder; the latter would rise at dawn on the day of the hunt and listen for the song of particular birds. Depending on where it came from, the hunters would set out as planned or postpone their expedition. Farming and foraging was woman's work, but hunting was an exclusively male activity. Because the Puyuma believed that even accidental contact with a woman's clothes the day before could bring about disaster, participants secluded themselves ahead of each hunt.[33]

Rukai tribesmen frequently hunted by themselves and were expected to stay within specific woodlands where the right to trap and shoot had been passed down by their ancestors. Such privileges are still recognized within the community. According to Kurtis Pei, one of Taiwan's foremost wildlife experts, the sizable non-hunting tracts between each man's hunting grounds, together with a custom of no hunting at all during late spring and summer (when hoofed animals breed), give the Rukai system a degree of sustainability.[34] This was true, he concluded, even after the tribe's post-1945 embrace of Christianity had freed hunters from the traditional restraint of bird divination. It also came at a time when most of the boars, muntjac, and serow (goat-antelopes, Taiwan's only native bovid) that were being taken from the district in Pingtung where he did his research were destined for nonindigenous consumers on the lowlands.[35]

Simple weapons and superstitions were not the only brakes on hunting. Storing meat was difficult, another reason why the Rukai preferred to hunt in the cooler months. Many aborigines alive today grew up in villages without electricity and can recall family members preserving strips of meat in salt or alcohol, or by smoking or sun-drying them. Visitors touring the highland indigenous village of Smangus are shown the chilly *Gong-sknux* ("flavor stream" in the Atayal language) that formerly served as the community's meat locker. The Paiwan delicacy *cinavu* (fermented millet and pork—some call it Paiwan sushi; among the neighboring Rukai tribe, it is *abai*) is wrapped in the sour, edible leaves of *Trichodesma calycosum*, and not simply to make it easier to handle. Like plastic wrap, the leaves help keep the food fresh a bit longer,[36] and they are said to prevent those eating it from suffering a bloated stomach. One of the ingredients in Paiwan *cinavu* is powdered taro, which the Paiwan also use to stuff mountain-boar intestines.[37]

Another preservation technique results in what the Atayal call *damamian*. Cured raw pork is placed on steamed rice in a container so fermentation can take place; within a month, it is ready to eat.[38] The Amis used similar techniques to preserve fish, eggs, and offal as well as meat.[39] The Bunun have an uncooked delicacy of their own: raw flying-squirrel intestines pickled in rice wine. Even now, Bunun hunters do not like to waste game that has spent too much time in the trap and begun to rot. They have no special name for this food—which they barbecue, then fry with some garlic and ginger—referring to it simply as *chòu ròu* ("stinky meat" in Mandarin). The squeamish, and the romantic, will prefer the Bunun's "love soup." Couples who share a serving of this blend of Chinese yam (representing men) and papaya (representing women) will, it is said, enjoy a more harmonious relationship.[40]

Hunting may have required elaborate preparations, but eating was seldom a formal affair. In 1715, Father de Mailla—a Jesuit who otherwise held indigenous people in higher regard than Han Chinese, because the latter bought and sold women—found the Puyuma "very dirty eaters, they have neither dishes, nor plates, nor bowls, nor forks, nor chopsticks. The food prepared for their meals is simply placed on a wooden board or a mat, and they use their fingers to eat, rather like monkeys." Field rat with a millet-wine sauce was an especial delicacy, he noticed: "They eat the flesh half-raw, and if it is even very slightly cooked, they find it excellent."[41] Earlier Han visitors had already observed that native Taiwanese scarcely cooked their fish and meat.[42]

Rodents are still consumed in some places. Indigenous people catch and cook mountain rats. In one corner of Chiayi County, a handful of non-aboriginal restaurants specialize in rats trapped in the area's sugar plantations. According to an Associated Press report that appeared in the *Los Angeles Times* on February 10, 2002, the flesh has "a rubbery, chewy texture and tastes like dark turkey meat with a bit of a gamey flavor."

After China was forced to open its doors to the West in the wake of the Opium Wars (1839–1842 and 1856–1860), hundreds of European and North American traders, travelers, and missionaries made their way to Taiwan. Most of their reports focus on the tattoos and head-hunting customs of the "savages," or the island's fauna, but a few are informative on the subject of what people ate.

William A. Pickering, later a senior British official in Singapore (where a street is named for him), worked for the Imperial Chinese Maritime Customs in what is now Tainan. Visiting aboriginal settlements in central Taiwan in 1866 and 1867, he found one hamlet "not in a very flourishing state as to food, so we had to be content with boiled millet and sweet potatoes, with a little dried venison. . . . At one house a honeycomb was produced in which the larvae predominated. As the others seemed to think this rather an advantage, I felt myself compelled to follow their example, and take the comb as it came to my share and munch it down, with a paste made of taro."[43]

Boiled millet and sweet potatoes does not sound very tantalizing, but as recently as the 1950s, it was reported that indigenous children for whom these were staples were less likely to suffer from thiamine deficiency, compared to Han youngsters on the lowlands who mainly ate rice.[44]

Men set out on long bear hunts with "nothing but a few balls of glutinous rice in their hunting wallets," Pickering wrote. He was not impressed by the obsession with stalking wild animals, noting, "In all the tribes that I have visited, the men never seem to think of doing anything but hunting, fishing, fighting, and constructing and ornamenting their arms."[45] At that time, the most advanced hunting weapons were muzzle-loading rifles. Since the Japanese colonial period, Taiwan has had very strict gun laws. The weapons used nowadays are not nearly as powerful as those available to US sport hunters.

Pickering found the etiquette in another village bemusing:

I was made to sit down beside the lady or daughter of the house, who with a large wooden spoon fed me with beans, millet, or broth, after just tasting each spoonful herself. With her own finger she picked out for me the choicest morsels of venison, pork, bear's fat or sausages. After the meal a long bamboo full of water was handed to me, from which to drink.[46]

In one indigenous community in the northeast in 1869, Edward C. Taintor found adults wearing Han-style clothing, and almost everyone able to converse in Holo (the language spoken by most of the settlers from China) in addition to their native tongue. Yet the way they ate was quite different from the Han. A family would sit on the floor inside their abode, "and making up little balls of rice with their fingers, convey them in the same manner to the mouth. Chopsticks seemed unknown."[47]

While touring Taiwan's southwest in 1871, and taking some of the very first photos of the region, Scotsman John Thomson[48] noted that "a plump rat is esteemed a choice delicacy" by the Siraya, who by that time were being fast absorbed by Han society. "These rats are cleverly caught in a simple and ingenious bamboo-trap, which was to me the most attractive article the houses of this simple people had to show." Bamboo was both an indispensable material and a foodstuff:

> The agricultural implements are many of them made of hard bamboo stems; and, indeed, the fishing net, the baskets of diverse shapes . . . the wine cups, the water ladles, the chopsticks, and finally the tobacco pipes, are all of bamboo. . . . So, too, are the water cans, the drinking jugs, and the rice measures. Hanging from the roof are a number of prickly bamboo stems supporting dried pork, and such like provisions. . . . The man who dwells there is feasting on the tender shoots of the plant.[49]

George Taylor—keeper of a lighthouse located on Taiwan's southern tip, fortified because it had been attacked more than once by irate aborigines—confirmed that as late as the final quarter of the nineteenth century, some indigenous groups still saw agriculture as a last resort, just as they had during the VOC occupation. "The Paiwan confined themselves strictly to hunting, leading a most idle life, tobacco and betel-nut being the only things cultivated. Wild pig and deer are so abundant that a big hunt once a month kept their larders sufficiently supplied," he wrote in 1888. Elsewhere, however, he was impressed by aboriginal cultivation of "millet, buckwheat, barley, hemp, and sugar cane, beautifying the landscape. . . . Close to the village many orange and peach trees stood, while each little house was surrounded by a small orchard containing tobacco, betel palms, orange trees, peach trees, and several other fruits I had never seen before."[50]

George L. Mackay, a Canadian Presbyterian missionary whose time in the north overlapped with Taylor's in the south, wrote an engrossing account of what he did and saw on the island. In *From Far Formosa*, he records some aborigines having a taste for ultra-fresh, raw meat[51] and that they often caught ocean and freshwater turtles.[52] Cooked with rice wine and mushrooms, turtle meat was a summertime delicacy until the 1940s.[53]

In a chapter on the island's foliage, he noted that pumpkins and squash grew well, as did cabbages and cucumbers. The last of these were usually pickled, he noticed; these days, cucumbers are often served raw as a salad with a little garlic, rice vinegar, soy sauce, sesame oil, and salt. Other common crops in the late nineteenth century were celery (never blanched, to Mackay's surprise), spinach, turnips, various beans, lettuce (always boiled), watercress, tomatoes, fennel, ginger, onions, leeks, and mint. He seemed especially impressed with a sedge known locally as *ka-pek-sun*: "The shoots, in the autumn, are used daily at meals. The roots, when sliced, is of a whitish color, with black spots. It is truly a well-flavored, palatable vegetable." Mackay also noted the importance of mustard greens ("this, when salted, is the staple vegetable among the peasants"[54]) and likely heard the Holo-language proverb *cha-bó-gín-á, kú chhài miā; cha-bó-gín-á, iû chhài chí miā* ("A girl's destiny is as insignificant as chives or mustard green seeds").

Touring rice-growing districts, he observed that following the second harvest in September or October, some farmers planted sweet potatoes, others mustard or oilseed rape. Part of the sweet-potato crop was cut up and dried under the sun for use throughout the year.

"During seedtime and harvest [the farmer's] wife rises at three o'clock in the morning, cooks rice and salted vegetables, prepares hot water for the men to wash with, and about four calls them up for breakfast. The men are in the field about five o'clock and work till ten, when a lunch of boiled rice and some salted vegetables is carried out to them." The first two meals of each day were often identical, but "At seven o'clock they return, wash . . . and sit down to a better meal, generally consisting of a tiny cup of hot liquor, pork, and fresh vegetables boiled with rice."[55]

SERPENTS, SQUIRRELS, AND SNAILS

Taiwanese a generation or two removed from the land associate hunting with the island's indigenous minority, and the prospect of feasting on bush meat is one reason Han tourists visit aboriginal communities.[56] Yet, well into the twentieth century, country folk of Han origin supplemented what they could grow or buy with game. Traps were set for the squirrels that are still common in forests and bamboo groves, and snares for the rabbits that nowadays are not frequently seen. Some households kept dogs for hunting.

Older farmers can remember a time when any beauty rat snake (*Orthriophis taeniurus friesi*) or Chinese cobra (*Naja atra*) they caught would be eaten with relish, often as a soup. Taiwan is home to more than fifty serpentine species; according to *Snakes of Taiwan* (www.snakesoftaiwan.com), six of them are dangerously venomous. But most have so many bones and so little meat that only the hungriest household would make them part of its dinner.

Restaurants that specialize in snake meat have never been numerous, but a small part of the populace continues to see legless reptiles as tonic food.[57] Gall (traditionally mixed with liquor and consumed raw because it is said to be good for one's eyes), snake blood, and snake penis can be ordered at specialist eateries on Taipei's Huaxi Street.[58] Not all of the meat in such places comes from farmed serpents; herpetologists report meeting amateur snake-catchers in Yangmingshan, the national park adjacent to the capital.[59]

The indigenous diet also included bats, crabs, grasshoppers, and snails.[60] Native freshwater gastropods can weigh more than an ounce each, but both of the principal species have become scarce in recent years due to the changing environment.[61] These days, the snails usually eaten are *Achatina fulica Bowdich* (Giant African snails), a species introduced to Taiwan from Singapore by the Japanese in 1932[62] and now common throughout the countryside. Even now, a good number of country folk are enthusiastic about this free protein. Farmers have an additional motive for eating them: giant African snails often damage vegetable crops and papaya and banana trees.[63]

Some aboriginal groups[64] and Hakka settlers used to boil snails in their shells straight after collecting. In Hakka villages in Taiwan's northwest, de-shelled native snails were once a common summertime food. Fried with garlic, ginger, chili, and a little soy sauce, they were garnished with locally gathered perilla leaves or basil. Basil is not native to Taiwan; it spread to the island in the seventeenth century, possibly brought by Hakka migrating from Fujian.

Down south, the preparation process skips the fasting, feeding with special foods, and purging periods favored by escargot eaters in the West. The snails are killed on the day of capture by smashing their shells, which are then removed and discarded. The flesh is washed in scalding water, and eggs and viscera are removed; country folk who have access to guava-tree leaves use them to scrape off the mucus. Oftentimes, the meat is cooked three-cup style (a cup each of soy sauce, rice wine, and sesame oil), but some prefer to sauté the snails with a little chili, ginger, oyster sauce, chicken stock, soy sauce, and rice wine. Because many wild snails are infected with *Angiostrongylus cantonensis* (a roundworm that can cause meningitis), high-temperature cooking is essential.

Because some consider the dark brown flesh of Giant African snails unappetizing, one contingent of snail farmers now concentrates on what they market as the Taiwan White Jade Snail, a pale-fleshed version created by selectively breeding albinistic and xanthic specimens.

Taiwanese have never regarded snails as a high-class delicacy, and more than a few would rather go hungry than consume gastropods. Frogs inspire far less revulsion, and they helped sustain at least one early Western expatriate. Recalling the 1865 visit of a delegation led by an American mercenary, Pickering wrote that the lunch they provided was "a welcome change from our customary fare of tough buffalo, skinny fowls, or curried frogs."[65]

One particular amphibian species is known to Holo speakers as *chúi ke* ("water chicken"), to Mandarin speakers as *tián jī* ("field chicken"), and to researchers as *Hoplobatrachus rugulosus* (East Asian bullfrog or Chinese/Taiwanese edible frog). These common names were not coined to save face; in Taiwan, there is nothing shameful about eating frog. Some say this species is so called because, when young, it sounds like a chicken, and the meat looks and tastes a bit like chicken. An alternative explanation has it that, during the Song Dynasty (960–1279), there was a ban on the consumption of frogs because they ate insects that would otherwise destroy crops or spread disease; to keep the authorities off their backs, frog-meat aficionados were forced to devise a euphemism. But as far as some are concerned, the term *chúi ke* is highly unsatisfactory: "It can also mean female private parts, so one of my aunts refuses to even utter these words. Instead she calls them *sì kha á* [four-leggers]," says H. M. Cheng.[66]

These days, most of the amphibians consumed in Taiwan are farmed bullfrogs, cooked three-cup style. In addition to eating frogs, the Amis people collect tadpoles for cooking in soups; a children's song celebrates the latter tradition.[67]

FORAGED FOODS

In the seventeenth and eighteenth centuries, it was said: *Chàp lâng lâi tâi saⁿ tī làk bông chit hôe thâu* ("Of every ten who reached Taiwan, just three remain; six are dead, and one has returned home"). This may have been an exaggeration. It is even possible the imperial bureaucracy encouraged horror stories of this kind, to put people off the idea of migrating to Taiwan, a troublesome frontier region as far as they were concerned. Whatever the death rate, life on the island was far from comfortable.

What imperial gazetteers called miasmic vapors was in fact malaria. Together with cholera, which arrived from time to time on ships from elsewhere, the mosquito-borne killer not only felled large numbers of Taiwanese but also cut swaths through the Chinese, French, and Japanese regiments sent to invade or subdue the island.[68] Chronic lawlessness was another problem. Settlers clashed with indigenous people; Hakka fought Hoklo (those who speak the Holo language); Hoklo from one part of Fujian battled Hoklo whose ancestors had come from a different part of the same province. In the 211 years preceding the Japanese takeover, there were 159 uprisings.[69] Because the migration of families across the Taiwan Strait was forbidden for most of the early Qing period, the Han population was dominated by men. Some were traders who came to Taiwan having obtained an expensive permit; others were single men inclined to drink, gamble, and engage in robbery.[70] Yet, compared to their relatives who had stayed behind in China, these frontiersmen at least enjoyed an abundance of food. The island was pestilential and sporadically unsafe, but fecund.

Those who knew what to look for and where to find it (skills sometimes learned directly from indigenous Taiwanese) could supplement their diet with wild taros and *Cordia dichotoma* drupes. After dry roasting, the former can be stored for two or three years; indigenous men liked to carry a few to sustain them during hunting expeditions. The latter is sometimes called fragrant manjack; it gets its Holo name (*phòa pò chí*, "shabby rags") because its leaves are often chewed to pieces by insects. The drupes, known in Mandarin as *shùzǐ*, are smaller than peanuts and yellowish-green when ripe. Archaeologists think cordia was consumed in quantity by the Siraya at least six hundred years ago, together with Job's tears, Chinese hackberries, and various beans.[71]

To modern palates, cordia drupes are unbearably astringent unless boiled and then pickled, a process that turns them brown. The flesh is soft and succulent, but the large pits frustrate some first-time eaters. In recent years, cordia—which some compare to an olive—has made something of a comeback. Driven by growing demand for lighter and healthier foods, the area devoted to commercial cultivation has increased. Many Taiwanese buy jars of pickled cordia in supermarkets for serving alongside steamed fish or for adding to omelets.

Cordia drupes are sometimes called pigeon peas or pigeon beans. Fresh and dried pigeon peas sustained certain aboriginal communities in the east, and in Hualien's Guangfu Township, there is a place whose name is derived from *vataan*, the Amis word for this kind of pea. On July 21, 2011, *Taiwan Today* reported that, as part of government efforts to give indigenous farmers more options, agronomists have developed high-yield varieties of vataan said to be good for stewing with pig's feet or cuts of pork. Bird's nest fern (*Asplenium nidus*) is regarded as an ornamental plant in much of the world, but for the Amis and Atayal it is a traditional food.

Black nightshade (*Solanum nigrum*) has always been popular, and a relative, shining-fruit nightshade (*Solanum photeinocarpum*), has caught on with consumers. Many think of these native plants as wild vegetables: both thrive even when

Pickled cordia drupes for sale in Taipei.
Katy Hui-wen Hung

neglected and—according to a report posted on Tainan District Agricultural Research and Extension Station's website—grow well during Taiwan's hot, humid summers when other domestic greens are in short supply.

Nightshade leaves and stems are often stir-fried with ginger, cooked in a porridge with shrimp or pork, or served in egg-drop soup. Egg or meat protein reduces the bitterness of the alkaloids the plant contains in abundance. According to Chinese medicinal theory, it can help relieve coughing and suppress inflammations. Among indigenous people, a soup that combines the leaves with tiny dried fish is a tonic for hangovers. In the old days, the dark purple mature berries were enjoyed as a substitute for candy or chocolate, but some say that eating too many can cause diarrhea or an itchy throat.

At least thirty-two poisonous mushroom species grow in Taiwan's forests and bamboo groves, but that does not stop the enthusiastic gathering of certain wild fungi. In rural parts of Tainan where *Macrolepiota albuminosa* grows especially well, it is better known by its Holo name, *ke-bah si ko* ("shredded chicken mushroom"), on account of its color and texture. So far, no one has successfully farmed *Macrolepiota albuminosa* because it grows only in obligate symbiosis with a particular termite species.

Between June and August, if there is a succession of rainy days with temperatures above 26°C, those who know where to look are able to gather several kilograms of *ke-bah si ko* each day. Fungus aficionados say they taste best when boiled with a little salt, with some going as far as claiming that no cultivated mushroom tastes as good.[72]

FRESHWATER RESOURCES

Just as they failed to make the most of the soil, the indigenous inhabitants showed little interest in the shoals of gray mullet that appeared along the southwestern coast each winter. By the Dutch era, if not earlier, fishermen from Fujian were exploiting this resource. Deveining the roe, salting it, drying it under the sun, and then pressing it to make a bottarga-like delicacy is a four-hundred-year-old Taiwanese foodway[73] recognized by the Slow Food Foundation for Biodiversity's Ark of Taste. The fish migrate from the eastern coast of China down the Taiwan Strait, hugging Taiwan's west coast to finally reach spawning grounds near Kaohsiung. However, the "rapacious and indiscriminate" and "illegal" behavior of Chinese fishermen is having a severe impact on the roe and other marine harvests.[74]

The aborigines showed more enthusiasm for fishing inland. Pickering saw indigenous people catch fish by tainting creeks with the roots of a poisonous creeper, probably *Millettia taiwaniana*.[75] J. B. Steere, a University of Michigan zoology professor who visited Taiwan in 1871, 1873, and 1874, wrote of lowland tribes using "a curious but very effectual way of fishing the shallow streams . . . by damming them and turning the water to one side of the channel, leaving most of the bed of the stream dry, and the fish and shrimps in little pools and under rocks, where they are easily captured."[76] Unfortunately, Steere was not able to enjoy much local cuisine on one of his expeditions. In a letter published in *Ann Arbor Courier* on June 12, 1874, complaining that his servant had left his knife and fork behind in Tainan, he recalled that for several days he "nearly starved, and had become pretty much savage in my method of eating," before replacements could be procured.

Rivers and creeks have paid an especially heavy price for Taiwan's development. Population growth, industrialization, and the concomitant pollution have massively disrupted riparian ecosystems. The freshwater Taiwan clam (*Corbicula fluminea formosa*) was previously so common that the Holo-language equivalent of "kill two birds with one stone" is *it kiam jī kòo, bong lâ-á kiam sé khòo* ("gather clams while washing your pants [in the stream]"). This clam species is seldom found in nature nowadays, due to the use of ammonium-based fertilizers and the rebuilding of irrigation ditches with concrete,[77] but there is some artificial breeding.

Yet local waterways are far from lifeless. Taiwan still has sixteen freshwater prawn species; thirteen are also found in the Philippines or Japan's Ryukyu Islands, but just a few overlap with prawn species in China or the Japanese Home Islands.[78] And according to the American expatriate angling enthusiast who blogs at www .taiwanangler.com, among the edible species often caught in Taiwan's rivers are the amur catfish, the sweetfish (*Plecoglossus altivelis*, which Taiwanese like to barbecue), the endemic *Spinibarbus hollandi*, the common carp, the Taiwan shovel-jaw carp (*Onychostoma barbatulum*), the skygazer (*Chanodichthys erythropterus*), various snakeheads, and *Zacco platypus*. In the mountains of central Taiwan, there is a remarkable fish that indigenous people used to eat but is now very rare and protected by the law. What the Atayal call *bunban* is notable for being the southernmost salmon in the world; *Oncorhynchus formosanus* (the Formosan landlocked salmon) clings to existence more than 1,740 meters above sea level, higher than any other salmon.[79]

INDIGENOUS FLAVORINGS

If any single ingredient distinguishes the cuisine of Taiwan's indigenous minority from that of the Han majority, it is *Litsea cubeba*. The fruit are known to Mandarin speakers as *shān hújiāo* ("mountain peppercorns") or, more often, *mǎgào*. The latter is derived from *maqaw*, its name in the language of the Atayal, the tribe most closely associated with this ingredient. Nowadays, few restaurants that present themselves as aboriginal do not have at least one menu item featuring maqaw—or, for that matter, mountain boar or wild greens.

In the West, the black peppercorns are used to make an essential oil called *may chang*. In Taiwan, they are usually dried before use in the kitchen, and sometimes crushed or ground, as noted in the maqaw entry on the Slow Food Foundation for Biodiversity's Ark of Taste website. Maqaw is often served with fish. The menu at Badashan, an indigenous restaurant in New Taipei's Bali District, includes maqaw sour-and-spicy prawns and a flying-fish fried rice dish with maqaw and XO sauce. (XO sauce is made of seafood; name notwithstanding, it contains no cognac.)

On January 3, 2017, the *New York Times* described the flavor of maqaw as "not only peppery, it's deeply fragrant, with a scent of lemongrass and citron, making it sublime on delicate fish." In his November 26, 2016, food column for *Taipei Times*, Ian Bartholomew declared that maqaw "combines elements of pepper, lemongrass, thyme, ginger and citrus oils"; however, while it provides "an interesting twist," he did not think it compelling enough to replace cheaper and more readily available alternatives.

Growing demand for maqaw in the first decade of the twenty-first century led to over-collection and its near disappearance from Taiwan's foothills. However, on December 20, 2014, *China Times* reported that government agricultural scientists are now able to artificially propagate *Litsea cubeba*. Propagation kits were sold to the public, and maqaw seedlings distributed to aboriginal farmers. Traditionally, maqaw has been sun-dried or pickled (and much of the pickled maqaw has been imported from Thailand), but in recent years an award-winning aboriginal restaurateur has pioneered the freezing of fresh peppercorns. According to Yabung Tally (see chapter 9), this method better preserves maqaw's lemony fragrance, and the "wet" peppercorns are easier to chew.

Yabung Tally had a hand in the revival of another ingredient. More than a thousand years ago, the leaves of the alianthus-like prickly ash (*Zanthoxylum ailanthoides*) were used by Chinese people as medicine and a substance to ward off evil. In recent years in Taiwan, however, what is known to several tribes as *tana* (and to Mandarin speakers as *cìcōng*; for Westerners, it is angelica leaf or prickly ash) has been marketed as an indigenous ingredient. An alternative name, translatable as "birds don't step on it," alludes to its thorniness, but the young leaves of this perennial are exceptionally rich in beta-carotene, vitamin E, and ascorbic acid. According to the website of the World Vegetable Center, they also contain useful amounts of calcium and iron. The Amis add chopped, de-thorned *tana* leaves to fish and chicken soups; the Puyuma have been known to fry them with snail meat. *Tana* or maqaw are sometimes added to tea, to give it a little extra kick.

Historically, *tana* was common in the Puli area and often used by the region's Thao tribe. According to the website of Seeland Monastery Farm, a sustainable-farming group in Sanxia, the young leaves are good for eating raw. Mature leaves can replace onions or basil in soups and omelets, and a December 5, 2012, entry on the blog *Food with Teacher Zhang* recommends finely chopping a few leaves and sprinkling them over a cold dish that is not remotely Austronesian but which epitomizes the Chinese and Japanese foodways that came to dominate Taiwan: century eggs and *hiyayakko* cold tofu.

2

❖ ❖

The Kitchen

A metropolitan area slightly larger than New York City, but so mountainous the majority of its seven million residents are squashed into an area smaller than New Orleans—this is Greater Taipei. Its three local-government divisions are the nation's capital (the population of which has grown eightfold since 1945), the encircling municipality called New Taipei, and the gritty port of Keelung.

Homes are small, and kitchens are cramped. Few have sizable countertops, let alone dedicated dining spaces, so meals are usually taken in the living room. Weekday dinners are often bought outside rather than cooked at home, especially if both the husband and the wife hold full-time jobs. Yesterday's newspaper serves as a tablecloth, and eating out of bento boxes means there are no dishes to wash. Yet, despite the long hours many people work (the fourth longest in the world, according to an October 6, 2016, report by *Focus Taiwan*), and the low cost and sheer convenience of eating out compared to preparing hot dishes from scratch, a great deal of home cooking still goes on. Some people enjoy preparing their own meals, of course, or are tired of what is available in the neighborhood. But a meaningful number of citizens switch on the stove because they worry that local food businesses may use unsafe ingredients, too much oil, or too much salt.

In three- and four-generation households, which are far more common in the rural south than in Greater Taipei,[1] kitchen duty very often falls to a woman over sixty. Despite the transformation of the diet since World War II, only one of the "seven necessities"[2] that Chinese tradition held to be essential can no longer be found in local kitchens. People who cook try not to run out of rice, oil, salt, soy sauce, vinegar, and tea—but of firewood they have no need. If any commodity nowadays counts as the seventh essential, it is sugar.

KITCHEN TECHNOLOGIES

Taiwanese prepare ingredients and cook with many of the same utensils as Westerners. In addition to cleavers, knives, ladles, spoons, spatulas, tongs, strainers, and a kind of shallow wire-mesh skimmer sometimes called a "spider," the well-equipped kitchen is sure to have at least one pair of cooking chopsticks. Roughly twice the length of normal chopsticks, these are always made of wood so that they do not melt, scratch non-stick pans, or (a possibility if made of metal) burn the cook's hands.

For most of the island's history, families that could afford them would buy cooking and eating utensils decorated with auspicious motifs. In Holo as it is spoken in the south of the island, the pronunciation of chicken and home are similar, so a chicken image meant a fortunate family. A fish symbolized bounty, while a shrimp represented prosperity. Butterflies and bats meant good luck. Pine, bamboo, and plum blossoms expressed noble sentiments. Grapes symbolized children and good fortune.[3]

In addition to woks, skillets, and stockpots like those used nowadays, until the 1970s many households owned steaming baskets made of bamboo. Hoklo people used these for oily rice, Lunar New Year treats, and sticky, heavy rice cakes like *âng ku kóe* ("red turtle cake"). Families originally from the mainland used them to steam wheat-flour buns. These days, you are more likely to see a steaming basket in a dumpling restaurant than someone's home. *Diàn guō* (see below) can handle most jobs, but for steaming something like a big fish, a stainless-steel basket atop a gas or induction stove is preferred.

The three-sided courtyard homes that once housed much of the population were equipped with wood-burning hearths made of brick or clay.[4] In the 1950s and 1960s, charcoal briquettes replaced firewood in many homes. In her preface to the first edition of *Mrs. Chiang's Szechwan Cookbook*, Ellen Schrecker recalls that, in Taipei in 1969, the eponymous Mrs. Chiang was used to cooking on an open fire.[5] Others began using kerosene stoves, sometimes using fuel obtained on the black market from American service personnel.[6] Parts of Taipei had running water as early as 1907,[7] but households elsewhere made do with brick storage tubs they topped up by bucket from the nearest well or spring.

A few countryside and indigenous families still use outdoor fires for stewing or roasting, but even in those households gas ranges are now standard. Electric stoves cannot deliver the instant, very high temperatures needed for wok frying. Piped-gas networks exist in some urban areas, but most homes depend on portable LNG (liquefied natural gas) cylinders. When the gas runs lows, a phone call is made, and within ten minutes a man delivers a fresh cylinder by motorcycle. Except for a few hours around dinnertime on Lunar New Year's Eve, replacement cylinders are available at all waking hours, 365 days a year. Only restaurants and street vendors keep spares, often chained together in alleyways, sometimes looking like a disaster waiting to happen. On July 19, 2017, *Taipei Times* reported a gas-bottle blast at a crowded Taichung eatery; one person died and fifteen were injured.

Ovens (gas or electric) are rare, and only a minority of households owns a microwave oven. As in the West, healthy eaters use blenders to make juices. Bread-making machines have caught on. Fitted kitchens come with an extractor hood above the range; this is essential for the comfort and pulmonary health of cooks who do lots of stir-frying.[8] But for millions of people, the one truly indispensable kitchen appliance is the *diàn guō* ("electric pot").

Calling this device a rice steamer fails to describe its versatility. It can be used to cook chawanmushi, fish, vegetables, stews, and soups. Reheating frozen steamed buns is a cinch. All a stressed office-worker needs to do when he or she gets home is put some leftovers in the steamer, add a little water, close the lid, and push the lever down. Burning food is nearly impossible. Because these steamers can keep rice warm long after cooking, food is seldom reheated for latecomers. So long as the rice is hot, the temperature of the vegetables and protein seems not to matter.

Just as specialized books and websites teach you how to make the most out of your microwave, *diàn guō liàolǐ* ("electric pot cuisine") has emerged as a form of cooking in its own right. Hundreds of recipes have been posted online or demonstrated on TV. One of these is salty egg and minced pork, a dish many generations of Taiwanese cooked in bamboo steaming baskets.

In Taiwan, one company above all others is associated with rice steamers: Tatung. Technical cooperation with Toshiba helped Tatung create a steamer that was easy to use, safe, and durable. For several years following its introduction in 1960, the Tatung *diàn guō* enjoyed a domestic market share of 95 percent.[9]

The original Tatung stainless-steel steamer is an iconic design. Over the years, the company has launched various models with additional features and functions; yet a version very close to the original in terms of shape and color continues to sell, in part because of its retro appeal. More than a few Taiwanese moving abroad for work or college have lugged a Tatung steamer all the way to the United States or Great Britain.

The steamer was not an overnight success, in part because the price (just under US$9 in 1960) represented a full two weeks' earnings for many Taiwanese. To catch the attention of housewives who had never seen such an appliance, Tatung's sales team conducted demonstrations at places like Taipei's Qingguang Market, just across the road from their corporate headquarters. Word of mouth, along with newspaper advertising (and television commercials after the country's first TV station began broadcasting in 1962), pushed annual sales to more than twenty thousand units by 1970, and total sales to thirteen million by 2011. But the company is aware that it can no longer depend on domestic demand, and it has turned its focus to India and Southeast Asia.[10]

Wu Shu-chen, first lady from 2000 to 2008, has recalled a poignant moment in her courtship by Chen Shui-bian. Visiting her dormitory in Taipei one day in the early 1970s, when both were college students, the future president mistook a cabinet for a refrigerator; because of his impoverished background, he was unsure what one looked like. By 1979, 90 percent of Taiwan's people lived in houses with refrigerators,[11] but even now few own a chest freezer. There is neither the space nor—because meals are often taken outside, and groceries can be bought every few days—the need.

Sales of kitchen gadgets like food steamers may shrink for demographic reasons. More and more people are living alone, and the around-the-clock availability of inexpensive hot food inevitably reduces their desire to cook. Many small apartments in Greater Taipei lack kitchens, and some single people see no reason to even own a refrigerator; hot coffee with milk can be purchased from any twenty-four-hour convenience store. The spending power of unmarried adults is prompting some restaurant owners who sell food traditionally enjoyed by families or groups, such as hot pot, to make their menus more single friendly, *Focus Taiwan* reported on March 27, 2017.

ESSENTIAL, YET NOT IMMUTABLE: SOY SAUCE

Soy sauce has its origins in China, but the first servings of this salty condiment to reach Taiwan likely came from Japan. In 1647, a letter listing the goods aboard a vessel sailing from Nagasaki to the Dutch East India Company's base in Tainan mentioned ten kegs of soy sauce. The term used by the letter writer was *soije*, based on the Japanese term *shoyu*, meaning soy sauce. The words *soy*, *soya*, and *soy sauce* later entered the English language from Japanese via Dutch, and the name of the soybean thus derives from the name of the sauce.[12]

As both a dip and a key flavoring when food is braised, soy sauce is regarded as essential to the cuisines of the Sinosphere. However, only since World War II has every household been able to afford it. In the past, many of those who could not fermented substitute sauces and pastes from shrimp or fish. For people living on the coast, this was also a way to utilize uneaten or unsold fish.[13]

Before the Japanese colonial period, Taiwanese soy sauces were made from local black soybeans that were steamed, salted, and left to ferment. The market is still dominated by locally made sauces, but as a result of Japanese influence, many are now made using yellow soybeans, and in some cases as much wheat or barley as soy. "Taiwanese people prefer soy sauces like those made in Kyushu or southern China. Those made in Honshu or northern China are significantly saltier," says Brian Chuang, a great-grandson of the man who founded Wuan Chuang Food Industrial Co. Ltd., one of Taiwan's most esteemed soy-sauce makers. According to Chuang, the company's general manager, in recent decades the average salt content of local soy sauces has fallen slightly from 15 percent to 14 percent.[14]

To accelerate fermentation, manufacturers of cheap soy sauces use hydrochloric acid instead of a traditional decomposing agent (*Aspergillus oryzae* or *Aspergillus sojae* mold). Their sauces are ready for bottling within a week, rather than the four to six months otherwise required, but have a sharp smell some find off-putting.[15] This is one reason why demand for sauces made the old-fashioned way remains strong.

"Customers get used to a particular flavor, perhaps because it was used by their mother or grandmother, so we may not change a particular formula for thirty years or more, one generation or even two," says Chuang. Whenever the company

Wuan Chuang employees stir salted black soybeans ahead of fermentation into soy sauce. *Wuan Chuang Food Industrial Co. Ltd.*

does release a new formula, consumers need a lengthy period to get used to it, he adds. Even though ketchup, mayonnaise, mustard, and other nontraditional condiments are widely available, Chuang asserts, "People certainly aren't using any less soy sauce, and they're buying better-quality soy sauces compared to before. That's especially true for households, but not so much for restaurants and food-processing factories."

The price of Wuan Chuang's premium sauce is seven times that of its main mass-market product. According to Chuang, some customers drive considerable distances to the small town of Xiluo—about 120 miles down-island from Taipei, and the company's base since its establishment in 1909—to purchase formulas that are hard to find in supermarkets.

The irreplaceability of *jiàng yóu* (as soy sauce is called in Mandarin; Holo speakers write it differently and pronounce it *tāu iû*) makes it an evergreen product. The industry is recession-proof but highly competitive. Chuang says it is still possible for small-scale manufacturers "to find their position in the market, in part because setting up a soy-sauce production line does not require much capital."

Black-bean sauces like those Wuan Chuang built its reputation on are nowadays referred to as *yīn yóu* ("dark sauce"), to distinguish them from formulas made with yellow soybeans. The former account for about 30 percent of the company's output and are priced 15–20 percent higher than competing products. But this does not translate into large profits, he explains. As part of Wuan Chuang's pro-local ethos, in 2009 the company began contracting local farmers to supply black beans, just as they did in his grandfather's and great-grandfather's times. Initially yields were poor, and the beans were very expensive. Nonetheless, the company persisted, and gradually increased the percentage of locally sourced black beans. Only in early 2017, by which time Taiwanese black beans were meeting around 85 percent of the company's needs, did Wuan Chuang begin to talk publicly about this policy, which the owners see as a Taiwanese tradition, not merely their family's custom. "We aspire to using only Taiwan-grown black beans, but that's hard to achieve," says Chuang. Few consumers choose products on the basis of "food miles," but being seen as a patriotic enterprise doing something for the welfare of farmers cannot hurt the brand.

In 2009, Wuan Chuang launched the first made-in-Taiwan organic soy sauce, and the raw materials it imports from North America and China are non-GMO. "Before 2014, very few soy-sauce manufacturers labeled their products as non-GMO, because there wasn't any reason to do so. But in the last few years, customers have begun to really care about this," says Chuang. In 2015 Taiwan's Food and Drug Administration ruled that bulk foods, packaged foods, and condiments that include 3 percent or more GM ingredients must be labeled as genetically modified;[16] since 2016, GM foods have been banned from school lunches.[17]

There are those who think quality soy sauce, like a good wine, gets better with age. Chuang knows a few customers who purposely store Wuan Chuang soy sauce long beyond the three years' shelf life printed on the label because they like how the taste changes. The difference in flavor is subtle, he says, "but I think real gourmets will understand and like it."

Brian Chuang's father is the company's chairman. Asked what it feels like to be heir apparent in a business that is a household name, the younger Chuang outlined his hope that he can "not only maintain, but also enlarge the scope of the business. To keep going as we have been, to preserve what we have, is honorable. I don't expect dramatic changes, but I do aim to expand the influence of our brand. Food is tied to soy sauce, so it's the obvious place to start."

Selling to companies that use soy sauce in food processing is of growing importance to Wuan Chuang, Brian Chuang says. He has invested in the Mazendo and Kokuraya restaurants (see chapter 7), both of which use Wuan Chuang sauces exclusively. Gratifyingly, other restaurants in which he has no business interest make a point of stating on their menus that they always use Wuan Chuang products.

Sean A. Hsu, general manager of the company that runs Mazendo and an old friend of Brian Chuang, describes Wuan Chuang's soy sauce in a way that probably explains its appeal to homemakers as well as restaurant bosses: "Because it's made with black beans, it has a taste of nostalgia. It's reminiscent of grandma's cooking."[18]

OTHER SOY-BASED CONDIMENTS

Like most soy-sauce manufacturers, Wuan Chuang also makes *jiàng yóu gāo* ("soy-sauce paste"). Made thicker and a little sweeter by adding rice starch, this brown paste is seldom used in cooking, but often appears as a dressing for breakfast crepes or fried dumplings.

Specializing in the production of *jiàng yóu gāo* helped another company establish itself as Taiwan's premier maker of "white" soy sauce. Until a few decades ago, the owner of Hsin Lai Yuan Food Co. Ltd. discarded the liquid left over after making soy-sauce paste or gave it away to households who used it to pickle cucumbers or cordia drupes. But when he began to sell the liquid—which is actually golden, not white, because yellow soybeans are used—to restaurants, the response (especially from those using it with seafood) was very positive. The company, now led by a fourth-generation descendant of the founder, began bottling it for retail sales.[19]

Some households keep a jar of fermented black soybeans (*dòuchǐ*) to flavor dishes constructed around bitter gourd or marbled pork and cucumber. Several companies make *dòufu rǔ*, a form of fermented tofu not to be confused with stinky tofu. Non-spicy versions are usually a yellowy shade of brown. *Dòufu rǔ*, which is often quite tart, is used in small quantities to jazz up rice gruel at breakfast time. A dash of it in the wok augments meat, water spinach, or eggplant with perilla seeds. Among those who try to eat healthily, there has been a revival of interest in making *dòufu rǔ* at home. This can be done by steaming store-bought tofu, sealing it in a jar with an equal amount of pineapple, some sugar, and a little rice wine or salt, then waiting three months.

OILS AND VINEGARS

Before Taiwan's industrialization was complete, countryside people fried with lard—often obtained from a pig they had raised themselves—while urban folk preferred non-refined peanut oil. Soybean oil was seen as inferior; it was usually relegated to burning in lamps, or blended with peanut or rapeseed oil.

This began to change in the 1970s, when the American Soybean Association coordinated efforts to market the surplus oil that was a consequence of increased soybean crushing to feed the country's rapidly expanding swine herds and poultry flocks. Realizing quality was an issue, the association also worked with domestic vegetable-oil manufacturers to improve refining facilities. By the early 1980s, they were claiming considerable success in winning over local consumers.[20]

Cookery teacher Jodie Tsao has vivid memories of the peanut-oil era:

> There were no convenience stores or supermarkets near our home by the Tamsui River when I was very young. When my grandmother or mother found out there wasn't any more oil in the tin in the kitchen, they usually sent me or another of the kids to buy some from the nearby grocery store. We'd run to the store with some money and the oil tin in our hands. When the owner saw me carrying the tin, right away she knew I needed some oil for my family. She'd open the lid of a big oil can, and refill my tin. The tin held about 400 milliliter [0.85 US pints]. I was too small to reach the counter, and not tall enough to see what was inside the big oil can.[21]

Taking your own bottle or jar to an oil seller for replenishment was called *dǎyóu* in Mandarin and *tán iû* in the Holo language; both mean "fetching oil." Soy sauce was sold the same way. Some of the vendors were mobile, but often to be found at places which now bear the name Youche ("oil/sauce cart"), of which there are at least five in Taiwan. This system generated less trash, to be sure, but had its drawbacks. One 1970 report characterized it as "a very primitive marketing method," noting how easy it was for retailers to adulterate refined oils with unrefined oils.[22] Yet, as Tsao points out, the behavior in very recent years of some cooking-oil suppliers has been highly alarming (see chapter 6).

Tsao remembers the stores near her home selling peanut oil, white sesame oil, black sesame oil, and camellia (tea seed) oil, all of which were produced in Taiwan. The first was for everyday cooking. The second, recalls Tsao, was occasionally used for adding flavor and fragrance to the dishes.

"Black sesame oil was always used for winter cooking and postnatal cooking," she explains. "Camellia oil was used not only for everyday cooking, adding fragrance to dishes, winter and postnatal cooking, but also for its great nutritional benefit." Cuts of chicken with the skin left on and basted in camellia oil are a popular dish in tea-growing areas such as Alishan.

As supermarkets replaced grocery stores, the "fetching oil" system disappeared. "People's diets also changed. Soybean oil became the most commonly used cooking oil. The old hand-pressed oils that people used to enjoy were expensive compared to mass-produced oils. And the manufactured oils were all nicely packed in clean bottles. Who would want to buy oil in a greasy old tin?" says Tsao.

Because cooking oil was precious, Tsao's mother used only tiny amounts: "She rarely deep-fried food, because it was too wasteful. Forty years ago, there were few overweight people. Many older people have told me that after they got into the habit of using soybean oil, their stoves became not only greasy, but also sticky, like they'd spilled glue. To remove the grease, they had to use very strong detergent. But when they used to cook with lard or peanut oil, the grease could easily be wiped away with some soap and water."

Tsao dislikes blended oils because "soybean oil doesn't add any fragrance or nutritional value to peanut oil or sesame oil." And she views the recent popularity of extra-virgin olive oils simply as things having come full circle: "People understand the nutritional benefits. They believe cooking with extra-virgin olive oil will protect their family's health. However, not many people realize that using high-quality oil was normal for hundreds of years. The oils in those old grocery stores were actually extra-virgin oils, as that was the only oil-making process people knew."

Food-safety scandals have revived the fortunes of artisanal oil makers, most of whom are second or third generation.[23] However, such businesses now struggle to source raw materials locally because of the ongoing contraction of agriculture (see chapter 5). More than 90 percent of the camellia seeds pressed for oil in Taiwan come from overseas.[24] All of the white sesame consumed in Taiwan is imported. Domestic production of black sesame—a key ingredient in three-cup recipes—has slumped in recent decades, now meeting barely 2 percent of local needs.[25]

What Mandarin speakers call *shāchá jiàng* is sometimes mistranslated as "satay sauce." The former counts as a distinct condiment, even though it evolved from the latter. Chinese who emigrated from the Chaozhou-Shantou region of southeastern China to Malaysia and Indonesia introduced satay to their hometowns, but replaced the crushed roasted peanuts with soybean oil. From there, this new sauce made its way to Taiwan, where it evolved further. The most popular mass-market version is Bullhead Barbecue Sauce (which is mostly soybean oil and flavored with ground fish and shrimp, garlic, powdered ginger, scallions, sesame, chili powder, salt, coriander, cinnamon, fennel, and pepper), sold in a silver tin nearly as iconic as the Taiwan Beer can. The company was founded in 1958 and began by selling *shāchá* powder, but not until the 1980s was the average consumer wealthy enough to buy the sauce on a regular basis.[26]

For Taiwanese chefs, cooking without vinegar is almost as inconceivable as living without soy sauce. Most keep at least two types on hand: a clear vinegar (*báicù*, "white vinegar") and inky *wūcù* ("black vinegar"). Both are made from glutinous rice. The former is pure; the latter gains its hue from the carrots, onions, sugar, ginger, spices, or other fruits and vegetables that are added. By some reckonings, the sodium content of black vinegar is twenty times that of white vinegar.[27]

Black vinegar appears in recipes such as noodles with braised cow's stomach. *Wūcù miàn* ("black vinegar noodles") is a simple dish often based around a type of thin noodle associated with and named for Tainan's Guanmiao District. These noodles are made without salt, then dried under the strong southern sun before packing.

White vinegar is a key component of the dressings for several of the cold side dishes known collectively in Mandarin as *xiǎocài* or *liángbàn*. One is raw cucumber with garlic; another is black wood-ear fungus seasoned with garlic, sesame oil, soy sauce, and sugar. It also provides the sourness in Taiwanese-style hot and sour soup (the Chinese name, *suānlà tāng*, is more accurately rendered "sour and spicy soup"). The hotness comes from white pepper, which overall is used more frequently than black pepper. Unlike mainland iterations, local hot and sour soup features an impressive amount of tofu, and wontons are seldom added.

As in other countries, most of the vinegar sold in Taiwan is chemically synthesized to reduce costs, rather than naturally fermented. Just as Wuan Chuang perpetuates time-honored soy-sauce-making techniques, vinegar makers like Kao Zhan Enterprise Ltd. carry the torch of tradition. Founded in 1903, the company is now based in New Taipei's Shulin District.

Since 2013, Kao Zhan has been led by a fifth-generation descendant of the founder who claims to follow the exact same procedures as his forebears. Only Taiwanese rice is used, and fermentation (which takes at least eight months for the company's Wu Yin brand clear vinegar) takes place in earthenware vats. Some of these containers are decades old; replacement vats are "matured" for two or more years before being utilized. However, the company does make some use of modern technology. The wheatgrass that workers stir into the steamed rice, which is said to impart exceptional flavor and nutritional value as well as promote acidification, is grown in a temperature-controlled cool room.[28]

THE EIGHTH ESSENTIAL?

Only dipsomaniacs guzzle the rice wine that cooks keep handy. Nevertheless, the role of this liquid is deeply rooted and goes far beyond masking the aroma of fish and mutton. It is, of course, a key element in three-cup recipes. A splash in the wok is thought to make fried vegetables look fresher and more appetizing. Rice wine is an essential wintertime tonic and dietary supplement. In her master's thesis on rice wine, Lee Ju-chi explains that, in the not too distant past, the liquid was credited with near-magical properties:

> For the people of Taiwan, rice wine is indispensable. When celebrating a birth, marking a death, worshipping a god or ancestors, rice wine is part of the offerings. In folk religion, rice wine is believed to ward off evil. It is one of the tools used by Taoist priests. Writing the logogram for "king" with rice wine on a child's forehead will drive away misfortune. And the older generation generally believes that wiping a stick of ginger moistened with rice wine over the head of a four-month-old baby's head can make its hair grow thick.[29]

The ways in which rice wine (in Mandarin: *mǐjiǔ*) has been deployed to season food and enhance appetites have changed as different regimes came to rule the island and with the subsequent arrival and integration of different ethnic groups. For years after 1949, many of the mainlanders who had fled to Taiwan expected to eventually return to their hometowns and did not try to adapt to the local diet. Thus, when better standards of living arrived in the 1960s and 1970s, and rice wine was no longer a luxury ingredient, there was a fusion of local *mǐjiǔ* and Chinese cooking styles.[30]

When Taiwan joined the WTO at the beginning of 2002, overnight the price of rice wine jumped more than fivefold. At the behest of US and EU trade negotiators, the island had agreed to tax all alcoholic beverages according to their strength, even if—as was apparently the case with locally produced *mǐjiǔ*—98 percent was used for cooking instead of drinking. The queuing, panic buying, and hoarding throughout the weeks between the increase being confirmed and it taking effect even made it to the pages of the *Los Angeles Times* ("Taiwan's Tempest in a Rice Wine Bottle," December 16, 2001). Before the year was out, several people had died of methanol poisoning after consuming bootleg wine.[31]

Many complained that, because this "critical seasoning" had become so expensive, during the crisis they could not afford to cook favorite dishes such as *shāojiǔ jī* (chicken stewed in a rice-wine soup that is set alight) or Lunar New Year specialties. Some cooks experimented with but were left unimpressed by Shaohsing Chiew (a very popular cooking wine on the Chinese mainland) and other alternatives.[32] Shaohsing "has a much stronger flavor and taste of alcohol, and is also a little spicy, which makes it unsuitable for many dishes, except stronger-tasting dishes such as drunken chicken, drunken prawns," and other slow-cooked meats, opines Taipei-born blogger-author Tsung-Yun Wan. She praises rice wine for having "a mild and refreshing taste, and I use it to season many Chinese and Taiwanese dishes."[33]

The majority still prefers Red Label Rice Wine (19.5 percent alcohol), a type of *mǐjiǔ* far older than TTL, the state-run company that makes it. Lawmakers cut the tax rate on distilled spirits in 2009 and again in 2010,[34] bringing the price back below US$1 for a 600 milliliter (76.8 US fluid ounces) bottle. The saccharification and fermentation methods used to make Red Label were learned from a Saigon winery in the late 1920s. The key ingredient is ponlai rice, mixed with water and hydrochloric acid, and then cooked until liquefaction occurs. After cooling, *Rhizopus delemar* mold is added. The raw wine is then blended with molasses alcohol in a ratio of 6:4 before bottling. Due to rice shortages, during and for a period following World War II the proportion was reversed, and the formula included taro and sweet-potato mash.[35] Cooking wine is no longer produced in Taipei, but the price cut of several years ago caused demand to bounce back, prompting TTL to open an additional production line in Linkou just west of the capital. In 2013 and 2014, the company's annual output of *mǐjiǔ* topped ninety million hectoliters, more than 40 percent higher than in 2006.[36] Potatoes and wheat products may be pushing rice off the dinner table, but cooking wine made from the grain appears to have a guaranteed spot in the kitchen.

A CAN OF THIS, A JAR OF THAT

Monosodium glutamate (MSG), the umami flavor enhancer sometimes said to cause "Chinese Restaurant Syndrome," may no longer be ubiquitous in home kitchens, but very few restaurant cooks do not keep a jar of it on hand. A few Taiwanese say that MSG gives them a headache or a raging thirst, but it has notable defenders, including head chefs at major Taipei hotels.

MSG contains much less sodium than table salt (12 percent compared to around 39 percent). As of October 23, 2017, the website of the Center for Food Safety, a unit of Hong Kong's government, advised the public to minimize their intake of MSG but noted, "When used in combination with a small amount of salt during food preparation, MSG has been reported to reduce the total amount of sodium in a recipe by 20–40 percent. Studies have shown that it is possible to maintain food palatability with a lowered overall sodium level when MSG is substituted for some of the salt in soups." This is highly relevant to Taiwan, where many adults suffer from vitamin D deficiency, elevating their risk of osteoporosis-related bone fractures. Sodium intake leads to urinary calcium excretion, further weakening the bones. Among men as well as women, Taiwan already has a higher rate of hip fractures than the United States.[37]

In a July 2016 article in *CommonWealth*, a respected Chinese-language magazine, Tan Dun-ci—the author of books on healthy eating—said MSG is one of just four seasonings she buys for her family. The others are salt, soy sauce, and sugar. (By not keeping some kind of chili sauce or spicy oil in the kitchen, she belongs to a small minority.)

There is no standard list of ingredients for the five-spice powder used on both sides of the Taiwan Strait, and some versions are made from more than five spices. This mix of cinnamon, cloves, fennel, white pepper, and turmeric and/or cardamom is widely used to flavor braised pork (*ròuzào*) and the meat-and-vegetable fillings of steamed buns (*bāozi*).

Many families keep a packet of *ròu sōng* ("pork floss") in the refrigerator. Made from pork that has been finely shredded and dried after stewing, it appears at breakfast, adding flavor and texture to rice gruel. Parents of young children gush about its magical power to transform green vegetables kids tend to reject into something youngsters are eager to gobble down. Like bacon bits, *ròu sōng* can be pressed into service as a topping for salads and pizzas. With mayonnaise and flecks of dried seaweed, it fills soft rolls that bakeries sell in the morning.

In the past, many housewives made their own *ròu sōng* from leftover cooked meat that was past its best. Few people bother nowadays, and some consumers prefer factory analogs made of fish or soy. The function of dried shrimp is similar to that of pork floss, although the taste is saltier and more umami. They are good for enlivening fried rice, omelets, and stir-fried cabbage, and some banquet chefs use dried shrimp as one of the ingredients replacing shark's fin in "Buddha Jumps Over the Wall" (see chapter 4).

Cooks utilize several different starches, such as tapioca or corn, so pan-fried pot stickers gain an extra crispiness. Sweet-potato starch thickens much of the thick soup (*gēng*) supped on the island. This term is frequently but inaccurately translated as potage; in a bowl of *gēng*, chunks of pork hand-kneaded with flour, or pieces of fish or squid, are intact and clearly visible, as are slivers of carrot, onion, and mushrooms. Unlike gumbo, *gēng* is not served over rice.

Canned or powdered soups are not as popular in Taiwan as in the West, but some form of homemade soup (*tāng*) accompanies most meals and is often drunk at the very end. It may be as simple as egg-drop soup, or clams with shredded ginger. People eating out by themselves frequently order a soupy entrée; beef noodle soup or *tāng miàn* (noodles in a clear soup with shallots, leafy greens, bean sprouts, and a little ground pork) are perennial favorites. But a conscientious host would never rely on soups to satisfy his or her guests. When Holo speakers feel something is lacking in substance, they may express their complaint through this idiom: *chit óaⁿ chhân lê, káu óaⁿ thng*—literally "one bowl of snails, nine bowls of soup."

3

❖ ❖

Iconic and Emerging Foodways

Han Taiwanese have traditionally categorized the foods they eat at mealtimes as either *fàn* or *cài*. The former, written with the character that can mean "meal" or "cooked rice," is not necessarily steamed white rice. In the past, the staple was often a porridge containing millet or sweet potato. The latter, represented by the logogram for vegetable, encompasses everything else that might appear on the dinner table: seasonal greens, eggs, meat, soups, fish and seafood, and the various cold side dishes known as *liángbàn*.

Until recently, *fàn* was the heart of each meal. This is why, when one Taiwanese asks another whether he has had lunch, the wording is literally "have you eaten rice yet?" In poorer households, the main function of *cài* (and soup) was to help the carbohydrates go down. Even now, a generous host might urge his or her guests to "eat more *cài*, eat less *fàn*."

Traditionally, each person started with their own bowl of rice and used their own chopsticks to dig into the non-staples (*cài*) placed in the center of the table. In recent years, more and more people have been replacing plain white rice with multigrain, or else skipping rice altogether. During the Qing and colonial eras, Taiwan enjoyed periods of sustained prosperity when the standard of living was much higher than on the Chinese mainland—as well as times when food was short, the most recent being the years preceding and following the end of World War II. Yet it remains true that, in the past four decades, ordinary folk have been able to enjoy a wider choice and quantity of *cài* than ever before. By the early 1990s, if not earlier, the average Taiwanese person was eating meat every day of the week.[1]

Where *cài* are being shared by friends or business associates rather than family, serving chopsticks called *gōng kuài* or a ladle are set out for each dish. The risk of transmitting infectious diseases is now widely understood, and using your own chopsticks to pick up slices of meat or chunks of fish is less accepted now than it was a generation ago.

Starting in the early 1980s, the authorities sought to reform food-handling practices in order to reduce the incidence of hepatitis. Roger Mark Selya, a University of Cincinnati geographer who did research in Taiwan, describes why change was needed: "Food servers rarely washed their hands during the course of a work day, and dishes were commonly washed in an open basin of cold, polluted water at the curbside without the use of any type of soap." However, he attributes the rapid improvements that occurred not to government policy but to consumer expectations. Better practices, he theorizes, "were adopted because during the mid-1980s Taiwan experienced an invasion of multinational fast-food chains such as McDonald's, and since these new establishments handled and served food in these ways, native restaurateurs and food sellers had to adapt in order to compete."[2]

The authorities instructed restaurants to use disposable tableware and asked citizens to bring their own chopsticks when eating out. The former policy was highly effective, but because so few people got into the habit of carrying a set of utensils, eateries found themselves giving out huge numbers of single-use bamboo chopsticks and flimsy plastic spoons. Government policy has since shifted 180 degrees; for environmental reasons, schools and other public facilities have been told not to use throwaway tableware.[3] Taiwan goes through an estimated five billion pairs of disposable chopsticks each year.[4] That number is expected to fall, as more and more eateries are providing reusable chopsticks and spoons for dine-in customers, and the carry-your-own cohort grows a little each time the media reports that disposable chopsticks have been found to contain toxic bleaching and mold-control substances.[5]

Office workers who bring lunch from home formerly used metal containers similar to Indian tiffin boxes; microwave-safe containers are now commonplace. Those who order takeouts are responsible for the production and disposal of millions of cardboard lunchboxes each week. Possibly the single most popular lunchbox meal is pork chop on rice (*páigǔ fàn*). The meat is marinated in a mix like that used to prepare *ròuzào* (see chapter 5), and then coated with cornstarch before frying in a skillet. More often than not, it is accompanied by three kinds of vegetable, one of which may be replaced by tofu or *dòugān* (dried tofu, described below). These are placed in individual compartments, so the juices from tomatoes cooked with egg or eggplant braised with garlic and basil do not soak into the rice.

Cooking *páigǔ fàn* is hardly prestigious, even when a restaurant is right to claim it as their *zhāopái cài* ("signpost dish," the Chinese equivalent of "chef's special" or "signature dish"). In recent years, the food industry has been guilty of overusing

三代福州意麵 老店

餛飩・福州魚丸・排骨

Families enjoy *yìmiàn* noodles at an eatery in Taichung, central Taiwan.
Rich J. Matheson

a couple of marketing terms. The first is *yǎngshēng*, often translated as "health-fulness" but closer to the Western concept of "wellness." More popular among educated city people than rural folk, it exists independently of the ancient healthy-eating notions that Han migrants brought with them from China.

The second is *gǔzǎo wèi*, "ancient, early taste," implying old-time authenticity. This should not be confused with *yuán wèi*, "original taste," an option presented by night-market vendors who think some customers may prefer no seasoning at all. *Gǔzǎo wèi* is an acknowledgment that few modern dining options are truly faithful to tradition. In many cases, it is also a claim that is hard to challenge, because so little was written about Taiwanese cuisine until recently. Recipes that were never recorded have been lost with the passing of a generation of old chefs. But some hope the flavors of the past can be revived. A March 4, 2011, article on the govern-ment's *Taiwan Today* news portal noted that "Taiwan's gastronomy is becoming ever more hybrid and sophisticated"; yet, at the same time, there are notable chefs eager to "take part in the renewal of old dishes, and the definition of a specifically Taiwanese cuisine." Robyn Eckhardt, who has covered the latter trend for the *New York Times*, brings an international perspective to the matter:

> As far as "fine" or "nicer" dining goes, Asian cities tend first to look to what Europe has, so menus are full of prosciutto, Italian basil, imported cheeses, and so on. Having lived or reported on food scenes in Hong Kong, Bangkok, and Shanghai over these years, I've seen that what is Western or foreign is considered "fancy" for a time, and what is local is not. At some point, most Asian cities seem to move beyond that, and chefs begin to take inspiration from what is around them—and, if possible, use local in-gredients. That's certainly been the case in Singapore, in Hong Kong, in Manila, and in Bangkok. And now Taipei has gotten past the foie gras, truffles and champagne phase.[6]

"LIVE BY THE SEA, EAT FROM THE SEA"

On both sides of the Taiwan Strait, people say "*kào shān chī shān, kào shuǐ chīs huǐ*"—that is, "Those who live in the mountains eat what they can find in the moun-tains; those who live by the sea eat [what they can gather] from the sea."

The gourmands of Taipei do not expect seafood to always come to them. They are willing to go to it, driving an hour or more to places like Fuji Harbor, tucked beside Taiwan's northernmost cape, or Zhuwei, a village close to Taiwan Taoyuan International Airport. The capital does not lack for seafood restaurants where fish and crustaceans are kept alive in display tanks until picked out by a customer. But just as many people believe they get fresher produce and better deals at traditional markets than supermarkets, there are plenty of folks who think eateries next to fish-ing harbors offer superior value compared to downtown establishments, and that the catch begins to deteriorate the moment it is taken from the ocean.

In front of a typical no-frills harborside restaurant, an array of plastic tubs linked by hoses contains the day's culinary prospects. Some customers specify in detail what they want; others place their trust in the staff. A degree of bargaining may be possible. Costs fluctuate from day to day and fish vary in size, so if there is a printed menu, prices are often expressed as a range. Skillful ordering can result in such delights as clams in brown garlic sauce with basil stems and leaves; pan-fried milkfish intestines (something that many Taiwanese refuse to eat, and so are often thrown away); grilled cuttlefish; king crab stir-fried with eggs and shallots; blue mackerel steaks in fish-head soup; sea-urchin steamed egg; and pan-fried sea bream.

Lobsters and crabs are special-occasion delicacies. Solo diners, those wanting comfort food, and people wanting a quick takeout meal often order seafood congee. The soft white rice comes with pieces of milkfish, a fish ball, a shrimp or two, a few clams, a couple chunks of squid, chopped vegetables—and non-oceanic ingredients like small strips of pork or pork liver.

Squid balls are white before cooking, whereas the typical fish ball is gray, then orange-gold if deep-fried, or off-white when appearing in a bowl of clear soup with a sprinkling of scallions and chopped celery. Unlike larger Fuzhou fish balls, which have a minced-pork core enveloped in fish paste, cross-sectioning a Taiwanese fish ball reveals no filling. Some fish balls are made from shark, others from mahi-mahi or swordfish.

A vendor cooks oyster omelets at Shilin Night Market, Taipei.
Craig Ferguson

Another everyday seafood dish is oyster omelet. This gooey delicacy, a mainstay of night markets in southwestern Taiwan, is usually known by its Holo-language name, *ô á choaⁿ*. Small oysters are cooked on a flat top, then covered with an egg batter that contains quite a bit of sweet-potato starch, plus bean sprouts and/or leafy greens (sometimes *Glebionis coronaria*, a.k.a. chop suey greens). Few vendors seem to care about the appearance of their omelets. Neither shape nor thickness matters, as long as the texture and flavor, slightly charred and enhanced by a sweet-ish ketchup-based sauce, is right. The sauce, called *hǎishān jiàng* ("sea mountain sauce"), sometimes incorporates miso paste.

THE HOT-POT CULT

Many types of congee, as well as crowd-pleasers like *guōshāo yìmiàn* (pot-cooked noodles with egg, pork, and clams), are reinforced with processed items that fall into the category *huǒguō liào* ("hot-pot ingredients"). Many of these contain crab, shrimp, or squid; others are taro or egg based. Proving the depth to which Western culinary influences have penetrated, some Taiwanese now add cheese-filled *huǒguō liào* to their hot pots.

The popularity of hot pot in Taipei can be attributed in part to the climate: in wintertime, it is unrelentingly damp and often colder than 50°F, so it is no wonder that the population embraces warming soups. Yet many hot-pot restaurants are busy year-round, because this is comfort food. Solo diners can get a fix at the hundreds of eateries that offer one-person pots. Preparing hot pot at home is a cinch because every supermarket sells *huǒguō liào*, pre-sliced meats, and a range of broth bases. Many households own a portable gas burner or hot plate so they can simmer food and eat at the same time.

Most hot-pot restaurants offer two basic options: a spicy broth or a milder soup usually made with chicken stock. The former is often Sichuan-style *málà* ("numbingly spicy hot"). At many establishments, customers can specify "mildly spicy," "medium spicy," or *zhòng là* ("heavy or seriously spicy"). There are also purely vegetarian soups, blends of medicinal herbs, and broths that draw on Japanese, Korean, and Thai culinary traditions.

Spicy-hot broths typically contain large cubes of tofu and pig-blood curd; these are eaten with relish by hot-pot aficionados. Segments of breakfast cruller dipped in a cauldron of *málà* soup are delicious but packed with calories. On December 17, 2014, *Taipei Times* passed on a warning from the authorities, reminding the public not to overindulge at all-you-can-eat hot-pot joints, as it is possible to consume three thousand calories in one sitting. Adding butter to give the stock an appealing fragrance bumps up the calorie count.

Nevertheless, hot-pot restaurants do appeal to some health-minded eaters. The diner is firmly in charge: If you like your cauliflower crunchy, you can have it that way, because you control exactly how long each item sits in the soup. You can fill up on lightly simmered asparagus, broccoli, cabbage, daikon, and mushrooms, eschewing carbohydrates. Some skip the dip altogether[7] or replace certain elements in the traditional mix of soy sauce, vinegar, garlic puree, and chopped shallots. Some add daikon puree, pomelo vinegar, or sesame sauce. Bullhead Barbecue Sauce, formerly a very popular hot-pot dip, has fallen out of favor as consumers try to reduce their salt and oil intake.

UNDERPINNING IT ALL: SOY

If soy sauce was the first soy product to reach Taiwan, miso was a close second. Kegs of this distinctive paste were arriving from Japan by 1654 at the latest,[8] but miso soup did not become commonplace until the Japanese era. Most of the soybeans Taiwanese farmers grew before the takeover were used to make oil for powering lamps. Of the small amount of soy planted for human consumption in recent years, most has become edamame, immature green soybeans boiled or steamed in the pod. Known in Taiwan as *máodòu* ("hairy beans," because soy pods have very fine hairs), they are usually enjoyed as a side dish.

Soy imports played a role in Taiwan's emergence as a food supplier of global importance (see chapter 5). Sugar production surged after plantation owners began applying Manchurian soybean cake (the residue once soybeans have been pressed for their oil) to their fields.[9] As late as 1935, it accounted for more than 40 percent of all commercial fertilizer used in Taiwan.[10] In the 1950s and 1960s, soybean cake was a protein-rich supplement for hogs, which were mainly fed sweet-potato leaves.[11]

Directly in the form of tofu, soy sauce, and soy milk—and indirectly in the form of meat from animals fed on soybean meal—Taiwanese now consume soy in far larger quantities than two generations ago. This change in diet was made possible by imports from the United States and Brazil and in part is the result of American influences. Not all of the latter were corporate or governmental: Some attribute the popularity of soy milk to Dr. Harry W. Miller, a surgeon-missionary from Ohio. Invited to Taiwan in 1953 to establish a hospital, he also set up what was the capital's only soy milk production line until the mid-1960s. By the 1980s, processed-food companies were selling millions of boxes of soy milk each year, in flavors including egg, peanut, and strawberry.[12]

At the same time as conscription was introducing beef to a generation of young men (see below), the standard military breakfast of hot, sweetened *dòujiàng* (soy milk) and *yóutiáo* (like an untwisted cruller, but never covered in icing or pow-dered sugar) was creating a habit that many carried back to civilian life.[13] In one sense, soy milk is like coffee. Even if the beans have traveled thousands of miles, the drink tastes much better if the blending, straining, and heating is done by an ex-perienced practitioner at the point of purchase. The difference is comparable to that between a latte crafted by a skilled barista and a can of Mr. Brown (see chapter 8).

Salty soy milk has a small but devoted following. Often served with a squirt of vinegar, a dollop of sesame oil, and a dash of red chili oil (these cause the soy milk to curdle and take on a consistency like that of cottage cheese), the mixture is usually topped with chopped scallions and dried shrimp. This delectable item—too dense and lumpy to properly call a beverage—can deliver a capsaicin jolt as good as any caffeine kick.

Tofu (the English word comes from the Mandarin, *dòufǔ*) appears in classy veg-etarian repasts as well as humble lunchboxes. Local versions of hot-and-sour soup feature as much (if not more) tofu as pork. The Taiwanese who like *chòu dòufu* ("stinky tofu") also love to acquaint their Western friends with this delicacy. In its quintessential form—deep-fried cubes served with a chili sauce and some crunchy pickled cabbage—it is one of the most frequently eaten *xiǎochī* ("little eats," or street snacks). Shenkeng, on the southeastern outskirts of Taipei, is Taiwan's stinky-tofu capital; here, one can enjoy the odoriferous soy food in all its multifari-ous glory. The entire *chòu dòufu* production procedure takes less than half a day, from making the tofu very early in the morning to soaking, frying, and serving. Soaking in fermented vegetable brine takes no more than three hours. (Fermenting the brine can take up to six months.) Certain types of stinky tofu are so fetid that first-timers have been known to flee for fear of retching.

Very soft tofu, sometimes called bean-curd pudding (*dòuhuā*), is a dessert tra-ditionally enjoyed with cooked soft peanuts and brown-sugar syrup. In recent de-cades, the range of flavors has grown to include tapioca balls, adzuki beans, mung beans, honeyed yam, pumpkin paste, and wolfberry agar jelly. Unlike in China, in Taiwan *dòuhuā* is almost never served salty. A few people buy plain pudding from the *dòuhuā* trucks that circulate through residential neighborhoods, to which they add homemade flavorings such as ginger and brown-sugar syrup.

Dried or firm tofu (*dòugān*) is especially associated with Daxi, an hour outside Taipei. Thanks to the softness of the well water in this historic town, tofu made here is a signature "egg-white" shade of white[14] and exceptionally good.

Two of Daxi's most esteemed *dòugān* makers are run by descendants of Ma-dame Huang Chiu Lu and use methods she introduced nearly a century ago. Huang learned that adding star anise and cumin to tofu before pressing and drying it into *dòugān* reduces the beany odor. She also invented *wūdòugān* ("black bean curd") by boiling tofu in a brown-sugar syrup for forty minutes. At least one Daxi *dòugān*

Bean-curd pudding (*dòuhuā*) with adzuki beans and a sweet sauce.
Rich J. Matheson

maker now buys Canadian soybeans, saying they are the most similar to the beans from Dalian in northeast China their ancestors used during the Japanese colonial era. The packets of dried tofu sold in supermarkets are fine for nibbling during long train journeys. But as you might expect, freshly braised artisanal *dòugān* served hot with a sprinkling of raw scallions is a gustatory pleasure in a different league altogether.

Dark squares of *dòugān* are a key part of what Taiwanese call *lǔwèi* ("briny taste"), comestibles sometimes eaten with noodles, but often bought from a roadside vendor and taken home as a late-night snack. At many hole-in-the-wall eateries, the choice is limited to pre-braised dried tofu and hard-boiled chickens' eggs, circular fish cakes (*o'lûn* in Holo, derived from the Japanese food term *oden*), seaweed, and *zhūxiěgāo*. The last, often directly translated as "pig-blood cake," is a rectangular black pudding bulked up with glutinous rice. Where the vendor has more space or expects more customers, he is likely to offer uncooked cabbage and lettuce, mushrooms, half cobs of sweet corn, quails' eggs, ducks' heads marinated in soy sauce and medicinal herbs, and offal such as slivers of cow's stomach. Some say *lǔwèi* is a kind of appetizer, because diners often tuck in before their entrées arrive.

Ordering is simply a matter of using tongs to place the things one wishes to eat in a plastic colander, then waiting for them to be chopped and briefly re-braised. The broth is a blend of stock, soy sauce, and aromatic spices. The precise recipe varies from place to place but typically comprises black cardamom, cloves, fennel, sand ginger, Sichuan peppercorns, and star anise.

LIKE THEY NEVER LEFT: JAPANESE FOOD IN TAIPEI

"Taiwan has the best Japanese food in the world outside Japan, but except for those restaurants operated by Japanese brands, a lot of 'Japanese-style' food isn't very authentic," says Mikiko Ishii, a native of Japan's Aichi Prefecture who has lived in Taipei since marrying a Taiwanese man in 2011.[15]

Taiwan's status as an exceptional overseas outpost of Japanese cuisine is not simply a consequence of history and proximity. Few societies show as much genuine warmth for Japan or as much enthusiasm for Japanese culture and fashions. Japanese restaurants are prominent among Taipei's most expensive eating places.[16] At the same time, as Taiwan-born anthropologist David Y. H. Wu points out, Japanese cuisine can be found in far humbler surroundings.[17] Factory-made sushi and instant miso soups can be found in every 7-Eleven convenience store. In most night markets, there is someone selling sushi they prepared at home and temaki (*shǒu juàn*, "hand roll" in Mandarin) they assemble on the spot. Most bowls of shredded turkey on rice, and many of braised pork, are topped by a slice of *takuan*, yellow Japanese-style preserved daikon.

"Since 2014, I've been amazed how many Japanese restaurants have opened branches in Taiwan. Some of them have just two branches in the world—one in Japan, the other here—so there are famous Japanese restaurants I can visit in Taipei, but not in Nagoya. I think this shows just how much Taiwanese people adore Japanese food," says Ishii, agreeing that Kokuraya (see chapter 7) is a good example of this trend.

Soon after Taiwan became a Japanese possession, Japanese commentators were remarking on how Taiwanese banquets were quite different from Japanese celebrations. Taipei-based food scholar Yujen Chen quotes a Japanese writer as noting that, compared to the colonizers, the Taiwanese focused on eating instead of drinking and preferred chatting to appreciating dance and song performances. Then as now, Japanese meals were delivered to individual diners on trays, instead of dishes being shared by everyone present. He also thought it worth mentioning that very few Taiwanese dishes featured uncooked items and, overall, they exhibited stronger flavors.[18]

Ishii, a part-time teacher of Japanese cooking and a food-and-travel blogger, has noticed some similarities between Taiwanese cuisine and Okinawa's food culture. "In both places, people like to eat sponge cucumbers, bitter gourds, pig's feet, pig's ears, and some other things that people in Honshu seldom eat," she says. However, she says that for Japanese, Taiwanese flavors seem quite sweet. She thinks the way in which ramen is enjoyed in Taipei shows a crucial difference between Taiwanese and Japanese taste buds: "Taiwanese people really love the noodles, but many of them don't like the salty soup, which is central to the taste of Japanese ramen." A number of Taipei's Japanese-brand ramen establishments provide hot water for the convenience of customers who wish to soften the umami flavor. "That's something I've never seen in Japan!" Ishii remarks.

Another Japanese citizen residing in Taiwan agrees with Ishii. "Taiwanese food tends to be sweeter than Japanese. It's probably because the soy sauce is sweeter. The soy sauce used in cooking and for sushi dipping is definitely sweeter here than in Japan. Taiwanese miso is also sweeter," says Yukiko Sato, who grew up in Kawasaki, Kanagawa Prefecture.[19]

Sato thinks there is a lot of mayonnaise in Japanese food in Taiwan, and that, when making sushi, Taiwanese use some types of fish that are uncommon in Japan. During the twelve years she has lived in Taiwan, the quality of the Japanese food available in Taipei has improved. "When I first arrived, I noticed the difference straight away. But now the quality is better, and sometimes just like eating in Japan. Also, there's a greater variety of sushi and noodles," she says.

Sato used to miss *yakiniku*, Japanese-style Korean barbecue. "Most of the Korean barbecue restaurants in Taiwan back then served a very limited choice of meats, all marinated in one kind of sauce that was much sweeter than the sauces in Japan," she says. "But now there are a lot of Japanese *yakiniku* restaurants in Taipei, as well as Korean ones, so I don't miss it anymore." Finding Japanese ingredients in Taipei's supermarkets has also become much easier, so Sato has no need to buy them online.

A far greater proportion of Taiwan's population eats Japanese food now than at any time during the colonial era. The rural diets of most Taiwanese during the colonial period "had little to do with either the Japanese or Taiwanese high cuisines," says Wu. Because of this, Japanese cuisine had snob appeal, and it helped "to create a class distinction among Taiwanese people on the basis on one's social, economic and educational standing. Those Taiwanese who were knowledgeable about and could afford to consume Japanese food would gain enormous cultural capital."[20]

Postwar politics helped Japanese foodways survive, despite the removal of almost all of the island's Japanese residents very soon after Tokyo turned the island over to Chiang Kai-shek's Nationalist Republic of China on October 25, 1945. Following its retreat to Taipei, the KMT government's attitude to Japan was ambivalent. The recent Japanese invasion of China could not be forgotten; yet trade with and investment from Japan was crucial to the regime's survival. For several years, the showing of Japanese movies and the broadcasting of Japanese music were banned altogether. However, nothing stopped restaurants from serving Japanese food to the many Taiwanese who had been educated under the colonial regime, so these became some of the few places where what Wu calls the "demonstration of nostalgia for cultural Japan" was possible.[21] Even meal-boxes were "a clear ethnic marker" during Wu's childhood:

When I was in elementary school and traveled by train from Taichung to Taipei (in the late 1940s and early 1950s), the most anticipated and rewarding part of the trip was to get to eat a Japanese bento at Hsinchu or Zhunan station, most famous at that time for their delicious bento. . . . Bento and cash were exchanged through the train windows. All the bento sold at the stations from north to south were almost standardized in a thin, rectangular wooden box containing half of a hard-boiled *shoyu* egg (Japanese-style), shredded red-colored cuttlefish or braised hard tofu cake [*dòugān*], and *takuan* [pickled daikon], served on a thin layer of rice. The bento box was thin and small (in contrast to the later mainland Chinese-style metal box), made of paper-thin wood slices. . . . Several mainlander friends of my generation who lived in northern Taiwan had never heard of such Japanese-style bento, although they too had traveled on trains.[22]

Taiwanese students ate their bento cold, in the Japanese manner, but schools dominated by *wàishĕngrén* "were obliged to collect student *biàndāng* in the morning, send them to the school kitchen, and steam them in huge steamers so that the students could enjoy a hot meal at lunchtime." In an era when relations between those who arrived in 1949 (some of whom looked down on Hoklo Taiwanese as bumpkins) and those whose families had been on the island for generations were not always amicable, food was sometimes a bridge between communities. "As the two groups of students carried lunchboxes containing different ethnic dishes, they often exchanged food items to satisfy their curiosities," Wu recalls.[23]

That said, Ishii's experiences in Taipei suggest that the mainland preference for hot lunches has rubbed off on a good part of the capital's population. Explaining that Japanese normally eat cold bento because they take them to their offices from home at the start of working day, she says, "Taiwanese people seem to hate cooled-down food. If their lunchbox is cold, they need to make it hot in a microwave or a *diàn guō*."

Taipei's Japanese culinary renaissance is not entirely driven by consumer demand. According to Yukiko Sato's husband, restaurateur Sean A. Hsu, a lot of individuals have opened eating establishments in the past few years, and a number of companies with no background in food have diversified into the industry. This has made the restaurant scene very competitive, he says. "You have to constantly make your food better and better, or your customers will outgrow you. Their palates become more refined. For Chinese and Taiwanese food, customers have a lot of experience. They want good food, but it's very hard to charge higher prices. The more unfamiliar the culture, the more you can charge, but there's less chance of repeat custom," Hsu explains. "Japanese cuisine, however, is in a very sweet spot. Taiwanese know Japanese food but they're willing to pay high prices for it. Also, the food costs aren't that high because there's an emphasis on original flavors. Because of these various factors, Japanese restaurants are doing quite well."[24]

A vendor in Taipei's Raohe Night Market specializing in temaki, Japanese hand-rolled seaweed wraps. *Craig Ferguson*

An exception to this rule is the way shabu-shabu is presented in Taiwan. Mikiko Ishii points out that in Japan, shabu-shabu is seen as an up-market eating option, but in Taipei what is advertised as shabu-shabu is sometimes available for less than US$5 per person. "Japanese normally use good-quality beef, but in Taiwan you can add anything you like, including tomatoes, corn, and fish balls," she says. In Taiwanese shabu-shabu restaurants, she points out, each person has a personal simmering pot, but in Japan everyone at the table shares a single pot.

Most of the curries served in Taiwan are neither Indian nor Thai (despite the substantial Thai population) but instead relatively insipid Japanese-style renditions. Curry rice—a dish that these days typically includes cubes of potato and carrot, as well as diced meat—was being served at Taipei restaurants and school canteens as early as 1909. Ahead of World War II, curry powder was a common seasoning, with Japanese brands advertising in local newspapers.[25]

In recent times, curry rice has become a comfort food that appeals to all age groups; its charm does not seem to wane. Hsu makes this dish at home, and his version is perhaps more sophisticated than that followed by many people. He replaces the potato with daikon, because the latter has a lighter and more refreshing texture. Other ingredients are onion (sautéed, then caramelized with clear honey) and a slice of bacon; these are cooked in a pot with the pork (already sautéed until brown and deglazed with white wine), water, tomato juice, the root and leaf sections of a celery, and a pair of bay leaves. Later, a carrot and half a daikon (both cut into cubes) are added, along with garlic and another onion. Ahead of the final simmering session, Japanese curry roux blocks, ginger purée, light soy sauce, and butter are thrown in the pot, along with sprinklings of instant coffee and black pepper.

One key difference between Taiwan and Japan can be seen in how those who work in restaurants are perceived. "Japan has a culture of apprenticeship and craftsmanship, so F&B professionals get more respect there than they do in Taiwan," says Hsu. Nevertheless, the links between Taiwan and Japanese food culture—Taiwanese have a foot in both kitchens, so to speak—are so strong that Taiwanese entrepreneurs have introduced several Japanese food chains to the mainland Chinese market. Taipei-based An-Shin Food Services Co. Ltd., for instance, manages MOS Burger restaurants in both Taiwan and China.

MODERN PLANT-BASED DIETS: NO LONGER TIED TO THE MOON

One facet of Taiwan's food culture that shows no obvious Japanese influence is vegetarianism. Between 12 and 16 percent of Taiwanese never eat meat, a rate two to three times that in Japan. Accurately estimating how many citizens are vegetarian is not easy, as some tallies include those who, under the influence of Buddhism, forsake meat on certain days each month. Most of these people are vegetarian on the first and fifteenth day of each lunar month; others purposely take no meat for six or ten days per month. Religious traditions prescribe temporary vegetarianism on certain occasions, such as after the death of a relative. Also, those who consult spirit mediums over personal matters are sometimes instructed by a deity to follow a meat-free regime for a certain period.

Few people below the age of fifty are part-time vegetarians of the traditional sort, even though Buddhism is thriving in twenty-first-century Taiwan. According to Vincent Goossaert and David A. Palmer, "The spectacular rise of vegetarianism among the Taiwanese middle classes since the 1970s can be linked to the rising profile of Buddhism as a self-assumed identity among the same classes. . . . Vegetarianism's closer identification with Buddhism raised the social prestige of vegetarian practice as a type of modern, socially engaged morality."[26]

Younger people who embrace the religion are likely to become 100 percent meat free, although "flexitarian" compromises are common. Young Buddhists may eat what they are given when visiting their meat-eating parents; the Chinese term for this kind is *fāngbiàn sù* ("vegetarian when it's convenient"). There are also some who practice *guō biān sù*, meaning that they will eat vegetables and soyfoods cooked in a non-vegetarian sauce but push any meat to "one side of the pot." The Ministry of Education has been encouraging schools to go vegetarian for one day each week since early 2010. By late 2012, more than twenty-three hundred educational institutions were regularly meatless.[27]

Traditional vegetarianism in Taiwan involves not just eschewing meat and seafood but also what are called the "five pungent vegetables." While eggs and dairy products are acceptable, chives, garlic, leeks, onions, and shallots should be avoided because they are said to cause irritability and sexual impulses. On top of this, they weaken the ability to concentrate, which is key to achieving the understanding and mental development Buddhists aspire to. (For similar reasons, many Buddhists do not consume alcohol or other intoxicants.) Some provide secondary justifications: these vegetables may hurt your stomach if you do not eat meat, and if you consume garlic or onions, you will give off a smell that distracts others engaged in ascetic training.

The growing visibility of vegetarianism from the 1970s on is not due to Buddhism alone. Until the 1970s, more than 90 percent of Taiwan's vegetarian eateries were run by adherents of I-Kuan Tao, the country's third-most-popular faith, but—according to Goossaert and Palmer—"they were almost always small, cheap, inconspicuous places." By the twenty-first century, many such restaurants were larger and more up-market. At the same time, "explicitly Buddhist ventures were becoming more visible . . . [and] the social cost of being a permanent vegetarian had considerably decreased since the 1970s."[28]

The fact that plant-based diets inspired by religion are well established in Taiwanese society is, as vegan restaurateur Mai Bach says, "a double-edged sword. Relatively few people are internally motivated to give up meat; they're simply following the rules of their religion. But overall, I think it makes promoting veganism easier. We have quite a few Taiwanese Buddhist customers who come by simply because they want something different from standard local vegetarian fare."[29]

Horrified by what she had learned about modern farming methods, Bach embraced vegetarianism in 2010, two years after relocating to Taipei from California. Yet, when discussing with Taiwanese people the vegan principles she now follows, Bach does not emphasize animal welfare. Instead, she explains that a vegan diet is the best option for both the humans who follow it and the planet they live on.

According to Bach, a lot of Taiwanese learn about veganism through the internet. Serena Yiin's images of vegan delicacies won her more than twelve thousand followers on Instagram (@serene_eats) before her eighteenth birthday.[30] "Thanks to social media, there's something of a convergence between Taiwan and the West in terms of young people's culture and beliefs. That said, we meet people of all different ages adopting this lifestyle," says Bach. Being vegan in Taiwan is not easier than in the United States, but, she adds, "it's certainly different.

In the US, a huge range of prepackaged vegan foods is available. On the other hand, people in Taiwan are less likely to judge you if your eating habits are non-mainstream."

Taipei was named Asia's most vegan-friendly city by PETA Asia, an affiliate of PETA US, in December 2016. Bach says the capital now has "between ten and twenty" vegan eateries, including Ooh Cha Cha, which she founded in November 2013. Describing itself as a "plant-based cafe," Ooh Cha Cha has brought the owners a raft of compliments—but little in the way of riches. "We want vegan food to be accessible in terms of price, so margins are low," Bach says. "We want to show a vegan diet is affordable as well as delicious. But we have to educate our customers that this kind of food is labor intensive, and how much preparation time is needed. We make everything from scratch, except bread. But a lot of people struggle to understand this, because they never cook."

According to Bach, around 15 percent of the produce used in Ooh Cha Cha is certified organic, while a further 50 percent is pesticide free. Much of the latter is sourced from one farmer in Tamsui. A lot of organically grown greens look moth-eaten when placed beside conventionally farmed vegetables, but Bach never rejects vegetables because of their appearance: "A lot of what we use is turned into smoothies, so this isn't an issue."

About half of the 150 or so different ingredients the restaurant uses are imported. When sourcing nuts from the United States, Bach faces a singular obstacle: the US FDA requires all nuts sold in the United States to be pasteurized, but she prefers unpasteurized cashews and almonds. "Cashews can be used to make great substitutes for milk, cream, and dairy-based sauces. We don't use any peanuts because allergies are common." Two food-supply issues are sources of frustration for Bach and her team. "I'd like to use hemp seeds, because they're tasty and full of protein, but they're 100 percent illegal in Taiwan.[31] Brazil nuts are, for some reason, prohibitively expensive."

Ooh Cha Cha serves burgers, including one with "bacon" made from eggplant. Meat-free burgers are acceptable to most American vegetarians; yet some of the items that appear in thoroughly local meat-free eateries dismay Western diners. Tour guide Muchin Lee, who has been sharing her passion for food and travel with Taiwanese and overseas travelers for more than ten years, says that a number of the Western visitors she has shown around Taiwan react with consternation to the "mock meats" that often appear in vegetarian feasts.[32] These items—made of mushrooms, soy, or wheat gluten—are shaped and textured so that they resemble pork ribs or kung pao chicken.

Some North American and European vegans, especially those motivated by a concern for animal welfare, find fake meats gross and morally disturbing.[33] People raised in Western Christian-based cultures are perhaps more concerned with orthodoxy than orthopraxy. For Taiwanese, by contrast, if your religion requires vegetarianism, forsaking meat is good enough. Tucking into something made to look and taste like a steak does not invalidate your piety.

BEEF WINS A PLACE ON TAIWANESE TABLES

The popularity in recent decades of beef is striking because, just a few generations ago, the consumption of bovine meat was anathema to Taiwanese of Han descent. This taboo has its roots in ancient China, where laws prohibited ordinary people from killing cattle.[34] In Pearl Buck's 1931 novel *The Good Earth*, the central character shows extreme reluctance to slaughter his ox for food, even when his family is starving. When asked why their parents and grandparents do not eat beef, many Taiwanese explain it in this way: Those who grew up on farms regard water buffalo and oxen not as dumb beasts of burden but as loyal coworkers on the land. Without oxen, pioneering farmers would have struggled to convert Taiwan's plains into rice paddies. A traditionally minded Taiwanese farmer is no more likely to feast on a bovine than his British counterpart is to eat his sheepdog.

Literature and folk songs from the eighteenth and nineteenth centuries celebrate cattle that are admirably loyal to their masters, even saving their lives by warning of impending earthquakes or other disasters. Eating an animal after it has labored in your service would be to invite karmic retribution; in stories where an ox is butchered for food, the farmer often suffers nightmares in which the animal takes revenge on him.[35] Cattle are regarded as intelligent; yet, if Taiwanese folk tales are to be believed, eating beef may turn you into a simpleton.[36]

By the second half of the nineteenth century, observance of this taboo was less than universal, the authorities dealing with several cases where cattle were rustled and slaughtered so the meat could be sold.[37] But it was not until after Japan's takeover in 1895 that mainstream attitudes began to change, even though the Japanese themselves did not have strong beef-eating traditions. Enforcing Buddhist and Shinto food restrictions, Japan's rulers issued a series of prohibitions against the consumption of various meats between 675 CE and 1687. Those who ate horse or beef were considered especially unclean. But dietary habits were among the Western influences that poured into Japan during the Meiji Period (1866–1912). After the emperor himself was seen eating meat in 1872, the old precepts were gradually forgotten.[38]

During the Qing era, bovids were bred for physical strength, not edibility. The Japanese authorities introduced foreign cattle suitable for meat production,[39] and established a network of hygienic slaughterhouses.[40] During the second half of the colonial era, some Taiwanese beef was canned for export. Colonization led to an influx of Japanese civil servants, military personnel, and entrepreneurs. But Japanese immigrants and expatriates were not the only people eating bovine meat; the level of beef production suggests a good number of Han residents had overcome their aversion by the 1930s, in part because rapid urbanization meant a greater proportion of the population no longer lived in close proximity to cattle.[41] After retreating to Taiwan, Chiang Kai-shek's regime instituted a system of conscription that is now being gradually abolished. For a couple of generations, every healthy male served two years in the armed forces and had to eat what he was given. Sometimes this included beef, so many men from families that did not eat bovine meat became familiar with it.[42]

Angus, Brahman, Hereford, and other strains were introduced following World War II.[43] However, customers ordering beef in cheaper eateries were likely to be served the darker meat of a buffalo,[44] as the number of cattle being slaughtered did not exceed that of water buffalo until 1976.[45] The habit was encouraged by senior officials like Hsieh Tung-min (Taiwan provincial governor from 1972 to 1978, then vice president), who called on people to eat more beef and drink plenty of milk for nutritional reasons.[46]

In 1960, annual per capita beef consumption was just 0.67 pounds, and domestic beef met more than 90 percent of Taiwan's needs. By 1988, when average intake had reached 4.4 pounds, most of the meat came from Australia and New Zealand.[47] Between 2003 and 2012, exports of US beef to Taiwan were stymied, first by BSE and then by disputes over US farmers' use of ractopamine, a feed additive.[48] In 2015, consumption was 13.45 pounds—not much higher than that for China. Sun Yin-rui is right to say that "the full acceptance of beef is an important milestone" in local culinary history;[49] yet the shift that has occurred on the other side of the Taiwan Strait suggests that even if the Japanese had never colonized Taiwan, globalization would have led to the islanders eating beef sooner or later.

At present, a vestigial aversion to bovine meat influences perhaps one in ten non-vegetarian Taiwanese, so the suburban steakhouses that attract extended-family gatherings typically offer a few pork and chicken alternatives. Steakhouses (or pizzerias) are also where many Taiwanese, especially those over forty, had their first taste of what Americans would recognize as salad: iceberg lettuce, sweet corn, shredded carrot, red cabbage, cherry tomatoes, and other items picked from a salad bar, typically slathered in Thousand Island dressing. Because older generations were rightly worried about parasitic contamination, until the 1980s "everything green was cooked, except wasabi," quips one long-term American resident of Taipei who was unable to dissuade his Taiwanese mother-in-law from frying the lettuce he had brought home.

Many steak restaurants offer sweet-corn egg-drop soup as an appetizer or as an all-you-can-eat feature of the salad bar. It is also sold in thousands of breakfast shops. Like many other modern eating habits, it would never have become so established were it not for imports from the United States. In 1992, to encourage Taiwanese people to make corn soup at home, Green Giant offered substantial cash prizes for the best recipes.[50]

Steaks are common, as are burgers,[51] but beef noodle soup is ubiquitous. The popularity of beef noodles in Taiwan is often attributed to the arrival of the defeated Chinese Nationalist Army. "Many of these soldiers were from north China. . . . After leaving the army, they had to support themselves. Because they had no other skills, they made noodles, and soon dominated the stalls selling beef noodles and dumplings. Many were Muslims who brought their beef-eating heritage to Taiwan," writes Sun Yin-rui.[52] According to Sun, in the early days, different parts of the city were associated with particular flavors. Certain streets near Taipei Main Station were dominated by families originally from Shandong, so beef noodles sold hereabouts tended to come in a semi-clear *qīngdùn* stew (a simple broth flavored with nothing but salt, soy sauce, and perhaps a little rice wine). Gastrophiles looking for Sichuan-style beef noodles headed to Yongkang Street or Taoyuan Street, between the Presidential Office and Ximending.[53]

These eateries also attracted plenty of citizens who felt they had little in common with either the refugees or the regime that had brought them to Taiwan. Among them was a young H. M. Cheng. "Most of those selling beef noodles were veterans, and they tended to congregate with people from the same province. Often they couldn't afford to rent a place, so in the evenings they took over sidewalks in front of residential buildings," recalls Cheng.[54] He has especially fond memories of China Mall near Ximending, which, between 1961 and its demolition in 1992, hosted dozens of mainlander restaurants: "We went there, not only for beef noodles, but also for *wàishěng cài* [mainland Chinese] flavors we couldn't get at home."

Some of the meat consumed in these places was American and arrived on the island in cans intended for US military mess halls.[55] Another American contribution came in the form of donated and subsidized flour. As beef noodle soup was emerging in Taiwan, American flour was helping establish ramen as a popular dish in Japan (which, like Taiwan, saw an influx of people from wheat-growing, noodle-making parts of northern China after World War II).[56]

There are some, however, who believe beef noodle soup as it is usually enjoyed in Taipei first emerged in Gangshan, two hundred miles south of Taiwan's capital. Military families, living there after relocating from China in the late 1940s, are thought to have created Taiwanese beef noodles by adding locally made hot soybean paste to a Sichuanese beef dish.[57] Soybeans had long been one of the area's principal crops, but fermenting them into a spicy condiment only began in the 1950s. (See chapter 10 for a beef soup recipe that uses soybean paste.)

One of the first entrepreneurs to make and sell the paste was Liu Ming-teh. Kicked out of the air force because he was propagating the then-proscribed religion of I-Kuan Tao, he initially sold small dabs of sauce wrapped in lotus leaves. The company he founded went on to win an island-wide reputation and is still going strong under his grandson's leadership.[58] By helping to mask the flesh's unpleasant odor, soybean paste also helped goat meat—often served in hot pots or as a soup with angelica root—emerge as a Gangshan specialty.[59]

The appetite for beef has not been matched by any great thirst for milk. "No butter, milk or cheese is made in north Formosa," grumbled George L. Mackay just before the Japanese takeover.[60] Unlike some of his fellow missionaries in the south, he had no dairy cows of his own. In 1896 the Japanese began establishing dairy farms to supply milk to their soldiers, especially those who had been wounded. During the colonial era, few Taiwanese other than hospital patients were able to drink fresh cow's milk, but canned condensed milk found a market because of its convenience, perceived nutritional value, and rich taste. Early imports came from the United States, but by the 1920s a number of Japanese brands were well established.[61] Among them was Morinaga & Co. Ltd., best known for a milk caramel candy sold in distinctive yellow boxes since 1913.

Fresh milk is available everywhere; yet annual per capita consumption of dairy products is a mere forty-six pounds.[62] More than nine-tenths of the fluid milk drunk in Taiwan comes from local Holstein herds, kept out of the sun and rain in barns, and cooled by enormous electric fans. There is no meaningful domestic production of milk powder, butter, or cheese. Despite the urgings of public health organizations, which foresee an osteoporosis epidemic as the population ages, it appears milk and cheese consumption has, if anything, fallen.[63] Many adults drink milk only when having a coffee, and they eat cheese only if it appears atop a pizza or a gratin dish. The number of Taiwanese who cite lactose intolerance as a reason for not drinking milk is surprisingly low,[64] and fewer than one in five respondents to the same government-sponsored survey claimed to dislike milk. A third said consuming dairy was not among their habits. Very few complained that milk is too expensive.

The intake of goat's milk is also low,[65] but Taiwan is one of a handful of countries (Malaysia and Singapore are others) where you can have fresh, pasteurized goat's milk—hot, lukewarm, or chilled, as per your instructions—delivered to your home six mornings per week. Taiwan's torrid lowlands are unsuitable for sheep, which were introduced to the island in the late 1960s. One of the few places they are raised is Qingjing Farm, more than a mile above sea level in the Central Mountain Range. The farm was established by Chinese Nationalist soldiers and their families who were relocated there from Burma and ordered to be self-sufficient.

TABOOS OLD AND NEW

As recently as the 1890s, there were instances of cannibalism not driven by simple hunger. James W. Davidson, a journalist who became the first US consul in Taiwan, was appalled by "the sale by the Chinese in open market of savage flesh." He attributed Han enthusiasm for this kind of food to a conviction that eating an aborigine's body conferred "strength and courage."[66] George L. Mackay witnessed the execution of an aboriginal headhunter: "Scores were there on purpose to get parts of the body for food and medicine. . . . The heart is eaten, flesh taken off in strips, and bones boiled to a jelly and preserved as a specific for malarial fever."[67]

Taiwan was not the only part of the Qing Empire where such ideas existed. Lu Xun's 1919 short story *Medicine* concerns the traditional belief that a steamed bun soaked in the blood of an executed criminal could cure tuberculosis. In the second half of the nineteenth century, Taiwan's indigenous people may not have feasted on the flesh of their enemies, but after making inquiries during his visits to aboriginal settlements, William A. Pickering concluded that some headhunters were indeed cannibals, "to the extent that they mix the brains of their enemies with wine and drink the disgusting mixture."[68]

Some Taiwanese cannot bring themselves to eat sashimi, and a surprising number say they despise the smell of carrots. The island has never had a significant horse population, so the rights and wrongs of consuming horse meat have not been an issue. More than a few city folk are repulsed by the idea of eating rabbit, but the only meats that are truly anathema are dog and cat.

Prehistoric Taiwanese regularly ate dogs (see chapter 1), but in recent centuries canine meat has never been a mainstream food, even though many of the refugees who followed Chiang Kai-shek to Taiwan came from dog-eating provinces. In 2001, Taiwan's parliament outlawed the sale of canine and feline meat. In 2017, the prohibition was extended to include consumption.[69]

The idea of eating dogs or cats horrifies almost every Taiwanese now alive. But that was not always the case, says H. M. Cheng, recalling the one and only time his uncle ate dog meat: "While in high school in the 1950s, he and a friend noticed a small shop advertising *xiāng ròu* ['fragrant meat,' a euphemism for cooked dog]. Overcome by curiosity, they ordered and consumed a plateful only to find out later it was actually dog meat. That was a Cantonese dish, previously unheard of in Taiwan. My uncle remains the only dog-eater in the family, and that was the only time—not because my uncle would not have tried it again, but because *xiāng ròu* disappeared from menus. There was a lack of supply, and when family pets started to go missing, the authorities cracked down."[70]

Shark's fin soup may yet join dog and cat meat on the list of proscribed foods. Homegrown organizations like the Environment & Animal Society of Taiwan (EAST) have for years been highlighting the carnage caused by finning and promoting alternatives. Yet their message has yet to sink in fully: the chief of Taiwan's Environmental Protection Administration was forced to apologize after he was seen consuming shark's fin at a luncheon, *China Post* informed its readers on April 10, 2017.

A HEADLINE ABROAD; A FOOTNOTE AT HOME

If any Taiwanese delicacy has caught the imagination of Western foodies in the past decade, it is the guabao (see recipe in chapter 10), iterations of which are now sold on both sides of the Atlantic. One of the better known guabao eateries in the United States is BaoHaus in New York City, founded by Eddie and Evan Huang; Eddie wrote the memoir on which the ABC comedy series *Fresh Off the Boat* is based, and he hosts the Viceland TV show *Huang's World*.

The oldest surviving restaurant menu to mention what some now call "the Taiwanese hamburger" dates from 1939,[71] and in its original form, the guabao is a slab of pork belly the size of a deck of playing cards served inside a wrap of shiny white steamed bread. Because the meat is heavily marbled with fat, several hours' braising in a thick gravy (water, soy sauce, rice wine, sugar, star anise, and perhaps some cinnamon) turns it neither dry nor fibrous, but rather melt-in-the-mouth tender. The pork is enhanced with fresh cilantro, pickled mustard greens, and a dusting of crushed peanut, ingredients that elevate the guabao over its Fujianese equivalent, the *khong bah pau* (pork and celtuce in a bun).

The way in which the bun envelops the pork has inspired a unique-to-Taiwan nickname: *hŭ yǎo zhū* (*hó kā ti* in Holo, "tiger bites pig"). Because many think they resemble purses overflowing with money, guabao are sometimes served during *wěiyá* banquets (see chapter 4), when Taiwanese bosses treat their employees close to the end of the lunar year. But these hearty delights are not eaten as often in Taiwan as their growing popularity overseas might lead one to believe; they are available in every town and city, for sure, but certainly not on every busy street, nor even in many night markets.[72]

A few outlets, including Taipei's Stone Master chain, offer nontraditional variants featuring crab salad and whole-wheat buns, but they scarcely charge more than street vendors. Gourmet hamburgers are an established part of Taipei's dining scene, but it seems that so far no entrepreneur has been able to persuade the Taiwanese public to spend US$8 on a deluxe guabao when the original can be had for less than US$2.

PREMIUM *XIAOLONGBAO*, FAST-FOOD POT STICKERS

There can be no doubt which restaurant in Taiwan has the highest international profile. Following two decades with a single location, on Taipei's Xinyi Road, just around the corner from the foodie hub of Yongkang Street, Din Tai Fung grew rapidly after 1996 into a chain with more than one hundred branches in East and Southeast Asia, Australia, and the United States. According to the company's Hong Kong website, a single Michelin star has been awarded to two of its Hong Kong outlets and a branch in Macau.

Din Tai Fung's US website attributes its impressive, if belated, expansion to being named "one of the top ten gourmet restaurants in the world" by the *New York Times*. This claim, since repeated by many media outlets—and still on the company's website as of December 7, 2017—is not quite accurate. On January 17, 1993, the newspaper published a set of reviews by ten food experts of "restaurants that inspire a pilgrimage." One of these was Ken Hom's tribute to Din Tai Fung. It has been pointed out that "nowhere did the newspaper claim that these eating establishments represented the best around the globe," and that none of the ten restaurants reported on were located in such "world-class centers of gastronomic mastery as Paris, London, or New York."[73]

Nevertheless, when a government-sponsored DVD describes Din Tai Fung's steamed broth dumplings (*xiǎolóng tāngbāo*) as "the most internationally renowned dish" on the island (*Savor the Flavors of Taiwan*, released by the Government Information Office in 2011), it is hard to dispute the claim. Few deny the company's commitment to quality and consistency. At several branches, customers are able to see just how much work goes into a single serving of the signature dish. Each dumpling has eighteen folds, all made by hand; it weighs twenty-one g, of which sixteen g is the filling.[74]

Another Taiwanese chain, unknown to all but a few of the tourists who line up outside Ding Tai Fung, sells far more dumplings. With nearly eight hundred outlets across the country by late 2016, Bafang Yunji is now Taiwan's most ubiquitous fast-food brand. The standardized menu goes beyond pan-fried and steamed dumplings (all handmade) with traditional pork and leek fillings. The kimchi- and curry-flavored pot stickers seem consistently popular; there are also soups, noodles, and fresh vegetables. Bafang Yunji does not advertise, relying instead on word-of-mouth[75] and media discussions of founder Lin Jia-yu's business philosophy.

Lin created the brand at a time when he was struggling to pay huge personal debts, and he has often said that this experience makes him eager to help the unemployed and impoverished improve their lives. In an article posted on the *Health for All* website in June 2012, he was quoted as saying that, because they face serious discrimination in the job market, he has a particular interest in recruiting men and women already in middle age. What is more, such people are unlikely to have the means to buy franchises, so more than half of those recruited in recent years have been loaned the initial fee by the company, after spending three months at head office proving they have what it takes to run a branch.

A CITY WITHOUT ETHNIC ENCLAVES?

In North American and European cities, certain neighborhoods are far wealthier than others, and the ethnic makeup in one part of a metropolis may be very different to that a mile or two away. By contrast, Taipei is strikingly homogeneous. Wanhua looks less affluent than Xinyi or Da'an, and the percentage of Western expatriates may be highest in Tianmu in Shilin District. But every street is shared by Mercedes-Benzes and old motor scooters.

Thanks to intermarriage and social mobility—not to mention the demolition of China Mall (see chapter 6) and all but a few of the military dependents' villages (*juàn cūn*) where soldiers, sailors, and airmen lived with their families—with each decade it gets harder to pinpoint particular Taipei neighborhoods as being dominated by the descendants of mainlanders who arrived with Chiang Kai-shek. An entire generation grew up in the military dependents' villages, eating the specialties of their fathers' (and sometimes mothers') native provinces. The buildings themselves were cramped and often jerry-built, some say because the authorities expected to retake the mainland imminently. If they had a bit of yard space, many servicemen's wives raised poultry or grew vegetables.

According to Yujen Chen, while China Mall and certain markets "were influential in spreading Chinese dietary culture into [native Taiwanese] family homes, which further contributed to the hybridization of dishes," the typical military dependents' village was "a relatively closed space where various Chinese dishes were preserved." Military families were entitled to monthly rations of rice, noodles, cooking oil, and salt; larger villages had their own markets and clinics. "For the villagers and their descendants, such relatively independent living conditions provided a safe environment where they could maintain their languages, customs, and collective memories of mainland China, as well as their food. Those who lived in these villages preserved many food habits and customs from their hometowns, including eating habits and festival dishes," Chen writes.[76]

The customs and cuisines within the military dependents' villages were as diverse as the huge country from which the 1949ers came. Inevitably, it was impossible or impractical to replicate some of the recipes these refugees brought with them. What are known as *juàn cūn cài* ("military village dishes") or *juàn cūn měishí* ("military village foods"), therefore, integrate mainland flavors with the characteristics of Taiwanese ingredients. Although it sometimes seems that many Taiwanese eager to try new things look abroad before exploring their own back-yard, the recipe-compilation website iCook (www.icook.tw) sums up mainstream opinion by describing this category of dishes as "a precious culture" that has "excited appetites in recent years."

In 2015, as part of the annual military dependents' village festival it sponsors, Taipei City Government's Department of Cultural Affairs issued a tourist leaflet that highlighted forty-some restaurants and stalls said to epitomize *juàn cūn* food-ways. Beitou had more than any other district, but the list included eateries in all twelve of the capital's subdivisions. Among the featured restaurants' specialties were beef noodles, *mántou* (steamed buns popular in Shandong), and *shuǐjiān bāo*. The last of these is a bun-sized dumpling stuffed with cabbage, leeks, pork, shallots, and sometimes egg and/or dried tofu, then fried in a big pan. Even in strongholds of the Democratic Progressive Party (DPP, the main party opposed to Taiwan unifying with China), local governments have promoted military-village cuisine. Across the board, it seems, *juàn cūn* fare is now cherished as an authentic Taiwan culinary tradition.

The postwar emergence of wheat-based foods as staples probably had more to do with US aid and trade than the demographic shift. Nonetheless, Cathy Erway is right to point out that, before the arrival of the mainland Chinese, "noodles in Taiwan were typically made of rice flour, and there were few dumplings or buns, with the exception of glutinous, rice starch-based ones," like *bah-ôan* (the Holo name of a circular gelatinous dumpling not much smaller than a CD).[77]

Clusters of Southeast Asian businesses can be found in the centers of Taoyuan, Taichung, and a few other places. Authentic Thai food can be had in ramshackle eateries on the edges of industrial zones, cooked by Thais for compatriots working in nearby factories. But Greater Taipei has just one genuine immigrant neighbor-hood: "Little Burma" in Zonghe District. Tens of thousands of people around the capital have Burmese roots. Some of them arrived as early as 1954;[78] others came more recently to attend university. Nearly all are of Chinese descent, and many fought as part of the KMT forces that retreated into what is now Myanmar after the Communists' victory. At Chiang's behest, some units were kept combat-ready for years. But, gradually, the soldiers and their dependents—which included Burmese wives and children born in Burma—were allowed to move to Taiwan, where many settled near Zhonghe's Huaxin Street.

But for the languages you see and hear, Huaxin Street resembles blue-collar neighborhoods throughout Taiwan. The buildings that line the street are mostly old apartment blocks; every first-floor unit is given over to a small business. A couple of clinics have notices in the Burmese alphabet as well as Chinese, and two or three of the vendors in the small morning market that occupies a side road label their produce in Burmese. Inside the grocery stores, shelves are filled with Southeast Asian cookies and packaged ingredients. Outsiders are mainly interested in the street's dozen or so restaurants. In some, the Burmese-language bill of fare is much more prominent than the Chinese-language menu. Mild curries, *danpauk* (biryani), and naan flatbreads are staples. Several of the eateries are halal establishments, so the default meat is chicken, rather than pork. Early-opening places put folding tables and plastic stools out on the sidewalk so customers can smoke while drinking sweet, Indian-style milk tea or coffee. In the mornings, the clientele is 100 percent male, and nobody looks younger than fifty.[79] The ex-soldiers from what is now Myanmar are dying out. But like many Chinatowns in the West, "Little Burma" is kept ticking over by tourism—the government promotes it as Nanyang Sightseeing Food Street—and by Greater Taipei's floating population of Southeast Asian students and laborers.

HAKKA CUISINE COMES DOWN FROM THE HILLS

Even if mainlanders and their descendants are seen as a coherent demographic, Hakka people constitute Taiwan's biggest ethnic minority. Upward of 15 percent of citizens are descended from Hakka pioneers who left Guangdong and Fujian in the eighteenth and nineteenth centuries.

Like their Austronesian compatriots, Taiwan's Hakka have become more confident about asserting their identity since political and social liberalization began in the late 1980s. Support and subsidies for their language and customs flow from the central government's Hakka Affairs Council (HAC). Since the early 1990s, Hakka cuisine has gone from being ignored by newspapers and TV stations to receiving considerable and usually positive media attention.[80] The government-backed Hakka TV channel, launched in mid-2003, broadcast more than one hundred episodes of a cookery program titled *Master-Chef of Hakka*, replacing it in summer 2017 with *Hakka Yummy*.

The terms often used to characterize Hakka food in Taiwan, "salty, fragrant, and oily," appear on HAC's website, and it replays a common explanation for this state of affairs: "It is salty so that it can be preserved for a long time and to replenish the salt that people lose during a day of hard farm work. It is fatty because the work that the Hakka people do requires a great deal of physical strength, and they need to supplement their physical strength. It is fragrant so that it can stimulate the appetite and be more filling."

Until recent times, of course, the majority of Taiwan's non-Hakka were also struggling to survive, and had equal need of physical endurance, but did not develop cuisines so heavy in oil and salt. Linda Lau Anusasananan, author of *The*

Hakka Cookbook: Chinese Soul Food from around the World, paints a more nuanced picture. She plays down the "fatty-salty" generalization, saying that it is "true for some dishes, especially those that use salt-preserved vegetables and fatty cuts of meat, such as pork belly. Although many [non-Hakka] farmed and did other physical work, the Hakka were forced to work longer and harder to succeed. That's because earlier settlers claimed the most desirable fertile lowlands. As migrants who arrived much later, the Hakka were left with scraps of hard-to-farm land that required extra labor to get crops to grow. Often this land was located in isolated and inhospitable areas where growing conditions were challenging. Salt acted as a preservative that allowed them to have a supply of food, no matter where they lived. Fat satisfied their appetite so they could work longer. Even after they migrated to other areas, they maintained a taste for preserved and pickled vegetables and fatty meats."[81]

Anusasananan traveled widely to research her book. In Taiwan, she says, she found that "some dishes were completely new to me; others dishes tasted familiar. The Hakka specialty 'pounded tea' known as *léi chá* had become sweet—I was told this was to attract tourists—quite different than the savory versions I had in Singapore and Malaysia." (*Léi chá* is the Mandarin pronunciation; few Hakka under the age of fifty speak their ancestral tongue fluently.) She was also impressed by the frequent use of local tropical fruits, recalling mountain greens with a passion-fruit dressing and fresh pineapple added to a pork stir-fry.

It is often said that the characteristics of Hakka cuisine are fundamentally inseparable from local geography, the economic resources of each community, and the social and cultural environment. There is a strong emphasis on pork and rice. Dry preserves give many dishes a unique aroma. Hakka people do more stewing and less frying than non-Hakka.[82] Inevitably, there was some overlap between early Hakka foodways and how the indigenous people fed themselves. The HAC website rightly says that modern-day dishes like pigeon peas and pork ribs, pumpkin rice cakes, and mountain bitter gourd represent "the re-application of the original ingredients by the original inhabitants." Mountain bitter gourd is smaller and even more bitter than its lowland equivalent.[83]

Hakka settlers in Taiwan learned to create sauces from cordia drupes and other naturally occurring or easy-to-grow items. The peels and flesh of sour mandarin oranges are seasoned with sliced chilies and salt, then cooked to become a flavoring that works well as a dip for meats, vegetables, and soy foods. On the whole, however, the hearty fare served up in the Hakka-dominated townships of Hsinchu and Miaoli does not appeal much to modern, health-conscious consumers.

With the help of the HAC, Hakka cuisine is being both repackaged and reinvented, in the process bringing to the fore some little-known delicacies. In a 2016 competition sponsored by the HAC and Taoyuan City Government, contestants were asked to cook silver needle noodles with shellfish, an ingenious combination because Hakka communities tend to be far from the ocean.

In China, the Hakka name for silver needle noodles is memorable but unappetizing: *lo-see-fun*, "rat's tail noodles." Taiwanese Hakka call them *mí thôi muk*, sometimes rendered *mee tai mak*, akin to the name in Singapore (*mee tai bak*). This name describes the method by which these noodles are made: rice paste is pushed through a sieve, then dropped in hot water for cooking. They are not quite the same as rice vermicelli (*mǐfěn*); fried rice vermicelli is popular in Hsinchu, which happens to be the place where a lot of this type of pasta is produced, because reliable winds facilitate outdoor drying. Like *bǎntiáo*, the much thicker flat noodles eaten in Hakka settlements down south, silver needle noodles are traditionally made from glutinous long-grain *indica* rice. These days, however, tapioca is often mixed in, because it is cheaper and creates a chewier texture. Producing *bǎntiáo* involves soaking the rice in water, then grinding it into rice milk. Tapioca is added so it thickens into a paste, after which it is steamed in a flat mold or on a tray. Left to cool, it forms sheets that resemble white bathroom towels, nicknamed *mien pha pán* ("face cloth" in Hakka[84]). These are cut into strips as thick as pencils and typically served with bean sprouts, scallions, a little pork, and some garlic sauce.

In another event, chefs had to make innovative use of Hakka-style pickles, including daikon, and Chinese mustard (*Brassica juncea*) in its pickled, salted, or dried-then-salted forms.[85] The older generation still does a lot of home pickling. In east Taiwan in particular, you do not have to travel far to see mustard greens, oilseed rape, or cabbage leaves spread on the tops of walls, destined to become *fù cài* or *méigān cài*, and then added to pork dishes or mixed into the fillings of steamed buns.

Around Lunar New Year or other festivals, Hakka people have traditionally made a range of steamed rice cakes called *bǎn* (see chapter 4). To broaden the appeal of these treats—which are promoted as being low in fat, salt, and sugar—old recipes have been jazzed up with new elements like lotus root, pumpkin, sweet potato, and taro.

HAC officials have been trying to bring the ethnic group's culinary achievements to the attention of gourmets beyond Taiwan. The HAC website describes more than forty "innovative Hakka cuisine" dishes in English. Among them are diced frog leg with bamboo shoots and romaine lettuce, and Persimmon Delight (blanched cabbage, minced chicken, dried persimmons, fermented mustard greens, wolfberries, and other ingredients).[86] And in 2017 and 2018, HAC dispatched chefs to North America, Southeast Asia, and Australasia to promote ten Hakka signature dishes. Among them are fried *bǎntiáo*, pineapple fried with wood-ear fungus (a distinctly Taiwanese combination usually cooked with sliced pig's lung), and eggplant stewed with sweet-scented basil. Sweet-scented or clove basil (*Ocimum gratissimum*, rather than basil, a.k.a. St. Joseph's wort, *Ocimum basilicum*) features in several Hakka dishes.

For all the talk of bringing Hakka food into the twenty-first century, there is steady demand for Hakka culinary classics such as the "four stewed and four fried dishes," known in Mandarin as *sì wén sì chǎo*. The single most eaten of these is Hakka stir-fry (*kèjiā xiǎo chǎo*), another of the ten menu items promoted by HAC's touring chefs. It is a mix of toothpick-sized strips of pork, squid, shallots, dried tofu, and celery, seasoned predictably with garlic, rice wine, white pepper, and soy sauce. Just as chop suey was created to use up miscellaneous scraps, Hakka stir-fry was originally a way to make an appetizing meal from foods left over after religious events. This explains the presence of squid; a century or more ago it was an extravagant victual for hill farmers living far from the coast, but a necessary component of offerings.[87]

IF GRANDFATHER WAS A GOOD BOY . . .

Dòuhuā is perhaps holding its own, but cookies, candies, and what Mandarin speakers call *dàn gāo* have in recent decades been pushing traditional treats into the background. (*Dàn gāo*, "egg cakes," are distinct from other *gāo*, some of which are savory, and/or consist mainly of intact grains of cooked rice.)

One of the goodies that Qing- and Japanese-era residents looked forward to was four-fruit soup. Many modern iterations of this old festival food contain no fruit at all, but rather mildly sweet balls made of taro or tapioca, and sometimes mung beans, adzuki beans, and/or peanuts. The "four" in the name originally meant four seasons, not four ingredients. Vendors who sell hot four-fruit soup in the cooler months often sell the same mix of items in the summer, but chilled and placed on crushed ice. The iced version is said to have been hugely popular with Japanese living in Taiwan before 1945, and not just because it featured fruits unavailable on the Home Islands. Until American condensed milk became commonplace, summertime four-fruit dishes were flavored with "banana oil," an artificial product that contained no bananas but had a banana-like smell, which Japanese gourmands considered quintessentially Taiwanese. Local bakeries now use banana extract.

As might be expected in a city where daytime highs of 95°F are not unusual between May and October, the range of iced desserts is broad. The "eight" in eight-treasures ice is not literal; in the words of *Spectacular Taipei No. 33*, an English-language brochure produced on behalf of the city government in the summer of 2013, when customers order this cooling delight, they "pick-and-mix from a choice of tapioca pearls, kidney beans, adzuki beans, mung beans, barley, konjac [konnyaku] jelly, coconut, and aiyu jelly."

Before the arrival of Chiang Kai-shek and his followers, Taiwanese tended to eat crullers with *xìngrén chá*, not soy milk. In English, the former is often called almond tea, even though it is made from apricot kernels rather than almonds and contains no *Camellia sinensis*. In Mandarin, *xìngrén* can mean either apricot kernel or almond; this ambiguity has confused shoppers in Greater China. Many have bought bags of *xìngrén* from California, believing them to be apricot kernels, only to later find they are almonds.[88] The former are coveted because, according to Chinese herbal medicinal theory, they can alleviate chronic coughs and relieve constipation. A September 23, 2014, report in the Chinese-language *United Daily News* went further, claiming that they are good for your skin. Apricot kernels can be divided into a bitter "northern" variety and a sweeter "southern" cultivar. Whereas the Cantonese usually mix the two, the Taiwanese prefer southern kernels and often add crushed peanuts.

The old fashioned *xìngrén chá*-cruller combination is said to be a favorite of Lee Teng-hui, and it is tempting to see a political angle in his rejection of soy milk. Lee changed the course of Taiwan's history by rising through the ranks of the KMT to become the first president actually born on the island. Within a few years, he had sidelined the party heavyweights (most of whom were mainlanders) who assumed they would be able to control him, and it became obvious that his true sympathies lay not with the Chinese Nationalist agenda, but with the pro-localization opposition.

A food-stall dessert in the days of yore, almond tofu has been promoted to high-class banquets and hotel restaurants. Made of apricot kernels ground up with peanuts, it contains neither almonds nor tofu. The nutty liquid is cooked; then milk, sugar, and cornstarch are added. When it sets, it has a tofu-like consistency. These days, it is often eaten with canned fruit.

Pineapple cake, which is now much more like a shortbread than a sponge, has long had a ritual function. Because the Holo pronunciation of pineapple has auspicious connotations, it was often given by a man to his future bride's family as an engagement gift. Over time the cakes have become smaller, and it is as a bite-sized goody that it really came into its own at the end of the twentieth century. Unlike stinky tofu and many of Taiwan's other signature delicacies, it travels well and is acceptable to nearly everyone.

Just as almond tea is not made from almonds, pineapple cakes are not always filled with pure pineapple jam. Some manufacturers add winter melon to adjust the taste and/or save money. However, cakes made by SunnyHills (founded barely a decade ago but by any criterion Taiwan's most successful pineapple cake brand) contain 100 percent smooth-cayenne pineapple grown in the Changhua area. The flour comes from Japan and the butter from New Zealand, but the eggs are local. Neither preservatives nor flavor enhancers are used, so the product's shelf life is a mere fifteen days.

SunnyHills is often held up as an example of what can be achieved with patience, long-term vision, and an uncompromising dedication to quality. The company does not advertise, nor does it pay commissions to travel agencies or tour guides who bring groups to its eleven outlets, of which six are outside Taiwan. Every visitor to a SunnyHills shop is greeted with a pineapple cake and tea in a porcelain cup.[89]

SunnyHills also makes castella cakes. In the sixteenth century, Portuguese merchants introduced this type of moist sponge cake to Nagasaki, then the only Japanese port open to foreign commerce. Like the Japanese passion for baseball, during the colonial period, castella cake traveled to and caught on in Taiwan. Apart from the flour, which is imported from Japan, the company prides itself on sourcing all other ingredients—eggs, longan honey, cane sugar, and aged plum sauce—from central and southern Taiwan.[90] Reminiscent of how Japan evolved from a consumer of Scotch into a major exporter, Taipei-based bakery chain Le' Old-Time Flavor of Taiwan has gotten shoppers in Singapore and Seoul to wait in long lines for its cheese-, chocolate-, pork floss-, and traditional-flavor castellas.

THE BAKERY BOOM

Pineapple cake becoming the default food gift when Taiwanese interact with foreigners is appropriate, as the modern pineapple cake was developed in the early 1950s by a Russian working with American flour and milk powder at Astoria Confectionary and Café. This culinary landmark is located roughly equidistant between Taipei Main Station and the former Japanese governor-general's office, now the Office of the President of the Republic of China. Founded in 1949 by six White Russian former residents of Shanghai with the help of Archibald Chien, who was not yet twenty, Astoria became a pioneering Western-style bakery. "We practically introduced birthday cakes to Taiwan," *Taiwan Today* quoted Chien as saying in an October 16, 2009, online report titled "Astoria, a Corner of Taipei's History."

The Russians, who had fled to Taiwan as the Communists tightened their grip on the mainland, are long gone, and Chien (who eventually became sole owner) handed control of the business over to his daughter some years ago. Nevertheless, Astoria continues to sell borscht, Russian soft candy, mazurka cake, and other items seldom seen in East Asia. But few Taiwanese know the real significance of the place. Donuts did not come to Taiwan from the United States, as many assume; Astoria was the first bakery to sell both freshly baked and deep-fried donuts. The Russians could not find cranberries or blueberries, and they rejected Chien's suggestion that they use candied fruit. In the end, they made fruit jam using oranges from Yangmingshan, the range of mountains immediately north of the capital. Chien later found papayas and carambolas suitable for jams.

Astoria's seasonal fruit jams are still star items today.[91] Along with vanilla biscuits and almond flakes, one of the three most popular handmade cookies was a
Taiwanese-style macaron.[92] While French macarons are made using egg whites, for
Astoria's early Taiwanese-style macarons (which have a drier texture) the entire
egg was used; the white and the yolk were separated, and each was then whisked
with granulated sugar. In that era, no Taiwanese (or Russian resident of Taiwan)
would have contemplated wasting anything as valuable as a yolk. What is more, the
eggs available then came from native *tǔjī* hens and were fairly small, so a recipe
using only whites would have been a shocking misuse of resources. Making one
butter sponge cake required eight *tǔjī* eggs.

European macarons did not catch on until some years into the twenty-first century, with the manager of the Taipei branch of a Parisian pâtisserie reporting that
families were buying the confections for *shōuxián* ceremonies. This ritual involves
the relatives (and often their friends) of a four-month-old baby stringing cookies
around the baby's neck, breaking off pieces, and then rubbing them on the youngster's lips in the belief that the infant will then stop drooling. Macarons are thought
to be ideal for this purpose because they come in different colors, making for appealing photos of the event.[93]

A shortage of walnuts and blueberries stymied the Russians' efforts to recreate
the rich fruitcakes they had baked before reaching Taiwan, but Chien persisted,
eventually making a longan-and-raisin version. He brought a chocolate cake to
market in 1961. Within a few years, Astoria was offering Taipei gourmets crois-
sants, chiffon cake, and Taiwanese-style Swiss rolls.[94] Speaking to a *New York
Times* reporter for a March 30, 2008, feature, Chien admitted that much of what
Astoria has sold over the decades was Russian by inspiration, if not replication,
and that this truth had to be disguised for political reasons. In the 1950s, Taiwan
was on the Cold War front line and ruled by a paranoid dictatorship that saw the
Soviet Union as an implacable foe. Astoria's Russian presence—and the frequent
gatherings of intellectuals—invited state surveillance. But perhaps the organs of
state were simply ensuring the safety of two regular VIP customers who had a taste
for Russian fare: Soviet-educated Chiang Ching-kuo (Chiang Kai-shek's son and
successor) and his wife, an ethnic Russian born in what is now Belarus.

Two of Taiwan's oldest confectionery businesses are still operating. Long Yue
Tang, in Dadaocheng since 1932, is best known for traditional items like mung-
bean cakes and their crumbly *yánméi gāo*, a sweet-salty plum cake. I-Mei was
established two years later and four hundred meters away at a location of tremendous historical significance. The former Da-an Hospital on Yanping North Road
is where Dr. Chiang Wei-shui (1890–1931) practiced medicine when not penning
insightful political essays or contemplating what he called Taiwan's "cultural mal-
nutrition" from a colonial jail cell (the Japanese authorities imprisoned him nine

times[95]). Such were his contributions to the development of Taiwanese democracy and civil society that a freeway is named after him, as is the road beside Taipei Brewery.

I-Mei is now a diverse food business with around one hundred stores and factories in Taiwan and Vietnam. After World War II, milk caramel made from fresh milk was a best seller, so the company set up its own dairy division in 1955.[96] It was probably the first shop in Taiwan to sell fresh milk to the public. According to the company's website, in the 1980s, I-Mei began supplying burger buns and dairy products to McDonald's, Kentucky Fried Chicken, and other fast-food chains. I-Mei crackers, cookies, and mooncakes are prominent in supermarkets up and down the country.

In the Holo language, bread is called *pháng*, from the Japanese *pan*, itself a loanword absorbed from Portuguese. Good bread was not widely available until well into the 1990s, but Vietnam War–era US military advisors stationed in Taipei could at least find some in Florida Bakery, founded in Shanghai but evacuated to Taipei in 1949. Florida currently has eight outlets around the city.

To Western palates, a lot of Taiwanese bread is sweet, perhaps because the Japanese introduced a preference for softer breads they treated as desserts rather than a staple. Bread is far more often eaten by youngsters for breakfast than with soup or cheese. Still, bakeries have been diversifying their offerings, in part because more bakers are learning the craft (and winning competitions) overseas. In their 2015 report on Taiwan's baking industry, business intelligence company Euromonitor International noted "growing demand for premium unpackaged/artisanal breads . . . with artisanal producers accounting for 65% of retail current value sales [in 2014]." They attributed this to artisan bakers offering wider assortments of types and flavors compared to factory bakeries, and to the common perception that unpackaged baked goods contain fewer artificial additives and preservatives.

4

❖ ❖

Offerings, Festivals, and Special
Foods throughout the Year

F ood offerings are an essential element of Taiwanese religion, which is variously described as Buddhism, Taoism, a system of folk beliefs, or a blend of all three.[1] When Taiwan was primarily an agricultural society, life was organized according to the lunar (actually lunisolar) calendar and the almanac. Aside from weddings, popular religion—which is seldom puritanical or doctrinaire—was for several generations the main distraction for rural folk.

"Social group[s] defined by residence and surname, and unified by religious allegiances, became the basis for much social activity throughout most of the history" of the villages in Tainan that anthropologist David K. Jordan studied in the 1960s.[2] Folk events where prayers for good harvests and abundant food were offered developed into rambunctious communal celebrations and colorful festivals. Many of the traditional rituals of Taiwan's Han majority were carried to the island in the hearts and minds of early settlers, first from Fujian and later from Guangdong. Generations later, despite periods of official discouragement and brief suppression during the Japanese colonial era,[3] these customs are largely intact.

The local pantheon, which largely but not completely overlaps with that worshipped in China before Communism, features thousands of gods, goddesses, immortals, and former mortals promoted to demigods. There are also minor deities believed to oversee a particular geographical location, outside of which they are unknown, and even a few animal gods. Believers express their respect for these supernatural entities by sacrificing incense, burning spirit money (a.k.a. joss paper, made of rice straw or bamboo in the old days), and placing food on offertory tables inside temples.

In Taiwan, as in many other countries, certain foods are given a particular meaning, and some items carry a clearly defined significance. A great deal of this symbolism is based on the homophones in which Chinese languages are awash. The Holo pronunciation of pineapple (*Ông-lâi*), for instance, is similar to that of "prosperity is coming" (*ōng lâi*). Asian pears are suitable for inclusion in temple offerings, because in both Holo and Mandarin their name implies "fortune flowing in." However, pears should not appear in a wedding banquet, because the fruit's Mandarin name (*lí*) is identical to "separate" or "go away" (*lí*). For the same reason, some people refuse to share a pear with a friend.

The second part of the Holo word for banana (*kin-chio*) is similar to that for "inviting" (*chiau*), making it an auspicious offering in most, but not all, circumstances. On September 11, 2017, *Taipei Times* reported that officials and fruit vendors were unhappy that, during the seventh month on the lunar calendar ("Ghost Month," see below), consumers were avoiding certain fruit. According to the newspaper, significant numbers of people were refraining from offering bananas (as well as pears, pineapples, and plums) "because the fruits' names sound like they are inviting ghosts in Holo. . . . Some so-called folklore experts kept spreading the belief, but it is actually a superstition that has cost fruit sellers serious losses [as one official said]." The words of another official were paraphrased as "The superstition is capricious given that the names sound different in Hakka or aboriginal languages."

Neither tomatoes nor guavas should ever be offered. Because humans cannot digest the seeds, and they come out in excrement, they are regarded as growing in filth; it would be disrespectful to present them to gods or ancestors. The fruit called Buddha's Head is kept away from offertory tables because its presence would be seen as sacrilege against the Buddha.[4]

Those hoping to conceive offer pomelos, because *yòuzi* sounds like *yǒu zi* ("have a child"). Grapes, muskmelons, and watermelons also symbolize fertility. Presenting longans indicates a particular desire for a son; the Chinese characters for *longan* mean "dragon's eyes" (*lóngyǎn*), and dragons are a symbol of both maleness and the emperor. Persimmons signal a desire for everything to go as planned. Now that imported apples are not particularly pricey, they are popular offerings, because in Mandarin the first syllable resembles the first syllable in "peace."

Not every type of food used in rituals is chosen because its name matches worshippers' goals. Jordan witnessed a rite that sought to exorcise a malevolent ghost from a fishpond. In addition to bringing effigies of two friendly deities to the pond, shouting, and letting off firecrackers, villagers threw handfuls of sesame seeds into the water. He was told this was done because the ghost would try to count them, but eventually give up in frustration and flee—and that any small seeds would do.[5]

As an offering, fruit by itself is never sufficient. Traditionally, three cooked meat or fish items and fruits that represent the four seasons should be sacrificed.

The proteins are usually pork, chicken, and fish; if five are offered, as is sometimes done at larger ceremonies, chicken eggs and duck are added. Occasionally crabs or other shellfish replace the eggs. Offering beef or dog meat is taboo: bovines were revered for contributing their labor to farming in the early days, while dogs were seen as loyal friends, even before the sale and consumption of canine meat became illegal.

When fowl are offered, usually the whole bird is cooked. However, during the Hakka Yimin Festival, a uniquely Taiwanese religious event in the northwest held around the end of each summer, minced chicken and duck are sacrificed.[6] Most Taiwanese also believe that fish must be complete when offered; cutting off the tail means you will have no descendants. Because they are sold with their tails already removed, cod and tuna are therefore unsuitable.

The head of a chicken being sacrificed should point outward, away from the worshipper and toward the effigy. For an offering of fish, the positioning depends on where in Fujian the worshipper's ancestors were from. People of Zhangzhou and Quanzhou descent generally have the fish's head closest to the god, while traditionalists whose families hail from Tongan do the opposite. Foods offered to gods should be lukewarm, to represent there being some distance between humans and their gods. But when sacrificing to ancestors, the foods are fully cooked and cut into pieces to signify a more intimate relationship.[7]

In the past, everything offered was eventually eaten. But in 2014, Taipei's Xingtian Temple and its branch temples in Beitou and Sanxia took the radical step of banning all food offerings because so much was being wasted. Previously, it had been customary for those who came to pray to present to the deities a dome-shaped rice pudding topped by a single longan. At the end of their visit, they would take the pudding home. However, after a consumers' group announced that many of the puddings contained dangerous amounts of preservatives, worshippers began leaving their offerings behind. The temple found it had to throw away about 1,000 puddings each day, so the management committee decided to abolish the practice. According to an August 26, 2014, report in *Taipei Times*, the decision upset many of the vendors in the neighborhood who made a living selling offertory items—but at least it put an end to the bizarre situation of people offering something to the gods they would not eat themselves.

THE ROLE OF RICE

For most of the past four centuries, the overriding objective for many Taiwanese was obtaining enough rice to feed their families. It would be surprising indeed if rice played no role in farmers' efforts to propitiate the gods and ensure bountiful harvests, as, deep in the heart of the traditional agriculturalist, there is the sense that each successful rice crop is a gift from nature. Each harvest is the result not merely of hard work but also of a profound relationship between the farmer and the gods he worships. The symbolic and literal importance of rice is obvious in the ways Han people express gratitude for their survival.

Fifty years of Japanese rule had a massive impact on local dietary culture, even altering the type of rice eaten with meals. During the colonial period, the *indica* rice cultivated by early Han settlers gave way to stickier ponlai strains developed to suit the Japanese palate (see chapter 5). But glutinous *indica* rices are still in demand for traditional rice-based delicacies used in wedding and funeral banquets, as well as folk rites. Glutinous *indica* creates the "Q" texture many Taiwanese adore. Food that is Q is more substantial than melt-in-the-mouth and has a delectable chewiness without being gummy.

The English letter Q appears in restaurant menus and on food-stall signs because no Chinese logogram represents this characteristic, even though there is a word in spoken Holo: *k'iu*. The enthusiasm for Q is why many people specify tendon (Mandarin: *niú jīn*) when ordering beef noodle soup, and it goes some way toward explaining the enduring popularity of oyster omelets and pearl milk tea. Cathy Erway puts it this way: "To say that a food is 'Q' is certainly a compliment. . . . Taiwanese eaters are almost as concerned with texture as they are with taste. Hence, we find examples of rather tasteless elements in dishes that only add textural appeal."[8]

Unfortunately, glutinous *indica* is not the most digestible of ingredients, so now it is common to mix in ponlai rice, sweet-potato flour, or potato starch when making what Mandarin speakers call *guǒ*. Some of these gooey treats are sweetish, but many have meat or mushroom fillings.

In Hakka communities, rice snacks called *bǎn* (in Mandarin) or *pán* (in the Siyen Hakka dialect) enjoy special prominence. There is a Hakka saying: *yit khoài pán tí sâm vón fan* ("a single glutinous rice cake is as good as three bowls of plain rice"). Sticky rice is a key ingredient of many Hakka snacks, one reason being that it satisfies hunger for longer periods due to its starch profile. Because many Hakka settled in remote locations, the ease with which sticky rice processed into a paste could be stored and transported was a definite advantage in the early days. When Hakka pioneers went to cut wood or clear land far from home, they would carry *pán* for sustenance. Present-day *pán* are made with various fillings and flavors, among them savory pumpkin, savory mung bean and ginger, sweet taro, and sweet mung bean and longan.

Rice cakes contain little salt or sugar and are said to epitomize the Hakka talent for combining their knowledge of everyday ingredients with culinary craft to create something mouthwatering. Hakka rice snacks make the most of the different qualities and textures of the various rices grown in Taiwan. The drier, harder, and looser character of pre-1895 *indica* varieties makes them ideal not just for rice noodles like *băntiáo* (see chapter 3) but also for more ornate dishes.[9]

Non-glutinous *indica* is the main ingredient in daikon cake and Hakka nine-layer cake. Carolyn Phillips describes the latter as "a charming confection of layers flavored with brown and white sugars, with a touch of banana extract to give it that quintessential Taiwanese flavor. . . . [The non-sticky rice flour] provides a softer, more delicate texture that practically melts on the tongue."[10] Two different batters are steamed, layer by layer, until there are nine in total. In addition to the original two-color brown/white sugar version, some vendors now make and sell decidedly nontraditional multicolored nine-layer cakes. Seven-layer cakes are also made, but only the nine-layer version has a ritual role, appearing during the Double Ninth Festival (the ninth day of the ninth lunar month).

One difference between authentic Hakka "grass cakes" and those made by Taiwanese of Fujianese descent is that the former often used *Artemisia argyi* (Chinese mugwort), while the latter utilized *Gnaphalium affine*, a kind of barley grass. Almost everything cooked with either of these two herbs takes on a grassy coloring. The traditional gathering season for *Artemisia argyi* is from the third day of the third lunar month to Duanwu Festival (a.k.a. Dragon Boat Festival) on the fifth day of the fifth lunar month. Thanks to its distinct smell, Han people have used it from time immemorial to repel evil spirits; it is also thought to keep venomous snakes away. In Hakka districts, copious amounts of *Artemisia argyi* are mixed into glutinous rice paste, then steamed to make bun-sized cakes with a refreshing, piney flavor.[11] In the past, these items were vegetarian, but now there are pork and shrimp fillings, as well as mushrooms or sweet paste. In Taiwan, *Gnaphalium affine* cakes are associated with Qingming Festival (celebrated 104 days after the winter solstice, on April 4 or 5), when Han people in many countries visit cemeteries and columbaria to sweep the graves of their ancestors and make offerings.[12]

In Hakka regions, it is customary to serve ciba during traditional festivals and family celebrations. The English term for this snack, made by pounding glutinous rice flour that has been steamed into a paste, is derived from its Mandarin name. The traditional preparation process is laborious and often done by several neighbors working together. Once the paste has the desired Q consistency, it is divided into egg-sized balls and coated with crushed peanuts, sesame seeds, or—and this is an old-time favorite in Hakka communities—brown sugar.[13] These days, an easier way of making ciba is preferred: grind rice into milk, remove the excess water, steam it, and then pound it into shape. According to the HAC website, the modern ciba "doesn't taste as good as it used to," but it continues to be provided at weddings, funerals, and Mid-Autumn Festival parties, and it is even used to lure people to political rallies.

One of the most endearingly named Hakka snacks is *ngiù vún súi*, "cattle bathe in water"; like ciba, it is a variation on mochi. *Ngiù vún súi* rice balls are served in syrup (hence the name), usually with peanuts. Like all Hakka rice cakes, making them involves repeated kneading, but that is what gives this category of foods their distinctive and delightful Q-ness.

KEY DATES ON THE HAN CALENDAR

The first day of the lunar year falls between January 22 and February 19 on the Gregorian calendar, and the Lunar New Year period is far more important than Christmas or December 31. Schools close for around three weeks. With the exception of some hotels, restaurants, and shops, business halts for several days. This time is spent feasting, visiting relatives, cleaning one's home, and presenting cash-filled red envelopes to youngsters and elders. Unmarried adults try to get back to their parents' homes in time for dinner on New Year's Eve. There is no customary dish for this occasion, certainly nothing synonymous with the event like turkey is for Thanksgiving and Christmas. Many families sit down around a hot pot, and then they relax in front of the television.

Traditionalists conduct certain rituals on the eve of the first day of the first lunar month. But preparations for the year ahead begin even earlier. In the seven days before the year begins, the Kitchen God, as he is known in English (*Zào Jūn*, "master of the hearth," or *Zào Shén*, "god of the hearth," in Mandarin), is believed to ascend to heaven. There, he speaks of each household's deeds and misdeeds to the Jade Emperor, Taoism's chief deity. To ensure a favorable report, family members propitiate him with sugary items that will make his utterances sweet, and perhaps some rice wine to make him forget their misdemeanors. Among the offerings may be *nián gāo*, made of glutinous rice that has been pounded into a paste and cooked in a wooden-box steamer. But this custom is disappearing, as very few homes built in the last half century have a hearth. Also, many of the people who do make some sort of offering save time and trouble by presenting supermarket candy.

Many of the old-fashioned steamed rice cakes eaten around the New Year are filled with sesame or peanuts and sweetened with brown sugar, as it is believed sweetness signals prosperity during the coming twelve months. But there are also savory versions flavored with radish, pork, or taro. Because they rise, cakes made from ponlai rice and yeast symbolize growing wealth. Combining taro paste and glutinous rice is also auspicious, as taro in both Holo and Mandarin sounds somewhat similar to "protect," with the implication being that you are protecting what is—in classical Han thinking, at least—your most valuable asset: your grandsons and your bloodline.[14]

On the first day of the lunar year, the traditionalist will offer to his ancestors the three proteins and four fruits mentioned above, plus six plates of vegetables, radish cake, or yeast cake. He will also sacrifice to heaven flowers, fruits, ginger, salt, rice cakes, candy, and very thin wheat noodles called *miàn xiàn* (in Mandarin) or *mīsua* (in Holo).

Lunar New Year festivities traditionally continue for fifteen days until the first full-moon night of the new year. In Mandarin, this final celebration is called *Yuánxiāo Jié*, but in English the event is known as Lantern Festival, because decorative lanterns of all shapes and sizes decorate public places. One food always associated with Lantern Festival is *yuán xiāo*, balls of glutinous rice flour cooked and served in a light syrup. They are often no bigger than grapes but may be nearly as large as golf balls if filled. A single bowl may contain balls of four or five different colors, depending on the ingredients used. One recipe on iCook (www.icook.tw) lists powdered black sesame, green tea powder, white chocolate, strawberry chocolate, and the paste of both purple and yellow sweet potatoes. On the winter solstice, a very similar dish, but called *tāng yuán* (Mandarin for "soup balls") and traditionally unfilled, is consumed.

Much as *yuán xiāo* is eaten around Lantern Festival, spring rolls (*lūn piá^n* in Holo) are the customary lunch when families gather to celebrate Qingming Festival. These are never deep-fried, but rather eaten as soon as the thin, translucent rice-flour wrap is folded around a mix of pork, dried tofu, strips of fried egg, and springtime vegetables: mung-bean sprouts, carrots, celery, chives, and leeks. Because the contents are sprinkled with generous amounts of sugar and ground peanuts, Qingming-season spring rolls are not necessarily healthier than the deep-fried spring rolls served in Asian restaurants in the West.

The fifth day of the fifth lunar month, Duanwu Festival, is when dragon-boat races are held on waterways and Taiwanese gorge on stodgy rice pyramids known as *zòngzi* in Mandarin. This foodway has a macabre backstory. More than twenty-three hundred years ago, during China's Warring States Period, the great poet Qu Yuan was loyal to the State of Chu. While in exile, he learned the State of Qin had captured the Chu capital. Distraught, he weighed himself down with rocks and leapt to his death in a river in what is now China's Hunan Province. It is said that when news of his suicide reached his friends and admirers, they rushed to the river-bank and began throwing rice balls into the water, so his body would not be eaten by the fish. The custom of eating *zòngzi*, typically filled with pork, mushrooms, and peanuts, seems to focus on the circumstances of the poet's death, rather than his literary works or character.

Nowadays, *zòngzi*—frequently likened to tamales—are enjoyed with hardly a thought for Qu Yuan. The custom is observed throughout Greater China; yet, even within Taiwan, the preferred filling, the shape, and the material used to wrap what are often but unsatisfactorily dubbed "sticky-rice dumplings" vary from place to place.

The north-south difference can be summarized like this: The long-grain rice used in the north is more Q, while the other ingredients are sautéed with deep-fried shallot, garlic, and soy sauce before wrapping, and even after steaming, they are still somewhat hard; fillings may include chestnuts, hard egg yolk, squid, and shrimp. Southern iterations are softer because the rice is soaked for longer. The filling invariably includes whole peanuts, and because the complete dumpling is boiled—rather than the protein being sautéed and then everything steamed together—you end up with a stickier dumpling that is often eaten with a dip.

In the south, *zòngzi* are usually wrapped in Ma bamboo (*Dendrocalamus latiflorus Munro*) leaves. The leaves of this common species can be used fresh or dried. Makino bamboo (*Phyllostachys bambusoides*) leaves are thought to be more suitable for the steamed *zòngzi* made in north Taiwan, and they impart an aroma like that of bamboo shoots. Some favor the long leaves of *Alpinia zerumbet* (shell ginger, although only the leaves and not the roots are used in cooking) on account of their fragrance.[15]

Traditional *zòngzi* have scant appeal to health-conscious urban folk, and this is probably the main reason why "Huzhou *zòngzi*," named for a city in China's Zhejiang Province, have caught on in Taipei. Thought to be less salty, and flavored with meat of a more appetizing hue and texture, they seem to appeal to people who consider conventional sticky-rice dumplings, in the words of a *United Daily News* taste-test article published on March 19, 2017, "not pleasing to the eye . . . nothing more than packets of oil . . . and even outright disgusting."

The Hakka minority has its own *zòngzi*, including sweet dumplings and ones made by grinding glutinous rice and ponlai rice, and then adding radish, fried shallot, dried shrimp, pork, and other ingredients. The latter are regarded as good for eating cold or hot.[16]

In the past, but hardly nowadays, the summer solstice was marked with offerings to thank the gods for a peaceful first half of the year and beseech them to ensure the second half went smoothly. Some families still eat *tāng yuán*, alluding to an old custom of sacrificing glutinous rice balls to celebrate harmony and unity. The balls' colors signified "as sweet as honey," and djulis (native red quinoa) was one of the ingredients used to add an auspicious tint.[17]

The seventh day of the seventh month on the traditional calendar is *Qīxì*, alternatively known as Magpie Festival or Chinese Valentine's Day. The event celebrates the tale of the Cowherd and the Weaver Girl, whose forbidden love saw them banished to opposite sides of the Milky Way. But each year on this day, a flock of magpies forms a bridge allowing the lovers to meet. Qixi was traditionally an opportunity for young girls to display the skills that would make them good wives, such as threading a needle in poor light. They also deep-fried thin pastries called *qiǎoguǒ*, made of flour, mashed tofu, and sugar. Tofu, which lends an extra fragrance, volume, and crunchiness, is absent from the pastries made in China during this festival.

The seventh lunar month is always busy in terms of ritual activity for another reason. On the first day of the month, the gates of Hell are believed to open and the spirits of the deceased return to the human world. Food and joss paper are offered to so-called "hungry ghosts," spirits of dead people who have no living descendants to provide them with comfort and sustenance; if not kept happy, they may cause havoc. This is the one time each year when the living are concerned not merely with their own ancestors but with all of the denizens of the afterworld. Because of the danger, during "Ghost Month" people avoid elective surgery, long journeys, getting married, opening new businesses, or moving house.

A couple of generations ago, "universal salvation" rites (known in Mandarin as *pǔdù*) were held throughout the seventh lunar month, rotating from one household to another until the end of the month. In recent decades, Pǔdù activities have been consolidated. On the first day of the month, the ghosts are invited; on the fifteenth, they are fed; and on the twenty-ninth, they are sent away. Getting the invitation just right can be tricky. Lanterns are positioned to guide the ghosts to the offerings, but if too many are hung, attracting more ghosts than can be placated by the food supplied, the unsatisfied spirits are likely to bring misfortune to whoever miscalculated. Below the offertory table, the thoughtful may place a bucket half-filled with water and a face cloth, so the spirits can wash their hands and faces.

The Zhongyuan Pudu on the fifteenth day is the most important ceremony, because that is when the gates of Hell are open widest and the danger is greatest. Zhongyuan Pudu rites became especially important in the early years of Han settlement, because many settlers perished far from home, without descendants to care for them in death. It was believed, therefore, that an exceptional number of wandering souls roamed the island, ready to cause calamities if not appeased.

Keelung is famous for the grandeur of its Zhongyuan Pudu festivities, but the placating of ghosts at this time of year is a highly visible custom throughout the country. On the same day, many families eat *tāng yuán*. The precise recipe varies from place to place, but a common denominator is the belief that the roundness of the balls signifies a complete circle of unity within the family.

Hoping to curry the hungry ghosts' favor, businesses as well as households prepare offerings, often of fruit that symbolize good luck, such as apples, oranges, pineapples, longans, and grapes. Tomatoes and guavas never appear among entrepreneurs' sacrifices, but the reason has nothing to do with the seeds they contain. In Mandarin, tomatoes are called *fān qié*. In formal situations (such as on government websites), guavas are known as *fān shíliú*, but in everyday parlance they are *bālè*. The *fān* in both names means "barbarian," because both reached the Sinosphere from the West,[18] and it has the same pronunciation as another Mandarin word that means "overturn." Accordingly, they are avoided, lest mischievous spirits take them as an invitation to capsize the enterprise. Similar thinking is evident during going-away dinner parties, when fish should not be turned over, for fear that something bad may happen to the traveler.

In recent decades, a great deal of packaged and processed nontraditional food has appeared on offertory tables. The August 2009 issue of *Taiwan Business Topics* noted that sales of Proctor & Gamble's salty snacks (at that time, the company still owned the Pringles brand) surge during "Ghost Month." When hospitality businesses sacrifice to gods and ghosts, cans of beer and bottles of imported liquor may replace or supplement the prescribed three tiny cups of rice wine.

The fifteenth day of the eighth lunar month is a time for families to get together and appreciate the harvest moon. Some English speakers call this event "Moon Festival," but Mid-Autumn Festival is the proper translation of its name in Chinese languages. Few people these days regard it as a time when they should worship Chang'e, the moon goddess, but they continue to enjoy the mooncakes and pomelos with which their ancestors honored her.[19] Long ago, a family would cut up and share a mooncake. The round shape represented the full moon, while the sharing stood for family harmony. Traditional flavors included mung-bean paste (often with a salted duck egg yolk or a similar savory treat), pineapple jam, taro paste, and sweetened adzuki-bean paste, the last sometimes having mochi at its center. Some modern mooncakes are touted as low-calorie or lard-free, or else tasting of green tea or tiramisu.

Throughout Greater China, mooncakes take various forms, but the round shape is universal. Typical Taiwanese mooncakes feature layered flaky, fluffy pastry; those with ornate lattice patterns on top are more like Cantonese mooncakes. Manufacturing mooncake gift sets is big business for companies like I-Mei. Over the years, individual mooncakes have become much smaller—more in response to consumer preference than due to corporate cost cutting—and the pastry cases more of a hybrid of traditional Taiwanese and traditional Cantonese. Flavors popular a generation or two ago, like longan and walnut, continue to sell well; yet there is never a shortage of exotic (and expensive) iterations.

Taipei W Hotel's limited-edition mooncake sets have received a lot of media attention, including an August 22, 2017, write-up on *Vogue*'s Taiwan website. That year's set included three innovative flavors inspired by some of Yilan County's most famous products: sun-dried kumquat in creamy custard; mango and chocolate bean-paste infused with Kavalan whisky (see chapter 8); and scallions grown in the town of Sanxing with XO sauce. Other selling points were eco-friendly packaging materials and adding a jump rope to every box, to encourage people to exercise. At US$43 for six cakes, they were certainly among the priciest on the market.

Several decades ago, many people could not afford to buy mooncakes from a bakery, so they made their own round and flattish "moon-ray cakes" (Mandarin: *yuèguāng bǐng*). The pastry was glutinous rice with some sugar, and the fillings were made from cheap ingredients: taro or a paste made by mashing up red-heart sweet potatoes.

The demand for pomelos during this season has enriched fruit farmers in Tainan's Madou District; their pomelos are renowned for their thin skins and sweet and juicy flesh. As explained earlier in this chapter, the Mandarin word for pomelo is an auspicious homophone, and pomelo tea is a popular drink.

Taro also has positive connotations at this time of year. The rhyming Holo idiom *khè bí hún ō', ū hó thâu lō* ("eat rice vermicelli with taro, make good headway") reflects a belief that having that particular dish increases your chances of getting a good job.

Since the 1980s, many families have celebrated each Mid-Autumn Festival by barbecuing on the street in front of their homes.[20] Few city folk have back or front yards; in any case, the public location makes for greater conviviality. Neighbors are invited to stop by for a sausage or two, and because most of the barbecuing is done the weekend before the festival, kids and teenagers run or bicycle from one classmate's home to another. Fish, peppers, and enokitake and King Oyster mushrooms are grilled in foil. Instead of hamburgers, slices of pork (sometimes with lettuce) are eaten between slices of white bread.

On or around the sixteenth day of the final lunar month (most years have twelve months, but sometimes a "leap" month is added), *wěiyá* celebrations are held through the length and breadth of the country. Originally, these feasts honored the earth god. Known in Mandarin as *Tǔdì Gōng* or *Fúdé Zhèngshén*, he is a deity who oversees a defined local area. From place to place, he appears in different manifestations; some are believed to be incarnations of local worthies, while others have entirely divine origins. Because he is also a god of wealth, he has a following among businesspeople.

In modern times, *wěiyá* banquets are simply occasions for employers to thank their workers for their efforts over the past year. These events can get quite raucous, as bosses toast employees and raffle prizes are distributed. Decades ago, when travel from one end of the island to the other was far less convenient, and most people worked a six-day week, it was also an occasion when those whose jobs took them far from where they grew up could begin to look forward to returning to their hometowns and villages for the Lunar New Year.[21]

Even if the earth god hardly gets a mention, food customs still influence the menu at present-day *wěiyá* gatherings. Oftentimes, steamed spring rolls are served, because the way they are rolled up makes people think of bundles of paper currency. As explained in chapter 3, guabao also appear at this time of year because their shape is deemed auspicious: not only do they look like cash-stuffed wallets, but the "tiger's mouth" is also believed to eat bad luck.

The local earth god may no longer take center stage at annual *wěiyá*, but he still receives offerings and attention throughout the year. On the second and sixteenth day of each lunar month, those who seek his favor or protection may offer him mochi (its stickiness means money will stick and accumulate) or sweet snacks for general happiness. Alcohol (*jiǔ*) is a homophone for long (*jiǔ*) life; pig's trotters are an alternative, and perhaps a more appropriate symbol of longevity, because the meat is moist and tender, and thus suitable for elderly people.

INDIGENOUS TRADITIONS

Along with songs and dances, and the ritual and informal consumption of home-made alcohol, food offerings form part of the ancient religious customs of Taiwan's indigenous tribes. Even though most aboriginal people have converted to Protestantism or Catholicism since 1945, fragments of pre-Christian rites appear in the festivals that continue to loom large in village life far from Taipei. In addition to attracting tourists and their dollars, these celebrations are recognized as among the few opportunities to build family and community cohesion and transmit tribal customs to the younger generation because many people working or studying in the big cities return home.[22]

Greater access to lowland foodstuffs has reshaped the indigenous diet in recent decades, making the traditional foods that appear during festivals all the more special, as they provide a glimpse of past foodways. Millet, formerly a staple (see chapter 1), is now seldom used outside festivals and tourist-oriented indigenous restaurants.

The Amis Ilisin, a multiday harvest festival, usually opens with the slaughtering of a pig for consumption at a meal to which everyone is invited. In this respect, aboriginal habits are not very different from those of Han people who settled in Taiwan's countryside and raised a hog or two on scraps, fattening it for the next special family or community occasion.

Atayal festival foods include honeycombs and mochi made of foxtail millet or dryland rice. Meats and fish (especially shovel-jaw carp) that had been preserved in salt and foxtail millet, as well as the meat of animals like wild boar and wild muntjac, were traditionally offered raw before being cooked and consumed.[23] Two items associated with the Atayal, because they are sold by eateries in Wulai and some other places, are *zhútǒng fàn* (a section of bamboo filled with glutinous rice and goodies like mushrooms) and a type of wrap made from glutinous rice and mashed bananas. Both are traditional and popular with tourists—but neither is a festival food.

SEASONAL SPECIALTIES:
WARMING FOODS FOR WINTER

Except for those lucky enough to escape to the mountains for a weekend, a Taiwanese summer means at least three months of daytime temperatures above 32.2°C (90°F), coupled with brutal humidity. Few lowlanders under the age of forty can imagine life without air-conditioning. Many older folk, however, fondly remember certain foods for their putative ability to help people get through the hottest months. Mung-bean congee was one; lotus-leaf porridge (said to be good for preventing sunstroke) was another. Along with bitter gourd, daikon, and tofu, these ingredients are categorized by practitioners of Chinese herbal medicine as cooling foods.[24]

Homes and offices may be fitted out to reduce summertime discomfort, but even in the twenty-first century, much of Taipei's population endures the low temperatures of winter in unheated buildings. Tried-and-tested culinary responses to chilly weather include "the three best friends in winter" (*suì hán sānyǒu*).

For many hundreds of years, Chinese people have talked about "the three best friends in winter": pine (a symbol of bravery), bamboo (representing modesty and integrity), and plum (on account of its flowers and fragrance).[25] But when Taiwanese gourmands speak of their three finest friends in wintertime, they are referring to a trio of popular dishes: lamb hot pot, ginger duck, and sesame chicken in wine. All three are regarded as *dōngbǔ* (special boosts or supplements for the colder months), and all three acquire much of their flavor from rice wine. When eating these delicacies, one can fully appreciate the distinctiveness of Taiwanese rice wine compared to Chinese and Japanese rice wines. The molasses blended into raw rice wine (see chapter 2) gives the liquid, and many of the dishes it is added to, a sweetish aroma.

Lamb, a warming food according to ancient Chinese medical theory, was an unpopular meat before the 1980s. Widely thought to stink, only after selective breeding and changes to the way the meat is prepared did it become a favorite. Lamb for hot pots is usually diced, but sometimes thinly sliced. Ginger duck, eaten as a soup or a hot pot, should be made with old ginger, which has more "heat" (in the traditional Chinese medical sense) than very fresh ginger. The duck should be male, as males are more forceful, and therefore able to impart more vigor to the diners. Almost every recipe calls for sesame oil or sesame seeds. The third can claim to be uniquely Taiwanese. Known in Mandarin as *máyóu jī jiǔ*, it contains ginger and gets part of its delectability from the unsurpassed quality of local sesame oil.[26] It is often cooked in straight rice wine, no water being added, and is the kind of dish the authorities warn people to avoid if they plan to drive afterward (see chapter 8).

BANDO

A Holo term that is starting to enter the English language, *bando* means the kind of jolly roadside banquet that has been a feature of life for generations. Many bando are wedding celebrations: the groom's family will hold one for their relatives, friends, and neighbors, and then the bride's family will hold another. Other bando feasts are tied to religious festivals, and some companies opt to have their *wěiyá* next to their factory instead of in a restaurant. Evening bando are often held in community halls, parking lots, and on campuses, but taking over a stretch of road and erecting tarpaulin-covered cooking and dining areas remains very common.

Bando means "to set (or manage) tables," and the number of tables is usually between ten and thirty—with ten or twelve people per circular table—but much bigger events are not uncommon. Before the Japanese colonial period, social development propelled the growth of bando culture. Communal feasts were an opportunity for new arrivals to make and reinforce social networks that could replace family and other connections they had left behind in China. Taiwan was then a volatile frontier society full of opportunity; for ambitious individuals, sponsoring a bando was an effective way to strengthen links with those who might help them climb the social ladder.[27]

Treating your neighbors showed generosity and brought prestige, and people were building their reputations this way well into the Japanese era. Taking home uneaten food has always been the norm—these days, plastic bags are placed on each table for that purpose—so by providing far more than your guests could possibly consume during the meal, a host could make an extra impression on attendees. In the more distant past, when traveling from one settlement to another could take many hours, certain deep-fried items—such as *jījuǎn* (see below) and taro rolls—were served specifically because they were easy to pack.[28]

At the bando of yesteryear, fried dishes were especially popular, because the price of cooking oil meant people seldom fried food at home. Most families subsisted on boiled and stewed dishes and looked forward to special occasions because they could gorge on oilier, fattier, and saltier cuisine. This, writes Yujen Chen, "can explain why these festival dishes are regarded as symbolic Taiwanese dishes nowadays."[29]

Long ago, bando were key events in rural areas for another reason. Neighbors would get involved long before the day of the feast. Oftentimes, preparations began almost half a year in advance. Because there were so few professional chefs, and none in the countryside, the host family had to locate and invite a talented cook for the event. The eventual success of a bando depended in large part on the cooperation of neighbors, and the exchange of labor and sharing of resources enhanced village solidarity. In northern and central Taiwan, Jordan writes, there was a custom of rotating feasts:

Traditional religion . . . included feasting systems whereby participating areas would celebrate the same festival on different days, each participating area taking its turn at providing a feast for all the others. Informants joked that it was possible to eat for an entire month at other people's expense, although the costs when one's own turn came could be crushing. Supporters . . . maintained that it promoted regional integration on the one hand, and was a merry romp on the other. Opponents pointed to lost labor and to the potentially baleful results of poor people making excessive sacrifices . . . to support excessively ambitious feasts. One official of Taipei City Government told me of one man having sold his daughter in order to pay for his share in a community feast.[30]

In the early 1980s, the government began pressuring temples to curtail this practice, regarding it as wasteful. Jordan believes it would in any case have waned, in part because the structure of the economy was changing. A growing proportion of the population had to work regular hours five or six days a week, precluding them from attending out-of-town events. What is more, alternative forms of entertainment were becoming available and affordable.

The decline of temple-related bando is likely one reason why Tang Cin-lu, a leading banquet chef in Kaohsiung, complains that whereas he used to be busy every single day, sometimes he now has just three bookings in a month.[31] But after years of apparent decline, interest in bando cuisine and culture appears to have revived somewhat, in part because of a locally made 2013 film that was a box office triumph, titled *Zone Pro Site: The Moveable Feast*.

A "zone pro site" is the chief of a banqueting team; this Holo-language term, which would normally be rendered *chóng pho 'su*, means "a professional master of culinary skills." He (the authors have not come across a female zone pro site) is responsible for selecting dishes after consulting with whoever is paying for the feast, controlling the workflow from the time the team arrives on-site, and supervising the actual cooking. Depending on how many tables are being catered, there will be a number of assistant chefs and apprentices. Much of the ingredient chopping, serving, and general kitchen chores are done by middle-aged female workers hired ad hoc. In the south, these assistants have the picturesque nickname *shuǐ jiǎo*—"water feet"—because they invariably get their feet wet as they squat down to wash vegetables and dishes in large metal basins arrayed across the asphalt.

An even number of tables and courses is considered auspicious, unless the bando is being held as part of a funeral, or the host requests certain dishes and the menu ends up having eleven or thirteen courses. In the past, an odd number would have been considered unlucky, but bando chef Lin Ming-tsan says that these days it is not uncommon, and it does not bother him; ten or twelve courses is typical, but a few events have sixteen or eighteen. When there are so many courses, halfway through there is an interval of sorts, and a sweet soup is served before the feast resumes. Bando often begin with a cold platter, then a theme dish that sets the tone for the entire meal. Expensive ingredients such as abalone appear in the first half of the event, in case guests get full and these items go to waste. Fish are not served late in the bando, because fish leftovers are not easy to wrap and take home.

An almost extinct bando practice plays a notable part in the climax of *Zone Pro Site: The Moveable Feast*. Modern-day bando crews arrive and leave in trucks that carry everything they need, including the stoves on which they cook and the tables where guests sit and eat. In the past, however, many of the utensils were borrowed from the banquet hosts (who might also provide ingredients and firewood), their relatives, or their neighbors. To thank everyone who helped out in this way, after the guests had left, an "end of banquet soup" (*cài wěi tāng*) was cooked up—typically with leftovers, daikon, and mustard greens—and shared out. This custom, which many remember as one of the most charming aspects of traditional bando, expressed gratitude, albeit with humble materials. "If you're happy, then the food is delicious" is how a character in the movie sums up the sentiment that makes for a successful bando.

Lin Ming-tsan, a leading "zone pro site" and one of the culinarians who helped with the making of *The Moveable Feast*, is the son of Lin Tian-sheng (1934–2010), perhaps the most famous banquet chef in postwar Taiwan and a man dubbed "a national treasure." When it comes to giving interviews, Lin is generous with his time. Because neither of his children have followed him into the bando industry, he hopes that his late father's legacy can be preserved through the media.

Lin's recollections show how some bando practices have changed. During the 1960s and 1970s, banquet chefs sometimes butchered pigs secretly to avoid a substantial hog tax; in this era of centralized slaughtering and food-safety scares, that would be unthinkable. But the habit of making fresh chicken stock at the beginning of the working day remains very much in place.[32]

Lin believes he is the only banquet chef in the country who still arranges and cooks in the old bando manner. He never serves beef or lamb, and he includes sashimi only if requested by the person commissioning the event. Since the 1960s, a large proportion of banquets have featured a sashimi course, but Lin has prepared sashimi only a handful of times, because it is not Taiwanese. However, like many in the catering industry, he has dropped shark's fin and pig liver. Tang Cin-lu, by contrast, thinks constantly refreshing his repertoire of dishes can help his business. He now offers clients shabu-shabu hot pot featuring giant grouper, kimchi, and tofu, as well as crispy battered *bāozi* stuffed with pork, garlic, scallions, dried shrimp and fish paste, with a salted egg yolk at the center of each one.

Bando cold platters have changed a lot over the past four decades, Lin says. In the 1970s, they typically featured cashew nuts, sausage, and shredded squid. Pig tongue and pig liver appeared in the following decade. In the 1990s, seafood started playing a major role, with abalone, jellyfish, lobster, mullet roe, and scallops

Some of the bando tools Lin Tian-sheng used during his career as a banquet chef.
Katy Hui-wen Hung

becoming favorites. Yujen Chen ties this enthusiasm for expensive seafood to rising prosperity and a willingness to spend a lot more on special occasions.[33] "The
first-course seafood platter is the key to increasing the value of a banquet. How
expensive a banquet is usually depends on the cost and quality, as well as the quantity, of the seafood," says Lin.

Pork, chicken, and goose were bando staples in the old days, but Lin's efforts
to preserve old flavors are hampered by changing livestock practices. "Meats
taste different now," he laments. "For example, the pork supplied to us used to
be from pigs ten to twelve months old. Now we eat pigs at the age of three and a
half months. It's the same with chickens, twelve weeks instead of twelve months.
Pickles that were preserved or fermented for forty days are now 'ready' in ten days.
How could the tastes not be different?"

Like many restaurant chefs, Lin continues to use old-fashioned bamboo steaming baskets as often as he can, rather than durable modern stainless-steel ones, saying the former are better at preserving food aromas. In the past, if no refrigerator
was available, meats and other items were kept fresh until needed by stacking up
square wooden-box steamers and placing a large chunk of ice in the box at the top.
Each of the boxes below stored a different kind of food, with meat and seafood
on the lower levels (because they may drip), and additional ice packed around fish
and squid.[34]

Lin Ming-tsan spent ten years in bando kitchens before he became a chef: "I was
washing dishes, chopping, and cutting. These skills are basic and necessary. Only
by going through this can a chef learn about service timing and organization, how
to manage a banquet, and how to manage an emergency situation. Knowing the
time it takes to chop and cut are all important, because as a chef you need to control
timing and monitor service from start to finish."

Since the 1970s, he adds, there has been a greater division of labor, and now the
chefs can concentrate more on devising dishes and cooking. Previously, the "zone
pro site" had to control everything: designing the menu, ordering and purchasing
ingredients, administration and financial management were all part of the job.

Zone pro sites feel the most pressure when they have to cater a midday banquet,
because that means their preparation time is even more limited.[35] Bando kitchens
must have drains because so much water is used for washing vegetables and other
ingredients; once, when he was working with his father ahead of a 245-table *wěiyá*,
Lin realized that the site had no drain. He and his colleagues had no option but to
dig a drain by hand before they could begin cooking. Other veteran caterers have
spoken of trying to prepare for roadside banquets during rain so torrential that their
tarpaulins collapsed, their stoves refused to light, and some of the live fish they
brought escaped down a drain when their tub overflowed.

A MASTER RE-CREATES OLD FLAVORS

One morning at the end of July 2017, Lin Ming-tsan and his team arrived at Taipei's Palais de Chine Hotel—where, in March 2018, the in-house Cantonese restaurant was awarded three Michelin stars—and began preparations for a thirty-seven-table, twelve-course feast filled to the brim with old-time Taiwanese flavors. There was more to this event than offering the capital's gourmets an exceptional dining experience; the hotel saw it as an opportunity for the kitchen staff to learn traditional bando recipes from the country's foremost expert, with an eye to possibly adding these dishes to its own menu.

The meal kicked off with a Taiwanese-style cold platter. Among the ten meat and seafood items were hog maw and pig's uterus. In olden times, both were common banquet foods. No longer viewed as particularly prestigious, they are now usually enjoyed in a roadside-vendor setting.

Lin takes pains to make clear the differences between his authentically Taiwanese version of the second course, Pig's Knuckle Wrapped in Angel's Hair (very thin wheat noodles), and how a Cantonese chef might prepare it: "First, the pig's knuckle is flavored with *cōng shāo* [large scallions and garlic cloves deep-fried separately, then combined into a single flavoring], plus ginger and chili. Apart from these, all I add is soy sauce, salt, and sugar, to keep the flavors as close to the original as possible. A Cantonese cook might well throw in medicinal herbs or star anise, but I don't use them."

A banquet without a fish course is inconceivable, and Lin's third delicacy was Five-Willows Steamed Red Snapper. His version has seven—rather than five—julienned ingredients: onion, pork, wood-ear fungus, carrots, bamboo shoots, green peppers, and red peppers. After thoroughly cooking the snapper by deep-frying, the fish gains a classic Taiwanese flavor thanks to a drizzle of white vinegar boiled with sugar poured just before serving.

The fourth course bore an ornate name: Phoenix on a Golden Carriage. The phoenix is in fact a sparrow, and the carriage is an egg yolk still in its shell. A hole is made in the egg and the white removed. Ham and thinly sliced mushrooms are put inside; the sparrow is then tucked in with its head sticking out. After topping up the shell with glutinous rice, the whole thing is steamed.

Farmers continue to trap sparrows with nets because they eat their crops, and no more than a few decades ago they would often grill and eat those they caught. Phoenix on a Golden Carriage, however, has fallen out of favor on account of its disturbing appearance, and it was only at the insistence of the hotel's owner that Lin included it. The hotelier had childhood memories of sparrows in the fields in the south—but given the response the dish got on this occasion, it will likely be replaced with another classic banquet dish if the hotel decides to re-create Lin's old-time menu.

For the following course, Taro Duck Casserole, the duck is cut up, tossed briskly in a ladleful of hot oil, and then set aside. Dried, sliced bamboo shoots are softened with hot water, then placed at the bottom of the casserole dish; one advantage of this ingredient is that it helps rid the meat of undesirable odors. The taro plays a thickening role, like that of potato in casseroles. Sugar, rice wine, and white pepper are used to season the meat, and chicken stock is added before the dish is steamed.

Course number six, Jumbo Shrimp Simmered in Sweet and Sour Sauce, is what Lin usually prepares in place of the eel dish his father would serve. Sections of cruller are a key ingredient in this dish. These create a crunchy texture; after they soak up the sauce, they can be eaten like flavorsome biscuits. Lin uses shrimp because he worries that the eels available in recent years could be too tough and have too much chewy skin for this kind of dish. It is the sauce that makes this dish stand out: the shrimp and crullers are cooked with tomato and coriander, then topped with a sweet-and-sour concoction made of pineapple juice, sugar, and five-spice sauce.

Each "zone pro site" has at least one *tshiú-lōo-tshài*, a dish of which the chef is particularly proud, and that he hopes can be served at every bando he caters. One of Lin's is Gold Whole Chicken Wrapped in Silver. The final part of the name comes from the aluminum foil in which the bird is sealed, while gold is the color of the corn kernels and Green Giant–brand canned cream-style sweet corn with which the chicken is stuffed. Lin prefers Green Giant because of its thick, creamy consistency. The chicken is boiled by itself for forty minutes, then another forty minutes after the corn (along with sugar, rice wine, white pepper, salt, and chicken stock) has been added and the bird wrapped in foil. Lin has been serving Gold Whole

Members of Lin Ming-tsan's team prepare Gold Whole Chicken Wrapped in Silver. *Katy Hui-wen Hung*

Chicken Wrapped in Silver for at least thirty years, including it as often as he can, because he thinks the name, together with the golden luster of the sweet corn and the meat, have such positive connotations.

The ninth course has been a bando classic since the Japanese period and is often requested because it symbolizes family unity and harmony. To make Buddha Jumps Over the Wall, *cōng shāo*, taro, and spare ribs are deep-fried hours in advance. The egg is crisped up earlier in the morning for the same reason, to avoid bringing any hot grease into the freshly prepared food before steaming. The soup is based on chicken stock, other ingredients being bamboo shoots, twenty chestnuts for a table of ten, an identical number of quail's eggs, enokitake mushrooms, sliced shiitake mushrooms, thinly sliced pork, the fresh skin of ocean sunfish (dried skin is insufficiently thick or fatty), cabbage, chili pepper, dried shrimp, and scallops.

The addition of taro makes Lin's Buddha Jumps Over the Wall decidedly different from Cantonese versions. Lin explains the taro is there not merely for the "old-time" flavor it adds; it also thickens the soup, so no cornstarch is needed. The removal of shark's fin from most banquet menus, circa 2012, is in Lin's opinion the most significant change in banqueting culture for decades. Fish skin provides the smell people expect from shark's-fin dishes, but the same effect can be achieved by using the juices left after soaking dried shrimp, he says.

Fried items are convenient for taking home and eating later, or sharing with those who could not attend the banquet. Even now, placing bags on the tables so guests can wrap food and carry it away is standard practice. Lin's *fú lù shòu pīnpán* ("fortune, fame, and longevity platter") consists of taro rolls, adzuki-bean pastries, and *jījuǎn*.

Novice students of Chinese reading the logograms for *jījuǎn* might assume it is made with chicken, but an alternative name in Holo, *to î kńg* ("leftovers [turned into] rolls"), leaves no room for misunderstanding. A few generations ago, according to Lin, feasts connected to temple events were all-day affairs. At these *liû chúi chhiòh* ("flowing water banquets"), people would come and go, and latecomers expected to be fed. The custom of turning leftovers into meat-based deep-fried wraps is the origin of the modern *jījuǎn*, he believes.

Lin's recipe lists ground pork belly, fish paste, sweet-potato starch, onions, and carrots. Sugar is one of the seasonings; some of the northerners present at the Palais de Chine found the *jījuǎn* too sweet for their liking, Taipei's flavors generally being more savory than those in the south. These days, the filling is rolled up in tofu sheets, made from the film that forms on the surface of soy milk when it is boiled in an open pan. In the past, *jījuǎn* were wrapped in pig's caul fat, itself a common leftover.

Lin's penultimate dish that day was Squid and Whelks with Garlic Hot Pot (see recipe in chapter 10). In Lin's opinion, this dish is a classic example of the type of food that was presented at "flowing water banquets," as well as *jiǔjiā cài*. Defining the latter term as "dishes served at liquor houses," Yujen Chen explains its significance to "the notion of Taiwanese cuisine" by referring to the dining-and-drinking establishments that thrived in the Beitou area of Taipei during and after Japanese rule. Because of its heavy taste, and the speed with which it could be put together, squid and whelks with garlic soup was considered an ideal menu item for customers who had had a bit too much to drink.

Compared to liquor houses in Dadaocheng and other parts of the capital, those in Beitou were more expensive and their customers wealthier. The businessmen who frequented them demanded delicate dishes, so the neighborhood became a place where old Taiwanese haute cuisine recipes were preserved. At the same time, liquor-house owners pushed their chefs to create new dishes in order to attract customers. However, as Chen notes, liquor houses were not highlighted as venues serving Taiwanese cuisine until the 1990s—by which time they had declined in popularity—and nobody used the term *jiǔjiā cài* before that decade.[36]

The meal culminated with Lin's regular banquet dessert, steamed mashed-taro pudding. This gets its old-fashioned flavor from a mix of shallots fried in lard, sugar, and a sauce that blends longans and adzuki beans.

EAT ENOUGH, EAT WELL, EAT SMART:
BANQUETS FIT FOR A PRESIDENT

After 1971, the year the Republic of China on Taiwan left the United Nations, and even more so from 1972, after Chiang Ching-kuo rose to the premiership, Taiwanese were appointed to more senior positions in the government. When Chiang become president in 1978, he chose a Taiwan-born KMT heavyweight to be his vice president. Six years later, the man who eventually succeeded Chiang became the number two. Lee Teng-hui, who has never set foot on the Chinese mainland, went on to oversee important democratic and *běntǔ huà* (localization) reforms during his 1988–2000 tenure as president.[37]

In 1992, for the first time ever, the legislature was entirely elected by the people of Taiwan. (Previously, many lawmakers had been appointed to represent places in China and thus buttress Taipei's claim that it was the legitimate government of all China.) Schoolbooks began to focus on the history and geography of Taiwan, rather than treat the island as a tiny part of China. Holo, Hakka, and aboriginal languages were encouraged rather than denigrated, and there was an upsurge of interest in local customs, especially foodways.

The state banquets laid on by the highest office in the land have not only reflected changes in dietary culture but also served as opportunities for leaders to articulate a particular vision of Taiwan. When Chiang Kai-shek was leader, the menu, furniture, decoration, and even menu font evoked classical China. Most of the dishes served were Jiang-zhe or Cantonese, but the first dish at each event was the Plum Blossom Assortment, a cold platter named for and shaped like the ROC's national flower.[38] In this era, seafood played a relatively minor role, although shark's fin was often a highlight. During Chiang Ching-kuo's presidency, banquets were fairly frugal. Under his successor, however, the booming economy meant that such events were no longer occasions to "eat enough," but rather as opportunities to "eat well."[39]

Yujen Chen has written that, after the Democratic Progressive Party's Chen Shui-bian became the country's first non-KMT leader, "state banquets became highly charged with symbolic references to indigenization and ethnic integration." The inauguration banquet of Chen Shui-bian—who is seen as an emphatically Taiwanese, rather than Chinese, politician—on May 20, 2000, was noteworthy for featuring local *xiǎochī* for the first time. Among them were two from Tainan, the incoming president's hometown: milkfish ball soup and *óaⁿ kóe* (see chapter 6). "Media reports highlighted that local snacks were receiving a national honor insofar as they were a main course at the state banquet, and the media praised the choice as an effective way to raise the status of local Taiwanese snacks," Yujen Chen pointed out.[40]

Chen Shui-bian's desire for ethnic harmony was expressed by the dessert: taro and sweet-potato cake. Taro has long been a code word for *wàishěngrén* ("people from outside the province"—in other words, mainland Chinese), whereas sweet potato is shorthand for *běnshěngrén* ("people native to this province," meaning descendants of pre-1945 arrivals). His second-term inauguration banquet in 2004 included ingredients from every part of Taiwan. Minority foodways were represented by indigenous millet mochi and Hakka glutinous rice; guests toasted with Kinmen kaoliang, drank tea from Alishan, and sipped coffee from Gukeng (see chapter 8).

During Chen's presidency, a "localized state banquet" policy was launched. Foreign dignitaries were entertained in counties far from Taipei, and the feasts showcased dishes synonymous with those places. In Chiayi, shredded turkey with gravy on white rice made an appearance. In Tainan, the menu featured *dānzǐ miàn* (see chapter 6). "In addition, ethnic integration [was] still a common symbol presented in these banquets," writes Yujen Chen, giving as an example a banquet held in Pingtung that included Hoklo, Hakka, and indigenous cuisines.[41]

Chen Shui-bian decreed that abalone and shark's fin should not appear in government-sponsored feasts. Under his successor, Ma Ying-jeou of the KMT (president from 2008 to 2016), environmental considerations were given even greater weight. Because there was an emphasis on "food miles," most dishes used local produce.[42]

Power then shifted back to the DPP when Tsai Ing-wen became not only Taiwan's first woman president but also the first female national leader in Asia who was not the widow, daughter, or sister of a previous leader. Tsai's taking the oath of office was marked by an eight-course feast designed so attendees could "taste the tastes of Taiwan." The event went beyond highlighting local ingredients like garlic from Xiluo in Yunlin and scallions from Sanxing in Yilan. Food safety was one of the issues Tsai had campaigned on, and every item on the menu came with a QR code so guests could use their smartphones to retrieve product origin and other information.

SITTING OUT THE MONTH:
POSTPARTUM RECOVERY CUSTOMS

For at least a thousand years, Han people have believed that, after giving birth, women should "sit out the month" (*zuò yuè zi*), so their bodies can recover from confinement. This practice shows no sign of tapering off, in part because appearance-conscious Taiwanese women think it can help a new mother regain her pre-pregnancy figure. In addition to dietary do's and don'ts, there are lifestyle restrictions. The women should neither wash their hair nor take showers, instead taking sponge baths and rubbing their scalps with a mixture of alcohol and warm water. They should not leave the house. Nor, according to some, should they read, watch TV, or stay in an air-conditioned room, as these actions are likely to leave them further depleted.

Food cooked for the mother of a newborn should not contain salt, MSG, or other seasonings, as these are thought to affect her ability to produce breast milk. In the past, mothers-in-law would prepare special meals, but because now many people live far from their in-laws—or their relatives lack the knowledge or motivation to do the cooking—spending the month being fed and cared for in a purpose-built *zuò yuè zi* center is common. Or, like Leslie Hsu Oh, they order a month's worth of meals from one of the specialist suppliers that have sprung up wherever there are Chinese people.

Oh, a US-born graduate of the Harvard T. H. Chan School of Public Health, observed *zuò yuè zi* customs only when her fourth child was born. Writing in the January 8, 2017, *Washington Post*, she noted "inconsistent results" as to the overall efficacy of practice. "On the plus side were findings that a long recovery period improved a mother's health-related quality of life and led to better bonding with her child. But . . . limiting physical activity for a month was bad for muscular and cardiovascular health and increased postpartum depression."

Oh found sitting out the month a positive experience, even if, by the "standards of traditional Chinese medicine, I probably didn't eat enough pork liver to replenish the blood lost during childbirth, pork kidney to heal back pain, and pig feet to increase my milk supply." Presumably, she did not obey the customary rule that no water be drunk during the first month. In the past, rice wine was used to make all beverages, soups, and medicinal decoctions.[43] Now, many women drink what is called "postpartum water," Red Label Rice Wine that has been reduced to one-third of its original volume by boiling off most of the alcohol. Factory-made "postpartum water" is sold online and in certain stores.

In Taiwan, women who have just given birth are provided with protein-rich dishes made with Red Label Rice Wine. Other indispensable elements of the postpartum diet are black sesame oil and ginger, and the definitive *zuò yuè zi* dish is native chicken with sesame oil (*máyóu tǔjī*). However, some think *wūgǔjī* ("black-boned" hens) should be used, because they are more nourishing and better for the mother's kidneys.

Chicken with sesame oil is also associated with *mǎnyuè yàn*, the traditional "baby shower" celebration when a newborn reaches the age of one month. It is important that the chicken be cooked complete with offal and entrails, to symbolize the child's completeness and perfection. At this event, the baby's name is ritually announced to his or her ancestors, and their blessings are sought.

If the infant is the family's first son or first grandson, they may celebrate by holding a banquet; traditionally, the first course is chicken with sesame oil. The maternal grandparents will present the baby with a set of new clothes, and the newborn's parents will thank them by preparing Eight Treasures Oily Rice with chestnuts, pork, mushrooms, scallops, peanuts, ham, dried shrimp, and carrot. This dish is considered auspicious because its name implies that the youngster will lack for nothing when he or she is older. There may be offerings of hexagonal red tortoise cakes, named *âng ku kóe* in Holo, that are made of glutinous rice flour. Double happiness wishing rolls (*shuāngxǐ rúyì juǎn*)—finely chopped fish, pork, shallots, water chestnuts, and shiitake mushrooms rolled up in thin sheets of egg and spring-roll wraps—are another culinary device for attracting good fortune.[44]

5

❖ ❖

The Farms That Feed Taipei

Without its farmers, meals in Taiwan would be dull and less healthy, and the country's food security situation much worse. Yet Taiwanese farmers are poorly rewarded. Since the early 1970s, agriculture has never accounted for more than 40 percent of the total income of the average farming household. In the same period, the total disposable income of farming households (one in eleven of all households in 2015) has fluctuated between 62 and 78 percent of that in non-farming households.[1] When the economy boomed between the 1960s and 1990s, many farmers—male and female alike—spent as much time laboring on construction sites as cultivating their fields.

A lingering sense of gratitude to the land that fed them and their ancestors motivates members of the older generation[2] but rarely inspires their children to pursue a career in agriculture. At the same time, this emotional attachment means landowners are reluctant to sell or lease plots they no longer cultivate. Around half of Taiwan's farmers are over sixty-five, and three-quarters of them think no one will take over their fields when they are gone.[3] But agriculture is hanging on, and cultivated land still accounts for more than 6 percent of Greater Taipei's surface area.[4]

Over the past half century, an expanding population and changing eating habits have left the island dependent on foodstuff imports. Wheat, corn,[5] and soy are grown in miniscule quantities, and less than 5 percent of the beef eaten is local.[6] Few countries have experienced such a rapid collapse in their ability to feed themselves. Before 1968, food production in caloric terms was roughly equal to

97

domestic requirements,[7] but within two decades self-sufficiency was below 50 percent.[8] Even before Taiwan joined the WTO in 2002, farmers faced foreign competition due to rampant smuggling from China of mushrooms, tea, and offal.[9] In 2014, the self-sufficiency rate recovered slightly to 34.1 percent, and the authorities hope to lift it to 40 percent by 2020.[10]

While the cultivation of genetically modified crops is not permitted,[11] the country imports dozens of GM food products, *Taiwan Business Topics* pointed out in its May 2015 issue. Because inheritance customs give the oldest son half of his father's land, with other sons (and sometimes daughters) sharing the remainder, farms have been getting smaller and smaller.[12] By the end of 2010, average cultivated land per enterprise was down to 1.9 acres,[13] with just one farmer in five having more than 2.5 acres.[14] One expert who praises Taiwan as "the world's best exemplar of high-tech, mechanized small-plot agriculture" believes government-sponsored efforts to achieve economies of scale are crucial to the future of farming.[15] An initiative called "Small Landlord, Big Tenant" was launched in 2008 by the Council of Agriculture (COA), the central government agency that oversees farming, fisheries, and food affairs. Despite its flaws, the policy has succeeded in making thousands of acres of land available to younger professional farmers,[16] some of whom are applying technological skills they learned in other industries.[17] Taiwan is unlikely to meet the majority of its food needs anytime soon, but the future that faces the island's farmers is slightly brighter now than it has been for some years.

PADDY FIELDS AND SUGAR PLANTATIONS

A lament occasionally heard in Taiwan: The island's coal, copper, gold, and oil deposits are too small to be profitably exploited, and barely a third of its land is flat. All this is true, but as far as the Fujianese pioneers who sailed across "the Black Water Ditch" in the seventeenth and eighteenth centuries were concerned, the island possessed a more desirable natural advantage—a climate ideal for growing rice.

According to ClimaTemps.com, the average temperature in Taipei is 70.9°F, and rain can be expected at least fourteen days per month throughout the year. In 1627, before Han settlers reached the area, a Spanish expedition to the mouth of the Tamsui River found the area was producing surpluses of rice.[18] Over the next quarter century, however, neither the Spanish nor the Dutch (who expelled the Spaniards from north Taiwan) had much success in getting the aborigines to trade or share foodstuffs.[19] To ensure a reliable supply of local grain, the Dutch East India Company encouraged agricultural colonists from Fujian to settle in the Tainan area from the early 1630s, and in north Taiwan by the late 1640s. The company also imported draft oxen.[20]

Winters in the south are significantly warmer and drier than those in the north. Securing water for their paddy fields spurred Han encroachment into the foothills, and the outsiders inevitably clashed with indigenous tribes.[21] Following Taiwan's incorporation into the Qing Empire in 1684, imperial officials were preoccupied with managing aboriginal-settler relations while maintaining order and balancing the books. When deprived of their hunting and foraging grounds, indigenous communities often resorted to violence and sometimes threw in their lot with "untamed" aborigines living in the mountains. But farmland could be taxed, and the authorities feared that if Han migrants—who entered Taiwan in substantial numbers, even during periods when immigration was forbidden—were prevented from making use of uncultivated land, they would rebel or embrace banditry. What is more, Taiwan's grain surpluses helped feed soldiers and civilians in Fujian.[22]

Inevitably, the pale of Han agricultural settlement expanded eastward throughout Qing rule.[23] Robert Swinhoe, a British diplomat who used his free time in the 1850s and 1860s to describe Taiwan's natural wonders, reported:

> The line of demarcation between savage [indigenous] and Chinese [Han] territory is at once observable by the fine wood-covered ranges that mark the hunting grounds of the original possessors of the island. The Chinese territory is almost entirely denuded of trees and cultivated on these interior hills chiefly with the tea-plant, introduced from China. The absence of the primitive wood has naturally wrought a vast difference between the flora and fauna of the two territories. Coarse grass has covered the cleared hills, and the place of the woodland birds, the deer, and the goat, has been supplied by larks and birds of the plain, and by pigs and hares.[24]

In 1903, nearly seven hundred thousand acres, just over half of the island's cultivated land, was paddy.[25] Over the following three decades, large-scale irrigation projects reshaped much of the landscape and led to a massive expansion in rice output,[26] especially in the southwest. Production peaked at nearly three million tons in 1976, and per-acre yields continued to increase,[27] even as per capita consumption fell. Before the Japanese era, annual per capita rice consumption may have exceeded 440 pounds.[28] Until the 1970s, the average Taiwanese ate about three hundred pounds of rice per year, but as living standards rose and imported alternatives became widely available, intake tumbled. In 1980, it was 223 pounds.[29] Since 2013, it has been barely one hundred pounds per person, lower than Japan's and less than half that in South Korea.[30]

Since the 1980s, realizing they are out of step with consumer tastes, many rice farmers have taken government subsidies to leave fields fallow or grow nitrogen-fixing legumes. More recently, some have switched to biodiesel crops or signed twenty-year afforestation contracts. By 2004, the land area of paddy had fallen two-thirds from its peak and was smaller than it had been a century earlier.[31] On

September 15, 2011, the COA's website announced that, as part of efforts to help rice farmers, as well as reduce wheat imports, government researchers had perfected the baking of bread using 80 percent rice flour, 20 percent wheat flour.

The first type of rice cultivated in Taiwan was *Oryza sativa javanica*, a subspecies suitable for dry upland fields. Dryland rice is now restricted to a few places in the central highlands and in the east; for many hillside farmers, fruit crops are far more lucrative. Per-acre yields of dryland rice average 30–40 percent of that of paddy rice, but *Oryza sativa javanica* cultivars continue to intrigue agricultural scientists because they require just one-fifth as much water.[32]

For the first third of the twentieth century, most Han rice farmers grew long-grain *indica* accessions (Mandarin: *zàilái mǐ*) that their ancestors had brought over from China. However, these were unpopular with Japanese consumers used to shorter, stickier *japonica* rice,[33] so the colonial authorities funded research to create *japonica* cultivars that would thrive in Taiwan's conditions. A quarter century of crossbreeding produced Taichung 65, the first in a series of disease-resistant, flavorful, and high-yield varieties known locally as *pénglái mǐ* (or ponlai rices).[34]

Short-grain *japonica* cultivars like the slightly chewy Kaohsiung 139 and the fuller-grained Taikeng 9 still account for around 91 percent of all rice grown in Taiwan, but less than half of the island's glutinous-rice production.[35] Their enduring popularity means Taiwan's rice is not merely different from China's, but also—because ponlai accessions have not gained significant acceptance overseas—somewhat unique in the world.[36] This adds a sliver of credence to claims that China-born politicians who "grew up drinking Taiwanese water, eating Taiwanese rice" deserve to be seen as true Taiwanese.[37]

Before the advent of ponlai, many farmers grew just one crop of rice each year. But, as the International Rice Research Institute has recognized, "An important feature of the ponlai varieties, in addition to fertilizer-responsiveness and insensitivity to temperature and day-length variations, is early maturity. This permitted a substantial increase in multiple cropping."[38] The island's multiple cropping index (number of crops/acre/year × 100) reached 189 in 1964, possibly the highest ever achieved in Asia. Many farmers still grow two consecutive crops of rice, then one of sweet potatoes, corn, or vegetables.[39] But many rice and taro farmers complain their crops are damaged by golden apple snails.[40]

Taiwanese long-grain *indica* rice is lauded by the Food and Agriculture Organization of the United Nations as having paved the way for the Green Revolution. The "historic discovery" of the sd1 semi-dwarfing gene by scientists in Taichung "revolutionized rice production in the world," and Taichung Native 1 was a precursor of the IR8 variety that after 1966 helped Cambodia, China, India, Indonesia, and the Philippines achieve self-sufficiency—and Australia, Myanmar, Pakistan, Sri Lanka, Thailand, and Vietnam become net rice exporters.[41] Long before the

IR8 breakthrough, pre-ponlai accessions contributed to the improvement of rice varieties in the Americas via the transfer of genetic material from Taiwan by the US Department of Agriculture.[42]

Taiwanese grain is now expensive by global standards, so farmers and farmers' associations are trying to add value to their crops, differentiate their products, and develop co-branding relationships. One of the country's airlines works with rice growers in Chishang, a district in the East Rift Valley that supplied grain to Japan's royal family during the colonial period. Entrées aboard EVA Air feature Chishang rice; according to the company's corporate social responsibility website, the company's in-flight menus extol the advantages of ponlai "specially selected to share the great taste of Taiwan rice with our international passengers and etch it in the gastronomic memories of these globetrotters."

Rice sustained Taiwan's population for centuries, but the drivers of the island's pre-industrial economy were not its paddy fields but its sugar plantations. A valuable export during and after the Dutch period,[43] sugar had become so lucrative by 1695 that an imperial official feared the island would not be able to feed itself because so much land was being used to grow cane.[44]

Japan was a major buyer of Taiwanese sugar long before they took control of the island in 1895.[45] The colonial authorities poured capital and know-how into the sector; by 1939, Taiwan was the world's number four source of sugar.[46] By value, sugar represented 74 percent of Taiwan's exports in the early 1950s,[47] but this ratio steadily declined as manufacturing came to dominate the economy. The importance of sugar was reflected in local speech; in Holo, *kam chià bô siang thâu tiⁿ* ("no cane is sweet from top to bottom") is a way of saying that life has its ups and downs.

Many of the larger fields in southern and eastern Taiwan were state-owned sugar plantations not long ago, but for reasons of topography as well as climate, little sugarcane was grown in Greater Taipei. The traditional cuisine of Tainan—for centuries a key sugar-growing area—is often said to be sweeter than that of north Taiwan.[48] As far back as the mid-seventeenth century, Han people living there used sugar to mask bad smells.[49] Sugarcane occasionally appears on dinner tables: harvested when still very short and soft, it can be boiled and then stir-fried with turnip, carrot, chili, and a sprinkling of cordia drupes.

International demand for refined sugar has left an imprint on Taiwan's landscape. But it seems the influence of the island's sugar-growing past on its cuisine is not entirely straightforward. Some older folk attribute the postwar popularity of sugar as a cooking ingredient to the tight control the authorities exercised over this commodity during the colonial period. Back then, diverting a single cane could result in serious punishment, so sugar seldom appeared in larders, even among families that grew cane. As a consequence, when the rules were somewhat relaxed after 1945, people were eager to enjoy this local product.[50]

DRAGON'S WHISKERS, BITTER LEAVES,
AND SWEET POTATOES

Official statistics do not reflect the scale and variety of vegetable cultivation in Taiwan. Many farmers who specialize in rice or fruit also produce seasonal greens that they share with relatives rather than sell. Rural folk who have moved into cities cultivate scallions or cilantro in balcony boxes and cabbages on roofs. The sweet-potato vendor selling oven-roasted tubers in a night market may well source from his uncle's field but never think to boast about traceability or food miles. That said, COA data is further evidence of Taiwanese diets becoming more like those in the West.

Domestic output of many vegetables, including bok choy and radishes, declined between 2006 and 2015, but carrot and potato harvests grew substantially.[51] Hypermarkets sell imported fresh carrots, lettuces, and potatoes. Many frozen, dehydrated and canned vegetables—especially tomatoes, cauliflowers, peas, and string beans—come from China. Competition from Chinese suppliers has driven some Taiwanese vegetable farmers out of business, *CommonWealth* reported in March 2013.

Surging production in a grab-all category that includes celery, chayote, edible amaranth, lettuce, spinach, water convolvulus, and some other leafy vegetables may be a consequence of plant-based diets becoming more popular. Over the past decade, yields of cabbages and bamboo shoots—by weight Taiwan's two main domestically grown vegetables—were stable.[52]

Taro production peaks during the cooler months, as does that of cabbages. But even at the height of summer, the latter are grown a mile or more above sea level in parts of Taichung and Yilan. Radishes, carrots, and burdock roots are harvested in the spring, while water spinach (in Mandarin *kōngxīn cài*, "hollow vegetable") is grown from March to December.

Sliced lotus root is served in salads, pickled, and stir-fried. There is something of a trend for oven-baked lotus-root chips. Mixing black sugar and powdered lotus root in hot water creates a paste; steaming it in a *diàn guō*, then fridging it for an hour or two, creates a delectable jelly best enjoyed with milk and a little honey. Despite its Chinese name (*shuǐ lián*, "water lotus"), the vegetable called crested floating-heart or white water snowflake is *Nymphoides hydrophylla*, a plant unrelated to the lotus; the spaghetti-thin stems can be sautéed with garlic, ginger, and/or sliced mushrooms. The orange buds of the daylily (*Hemerocallis disticha*) are also used as a vegetable. They can be cooked in soups with pork ribs, mixed in with rice vermicelli, or battered and deep-fried to make a kind of tempura.

The stringy white flowers of the betel-nut palm (widely grown for its berries, which as in Southeast Asia are chewed as stimulants rather than eaten) are highly palatable when lightly boiled and added to salads, or stir-fried with pork.

Significantly more expensive, because it can only be obtained by chopping down the palm, is betel-nut heart. This is the sweet and succulent center of the trunk. It resembles bamboo shoots in color and texture, and the alternative Chinese name, *bàntiān sǔn*, implies that it is a type of bamboo.

Like burdock and wasabi, chayote was introduced to Taiwan during Japanese rule.[53] This low-maintenance food plant is abundant between April and October. Its shoots and leaves, which go by the memorable Chinese name of *lóngxū* ("dragon's whiskers"), are eaten at least as often as the gourds. When serving a plate of hot chayote or vegetable fern (the latter, *Diplazium esculentum*, is listed in the Slow Food Foundation's Ark of Taste under its Chinese name, *guòmāo*), some Taiwanese like to add a raw egg yolk to give the dish a smoother and moister texture.

Other commonplace vegetables have been given colorful nicknames. *Lactuca indica*, Indian lettuce or swordleaf lettuce, is usually known as *A-cài*, with the Roman capital *A* appearing before the Chinese character for vegetable. The *A* comes from the Taiwanese pronunciation of its original name, *e-á-tshài*. Other names for it are *é-cài*, or "goose leaves" because it was often used to feed geese, and—giving a clue as to why it was used as animal feed—*khú-chhoi*, or "bitter leaves" in the language of the Hakka minority. *Lactuca sativa Linn*, closely related to the lettuces North Americans usually eat, is often called *dàlù mèi*, literally "mainland [Chinese] younger sister." The cultivar was introduced to Taiwan from China in the early 1990s and initially dubbed *Guǎngdōng A-cài*, but market vendors soon adopted a catchier term, one that local media originally applied to young Chinese women trafficked into the country to work in the sex industry.

The sweet potato arrived in Taiwan before 1603, when Chen Di (see chapter 1) saw it cultivated by indigenous people. Several decades later, it helped feed Koxinga's army as they besieged the Dutch. In the early eighteenth century, a dock in Tainan was called "Sweet Potato Port" because *Ipomoea batatas* was a major commodity shipped from there to Fujian. Back then, its Chinese name meant "barbarian's potato" (Mandarin pronunciation: *fānshǔ*). Well into the twentieth century, there were times when sweet potatoes were all that stood between a good number of Taiwanese and near starvation. Because of this, the generation now passing on regarded them with sincere gratitude. The Holo-language proverb, *chiàh han-chî bô chhûn pún sim*, can be translated as "Those who eat charity sweet potatoes too freely show no gratitude and never remember favors."

These days, the preferred term for sweet potato is the more politically correct *dìguā* ("soil gourd"). May Yu-Hsin Chang, CEO of the Taipei-based Foundation of Chinese Dietary Culture, has called it a "versatile crop which can be grown all year round, on both wet and dry ground. Many varieties . . . are grown in Taiwan, and these are locally referred to by various names, for example 'yellow sweet potato' and 'red-heart sweet potato,' based on the different color of the flesh."[54]

For the first half of the twentieth century, the poorer the family, the greater its dependence on sweet potatoes to eke out expensive rice. During World War II, the Japanese authorities imposed rice rationing and requisitioned grain for their armed forces, leaving many Taiwanese civilians again dependent on sweet potatoes. After 1945, the KMT diverted rice to their armies battling the Communists on the mainland, then—following the retreat of 1949—to feed their supporters on the island. Despite the negative connotations, for some older Taiwanese, sweet-potato congee and grated sweet potato are comfort foods that evoke nostalgia.[55]

Although their parents probably saw them as sustenance for the poor, and their leaves as something only pigs would willingly eat, health-conscious urbanites now seek out sweet potatoes—especially since Taiwanese crop researchers have come up with tastier, less starchy cultivars, some of which also have vitamin-rich leaves that are excellent for stir-frying.[56] Previous generations called the aboveground part of the sweet-potato plant *ti chhài* ("pig leaves"), because it was usually chopped up and fed to swine.

Making the most of this trend is Taiwan Sweet Potato International Food Co., which works with contract farmers in Yunlin and sells throughout Northeast Asia. To meet consumer expectations, the company discards any tubers that are not pleasing in terms of shape or color, that were nibbled by rats or insects, or that retain too much moisture after a month's storage. Customers are encouraged to eat the whole potato, skin and all, rather than peel it like most Taiwanese. But some things never change: sweet potatoes that fail quality control are turned into animal feed.[57]

SWEETNESS FROM THE HILLSIDES

The topographical and climatic variations that give Taiwan its spectacular biodiversity make possible the growing of temperate as well as tropical fruit. But apart from some peach farms in the mountainous interior of Taoyuan—an appropriate location, the toponym meaning "peach garden"—there are few orchards or fruit plantations north of Taichung. More than twenty types of fruit are grown domestically in significant quantities, and for several years total annual fruit production has been stable at around 2.85 million tons.[58] For its land area, Taiwan produces twice as much fruit as California.

In 2015, mangoes were the number one fruit crop by planted area. Most are Irwin mangoes, which turn a purply orange-red as they ripen between May and August and are filled with juicy orange-yellow flesh. Irwins have been grown in Taiwan since 1954, when they were brought in as part of a US aid package.[59] So-called "native mangoes" are smaller, have yellowish-green skins, and ripen earlier in the year; they were introduced during the Dutch era.

Bananas were second, while longans, lychees, pineapples, and watermelons jostled for third place. The delicious flavor of Taiwanese pineapples is the result of considerable labor. Several weeks before harvesting, a canvas sleeve is placed over each fruit to protect it from the harsh sunshine; some farmers use plastic collars made specifically for the purpose, or old newspapers. Around fifteen pineapple cultivars are grown in significant quantities; in the 1960s and 1970s, improved varieties including Tainong 4, 6, 11 (the perfume pineapple), 13, 16 (the honey pineapple), and 17 (the diamond pineapple) largely displaced the smooth cayenne.

Other important fruits include guavas (another Dutch-era arrival), Japanese apricots, Asian pears, pomelos, ponkan mandarins, liucheng and tankan oranges, and sugar apples.[60] It is surely no coincidence that peaches, plums, and grapes reached Taiwan right after the expulsion of the Dutch, as this period was marked by an influx of Han from different regions of China.[61] Plums are sometimes used to flavor hot dishes; chicken fried with sesame and then drizzled in a sweetish plum sauce is one of several plum-based dishes popular in Meiling ("Plum Ridge"), a mountainous corner of Tainan. During the colonial era, Japanese scientists made an organized effort to identify which trees and plants were able to thrive in Taiwan's climate, and it was during Japanese rule that apples, avocados, passion fruit, and sapodilla were first grown on the island.[62]

Indigenous farmers in Kaohsiung harvest plums.
Rich J. Matheson

Between the 1930s and the mid-1970s, when Panama disease began to decimate Taiwan's Cavendish plantations, bananas were an especially valuable cash crop. In some years, eight out of ten bananas eaten in Japan came from Taiwan, and 9.5 percent of Taiwan's export earnings came from foreign sales of the fruit.[63] There were times when pineapples made more money than bananas. In 1960, for instance, when agricultural goods brought in almost three-quarters of Taiwan's foreign-exchange earnings, canned pineapple represented 5.2 percent of all exports by value.[64] But in the past quarter century, the number of consignments going overseas has been negligible. On the whole, Taiwan's fruit—like the country's rice and pork—is no longer internationally competitive. Since 2013, the country's most successful fruit export has been the atemoya (a hybrid of the sugar apple and the cherimoya also known as the soursop), but the fragility of this trade was made clear by *CommonWealth* magazine in August 2015.

Fortunately for fruit growers, domestic demand is consistent, in part because of religious customs (see chapter 4). While claims that Taiwanese eat more fruit per person than any other nationality are almost certainly wrong,[65] it may well be true that they have the highest per capita consumption of commercially sold fresh fruit in the world and that they eat a wider variety of fruit than any other nationality. Because there is a custom of gifting pricey fruit (often South Korean pears or kiwis from New Zealand) to relatives, employees, and business associates, we believe Taiwanese spend more on fruit, relative to their incomes, than North Americans or Europeans. One reason, perhaps, is that fresh local fruits are available twelve months a year. Liucheng and tankan oranges are abundant before the Lunar New Year, after which there are tomatoes and then watermelons. The appearance of mangoes coincides with that of pitaya. The pineapple harvest begins in June; by the time it tapers off in late summer, there are wendan pomelos to enjoy. Bananas and papayas see the consumer through to the end of the calendar year.

The public also shows a willingness to try unfamiliar fruit, not all of which are imported. In the past few years, the Taiwan native kiwi has caught the public eye, with one farmer offering his crop through Buy Directly from Farmers. BDFF is a social enterprise that, according to its website, aims to build "a harmonious relationship between the city and countryside . . . [and help] people understand how their lifestyle and eating habits impact the environment . . . [while providing] youth with viable options in their hometown for a sustainable and promising future in agriculture."

Jabuticaba, which Taiwanese people call *shù pútao* ("tree grapes"), is gaining ground because it is said to contain more than fifteen nutrients. What is more, VegTrends.com claimed on October 1, 2014, that very few pesticides are needed because of its natural resistance to bugs and diseases. Taiwan's first jabuticaba trees were planted in the 1960s, but because the berries only appear on old-growth trunks and branches, there was no fruit to enjoy until many years later. According to Tom Chen, the growing popularity of jabuticaba is further evidence that, starting around 2005, Taiwanese culinary priorities began to shift, from taste and cost, to how healthy a product is perceived to be.[66]

A few Taiwanese gather wild mulberries and cherries, but perhaps the only fruit still harvested from natural woodlands on any scale is the aiyu fig, an endemic sub-species of *Ficus pumila* that thrives at between four thousand to about six thousand three hundred feet above sea level. Each year, the government auctions off rights to collect these pear-sized figs from national forests; successful bidders then hire indigenous villagers to do the picking, usually around October. Because the work is usually in remote locations and often involves climbing high up trees, experienced pickers expect to be paid about three times Taiwan's minimum wage, *Apple Daily* reported on May 23, 2016.

In the language of the Bunun people, aiyu is known as *tabakai*; the Rukai call it *twkunuy*; it is *runug* to the Truku; and the Saisiyat know it as *rapit*. Among the Tsou, for whom it has long been a key source of income, its name is *skikiya*. After the fruit are dried, the fig seeds are soaked, then massaged through a juice-straining bag to release the pectin. The slimy gel sets into a jelly that is usually served with a little honey, a few slices of lemon or lime, and some ice. This low-calorie treat, hardly known outside Taiwan and Singapore, is both extraordinarily refreshing on hot days and an effective palate cleanser after greasy night-market snacks.

THE HOG ECONOMY

Taiwan's postwar economic history is littered with industries that led the world for a brief period, then crashed. Most failed because their costs rose and foreign competitors got organized, but the woes of the country's swine farmers started with the return of foot-and-mouth disease in 1997. The outbreak resulted in the loss of nearly four million hogs and sixty-five thousand jobs. One estimate of the total cost, including vaccinations and compensation, is US$6.6 billion.[67] Japan, the main overseas buyer of the island's pork, banned Taiwanese pig meat. Since then, Taiwan has not come close to regaining its status as the world's number two exporter of pork, behind Denmark but ahead of the United States.[68]

The disease likely arrived via live pigs smuggled from China. Whatever the cause, not until mid-2017 did the World Organization for Animal Health restore Taiwan to its list of FMD-free zones.[69] One bio-security weak point is the government-sponsored, island-wide collecting of leftovers from urban households for use as pig feed.[70] With the exception of coffee grounds, corn husks and cobs, the shells of crustaceans, egg shells, fish and seafood, fruit pits and peels, herbs (all of which the government urges people to compost), and large bones, pretty much everything can be tipped into the designated food-waste barrels on the backs of garbage trucks—and that includes raw fish, meat, and internal organs; pasta; expired flour and powder; soyfoods; and sauces like chili sauce and bean paste. This policy, lauded by environmentalists, recycles about two-thirds of the country's food waste.[71]

The FMD crisis had no long-term impact on pork consumption. Per capita intake, which has hardly changed since the 1990s, is substantially higher than in the United States, and double that in Japan.[72] Taiwan's most popular pork-based dishes show no sign of fading away; yet anecdotes suggest that the ways in which people consume pork are changing. It seems large chunks of marbled pork (*lŭròu*), braised in a thick gravy with hard-boiled eggs (*lŭdàn*), are not eaten as often as before, but pork-filled dumplings have become more popular.

Taiwan's default meat and what was, until recently, the essential carbohydrate come together in the dish likely served more often than any other in roadside eateries: *ròuzào fàn*, also called *lŭròu fàn*. The first of these terms means "minced meat on rice." The second is often translated as "braised meat on rice," and though it is not explicit in the name, the pork is almost always minced. This blue-collar favorite is made by braising finely chopped pork in roughly equal amounts of soy sauce and rice wine, to which water, garlic, and a generous amount of shallot confit are added. This gravy is seasoned with some sugar, a little five-spice powder, and a bit of white pepper. A key ingredient, added near the end of the braising, is pigskin; the collagen in it gives the sauce an ideal level of viscidity.

Once the sauce is ready, serving a portion requires only the few seconds it takes to scoop white rice out of the steamer and spoon the meat sauce on top. Both diners and kitchen staff appreciate this quality, and speed is surely one of the reasons why hundreds of thousands of bowls of *ròuzào fàn* are wolfed down each weekday lunchtime in Taiwan. But a single portion cannot come close to satisfying a hungry truck driver or construction worker, so most order a soup (often clams and ginger in a clear broth) and a plate of whichever vegetable is in season, wok-fried with crushed garlic.

As recently as 1966, four out of every five rural households kept a hog. At that time, more countryside families owned pigs than cars or motorcycles. Meat was not the only attraction; one sixth of the animals' economic value was the manure they produced.[73] Strict enforcement of water-pollution rules is one reason the industry has consolidated; according to a March 11, 2009, *China Post* report, over the previous eight years, more than four thousand pig farms had been shut down for this reason. The average piggery is much smaller than in the United States,[74] but in parts of south Taiwan the number of hogs per square mile is triple that in North Carolina's "swine alley."[75]

During the Japanese colonial era and just after World War II, hog-breeding efforts centered on crossing Berkshire boars with native sows. From 1959 on, US economic aid saw the introduction of Yorkshire, Landrace, and Duroc boars. The latter two breeds are used to eating corn, not the sweet-potato leaves and sundry leftovers traditionally used to fatten pigs in Taiwan, so the promotion of hybrids led to a dependence on US feed grains.[76]

Knowing it is only a matter of time before Taiwan fully opens its market to US and Canadian pork—and that the traditional preference for fresh rather than frozen pork does not hold true for younger consumers who shop in supermarkets rather than morning markets[77]—the authorities have been funding research into local black pigs. These animals, also known as "black-haired" pigs, are thought to have mixed South Chinese/native Taiwanese ancestry. Compared to mainstream breeds, they take longer to mature and thus are more expensive.[78] Their skin is thicker, but their meat is softer and fattier, and thus especially suitable for braising.

Since the FMD crisis, a small number of pig farmers have turned their backs on foreign breeds and now focus on raising black pigs. As slow-food concepts gain ground in Taiwan, these farmers hope that talking up native flavors and eco-friendly "scavenger feeding" will help them hold out against foreign competition.[79] One of the country's largest pig-farming operations belongs to Taiwan Sugar Corp. To boost revenue and reduce the carbon footprint of their piggeries, the state-run enterprise is installing equipment to convert pig dung into biogas and covering the roofs with photovoltaic panels.[80]

Just as FMD hobbled the hog industry, outbreaks of avian flu have driven poultry farmers out of business. Chicken, duck, and goose populations have declined since 2004, and imports—especially of broiler meat from the United States—have grown apace.[81] Many of the rural families who fattened a pig at home also raised a few geese on scraps, and not simply to provide additional food. According to countryside lore, having a goose or two patrol the perimeter of your homestead is even better than keeping a guard dog. What is more, goose excrement repels the snakes that populate Taiwan's foothills.

Turkey production grew more than tenfold between 1945 and 1976 because it was cheaper, pound for pound, than chicken. But by 1995 it had declined to less than a third of its peak, after Taipei was pressured by Washington to accept American imports to restore balance to the US-Taiwan trade relationship.[82] Nowadays, much of the meat used for shredded turkey with gravy on white rice—a dish associated with Chiayi—is imported. And just as FMD did not put people off their pork, H5N2 has not depressed chicken consumption, which, at seventy-one pounds per person in 2015 (according to statista.com), is high by Asian standards but lower than in the United States.

A lot of broiler meat gets deep-fried in night markets, popcorn-style (*yánsūjī*) or in the form of hand-sized cutlets. The former is breaded and seasoned with liberal amounts of garlic, soy, and five-spice powder. The latter are often marinated overnight in a blend of soy sauce, rice wine, sugar, onion, and minced garlic; some cooks use sweet-potato flour instead of wheat flour. The meat of local non-broiler varieties known as *tǔjī* ("native chicken"), *wūgǔjī* ("black-boned chicken"), and *fàngshānjī* ("free-range [in the mountains] chicken") is somewhat tougher and preferred for dishes like sesame oil chicken and soups in which the meat, skin, and bones are simmered with herbs.

Barrel-broiled chicken remains a countryside favorite, but poultry cooking methods have changed as the population has become more health conscious. There has been a very large decline in the number of people who say they fry meat or poultry in oil all or most of the time. At the same time, the proportion of those who habitually eat poultry skin and fat has fallen.[83]

Ducks are raised for both meat and eggs, with Yilan County being especially famous for smoked and dried duck meat. This foodway, it is no surprise to learn, developed when there was a need to preserve older, tougher duck meat. The county is notoriously wet, and, in the early days of Han settlement, floods sometimes frustrated farmers' efforts to grow rice. Whenever this happened, the pioneers released ducklings into their inundated fields. Thanks to the shrimp, fish, and insects that abound if pesticides are not sprayed, the birds thrived without human feeding. Their excrement nourished the land. So that they could store or sell surplus meat, farming families developed a special preservation process that some still follow today. Once they have been de-feathered and the internal organs removed, the carcasses are washed, flattened, and stretched on bamboo frames; then they are pickled in salt for seven days. After a period of outdoor drying, avoiding bright sunshine, the birds are dried in a charcoal oven, then finally baked with sugarcane to give them a sweet taste and an appealing golden color.[84]

AN EGG A DAY

The availability of cheap, soy-based poultry feed led to a massive expansion of egg production and consumption. The number of eggs eaten per capita is eight times what it was in 1961;[85] yet the COA's website says Taiwan is self-sufficient. For many schoolchildren, breakfast is an egg over hard with a little ketchup and some julienned cucumber, served between two slices of white toast—or a *dànbǐng*, an egg spread over a crepe, sometimes with bacon or canned sweet corn. Scrambled eggs do not appear until lunchtime, when they come with stewed tomatoes and a sprinkling of scallions.

Commuters dashing for a train might grab a "tea egg" or two from a convenience store. These are hard-boiled in water to which soy sauce, salt, star anise, and black tea have been added. The flavor enhancers may include sugar and/or MSG. Some of those who make batches at home use supermarket premixes; others do everything from scratch and claim that a generous splash of Coca-Cola makes all the difference. Visually, the result is much the same, whatever the ingredients: peeling away the cracked shell reveals stains and marbling that some find off-putting but many find appetizing. Far less common are "coffee eggs" (goose eggs steeped in a blend that includes granulated coffee).

Another type of braised egg is the "iron egg," a specialty of Tamsui. These desiccated chicken eggs are usually vacuum-packed and eaten cold several days after preparation. Foodies looking for hot quail eggs should head for a night market and seek out a vendor spooning dollops of quail-egg/batter mix onto a takoyaki grill.

RAISING FISH ON LAND

As befits one of the world's great fishing nations, the Taiwanese have a strong appetite for seafood. The island's pelagic fishing fleet ranks number one in the world for Pacific saury production,[86] number two for tuna, and number three for squid.[87] According to some tallies, more fish than pork is eaten.[88] At around seventy-seven pounds, Taiwan's annual per capita seafood consumption has overtaken Japan's[89] and is more than quadruple that in the United States.[90] But more impressive to visitors than the jiggers that go all the way to the Falkland Islands to catch illex squid are the fish farms that dominate several districts on the west coast.

In the second half of the twentieth century, aquaculture entrepreneurs resculpted the landscape almost as dramatically as Taiwan's rice farmers. By the early 1990s, 1.5 percent of the island's land area was given over to brackish-water ponds in which fish and hard clams are raised or networks of bamboo on which oysters are cultivated in shallow seawater.[91] In some places, paddle-wheel aerators outnumber humans. Compared to other parts of crowded, lush Taiwan, the lack of buildings and foliage in these dead-flat regions is slightly eerie. Even in winter the sun is strong, and every few years each fishpond is completely drained so sunshine can disinfect the mud.

Tilapia fillets sterilized with ozone and then frozen with liquid nitrogen are exported to North America and the Middle East; grouper are shipped on living-fish carrier vessels to China; and live eels go to Japan. The farming of black tiger shrimp for export boomed in the 1980s; at one point Taiwan was responsible for 12 percent of global shrimp culture production. The industry crashed due to viruses, a problem exacerbated by very high stocking densities.[92] Milkfish is another key product, but most of it is eaten locally.

A market vendor in Donggang, south Taiwan, weighs a squid mantle filled with fish roe. *Steven Crook*

Tilapia, which many Taiwanese call Wu-Kuo Fish in honor of the two men who smuggled tilapia fry back to Taiwan from Singapore in 1946 following wartime service with the Japanese, has fallen out of favor with local consumers. Because it was an important source of cheap protein after World War II, and the fry were often fed on duck droppings, it is now associated with poverty.[93] Taipei citizens trying to make a good impression on guests are far more likely to serve or order Norwegian salmon than tilapia. Yet tilapia may make a comeback; those raised in seawater do not have the unpleasant earthen taste associated with their freshwater cousins, and they are being marketed not as tilapia but as *Táiwān diāo* (Taiwan snapper).

Taiwan's aquaculturalists have been criticized for imposing external costs on society in the form of water pollution and land subsidence, the latter caused by the over-extraction of groundwater to fill fishponds.[94] Mariculture avoids some of these problems, and so far, cobia has been the main cage-cultured saltwater fish. Meaningful expansion is difficult because nets and cages positioned in the ocean around Taiwan are vulnerable to typhoon damage. Local researchers may yet find solutions, however. They have already made important breakthroughs in the artificial fertilization of shrimp, black mullet, and other species[95] and have discovered that tilapia fins can replace shark's fins in shark-fin soup.[96]

FARMING TRENDS: SMART, INDOORS AND ORGANIC

Frank Tai defies the stereotype of the poorly educated, elderly farmer. The land he uses, two hours' drive south of Taipei, once belonged to his father, but he was born in 1970 and holds a bachelor's degree in microbiology from one of Taipei's better universities. His farm is no longer Asia's largest producer of golden-needle (enokitake) mushrooms, but it remains Taiwan's number one supplier of esculent fungi. With the help of 150 employees, he ships twenty-five to thirty-five tons of mushrooms every day.[97]

Taiwan-grown mushrooms for sale at a roadside in Greater Taipei.
Steven Crook

Thanks to American assistance, large-scale mushroom production took off in 1960, and by 1963 the island was the world's number one supplier of canned and bottled mushrooms. Exports peaked in the late 1970s with annual earnings of more than US$100 million[98]—a fabulous return on the US$82,574 that USAID had invested in the development of sanitary harvesting and canning practices and the construction of processing facilities.[99] Tai's family, and many of their neighbors in Taichung's Wufeng District, were in the thick of it, cultivating white-button and wood-ear mushrooms in grow bags. The former, a species introduced to Taiwan specifically for export, was so unfamiliar that it was dubbed *yáng gū* ("Western mushroom").

By the late 1970s, Chinese and South Korean growers were eating into the white-button trade. Taiwanese farmers responded by switching to species popular with local consumers, such as straw mushrooms, shiitake, and shimeji (willow mushrooms), and benefited from a surge in domestic demand; in little more than a decade, the consumption of edible fungi appeared to more than quadruple.[100] These days, almost all of Tai's output goes to domestic customers, and the bulk is sold fresh. Dried mushrooms offer quite different flavors and textures compared to fresh ones, he says, but drying mushrooms is often a response to fluctuations in demand. Because so many mushrooms are eaten in hot pots, winter prices are typically double those in the summer.

Tai's cousin Chu Rui-Jong is another second-generation mushroom farmer in Wufeng. He did not originally plan to follow in his father's footsteps, working as a car mechanic in Taipei before returning to his hometown.[101] Compared to his father, Chu devotes less land to mushroom production but regularly achieves output ten times' greater. He especially enjoys enokitake omelet (cooked the same way as the classic Taiwanese radish omelet) and King Oyster mushrooms in rice wine–based dishes such as three-cup chicken.

Both men grow all their mushrooms indoors, thus maintaining full control over temperature and other factors. Because Tai keeps his enokitake sheds at 41°F, his operation is energy-intensive but otherwise eco-friendly. If the polypropylene bottles in which he grows mushrooms—he has more than six million such bottles, on which he spent more than US$2 million—are not exposed to sunlight, they should last at least twenty years. The substrate he uses for golden-needle mushrooms is three parts sawdust, one part rice bran. The latter is a byproduct of rice cultivation; the former is made from hardwood trees (to best replicate the rotting logs on which mushrooms naturally grow), uprooted and washed out of mountain forests during typhoons and then sold off by the government.[102] Spent substrate is used to grow other types of mushrooms, or flowers. There is not much physical waste, therefore, and only small amounts of water are used.[103] Maintaining 90 percent relative humidity is straightforward, because the growing rooms form a closed system. There is no need to wash the mushrooms prior to packing, as the conditions in which they were cultivated ensure that there is neither mold nor infestations. The only chemical Tai uses is calcium hydroxide, $Ca(OH)_2$, also known as slaked lime, to adjust the natural pH value of sawdust from 5.5 to between 9 and 9.5.

For both farmers, finding and retaining workers is a serious challenge. Unlike manufacturing and construction companies, agricultural enterprises are not allowed to hire foreign labor, which has forced them to embrace mechanization. Chu says farmers like himself should future-proof themselves against climate change by investing in high-tech equipment that can control temperature, humidity, and light. He points out that farmers who use more traditional techniques to cultivate abalone (gray) and shiitake mushrooms near Puli (about twenty miles east of Wufeng) have reported declining yields due to shifting weather patterns.

Producers of other crops are going even further. More than three dozen companies cultivate leafy greens indoors.[104] One site ships up to sixty thousand heads of lettuce a day, making it possibly the largest plant factory in the world. However, because that facility is not completely insulated and sealed, output is influenced by the seasons, and the greens cannot be marketed as ready-to-cook or ready-to-eat but instead cook-after-washing / eat-after-washing.[105] The majority of plant factories are far smaller but more advanced, equipped with what some in the industry call the "essential five" features: epoxy floors, airtight thermally insulated walls and roofs, air showers (to reduce particle contamination), air-conditioning, and carbon dioxide enrichment.[106] Rather than solid substrate, high-value crops like *Carpobrotus edulis* (Hottentot-fig or South African ice plant) are grown in nutrient solutions through which the plant's saltiness can be adjusted.

Few countries are better positioned for, or stand to gain more from, controlled-environment farming, which is also known as "Agriculture 4.0." Taiwan's world-class photonics industry makes LEDs that perfectly imitate the cycle of day and night, and the country's scientists have developed a space-efficient device that permits the automated, non-destructive and continuous monitoring of a plant's weight, accurate to 0.1 g.[107] Tropical storms and typhoons destroy millions of dollars' worth of crops each summer—according to a July 9, 2016, report on the *Focus Taiwan* news portal, that month's Typhoon Nepartak caused agricultural losses of US$24.1 million—and they are expected to become more severe. Each time a food-safety scandal erupts, the number of consumers willing to pay a premium for traceable, pesticide-free vegetables grows. Residential and infrastructure developments continue to chip away at farmland, while scores of former factories lie idle. Repurposing the latter as vertical farms would make economic as well as environmental sense.

When it came to establishing a regulatory framework for organic food, Taiwan was late to the table.[108] The first set of official organic standards—for livestock as well as plant crops—was announced in 2003, but certification was merely "recommended."[109] Because these rules did not penalize deceptive labeling, many buyers of organic food preferred imported produce.[110] Not until early 2009 did the law stipulate that only food certified by an accredited certification organization could be sold as "organic."

Government-supported research into chemical-free agriculture began in 1989, and the COA established plots where organic farming methods could be demonstrated in the mid-1990s. Soon after, the COA started certifying farmland as "under organic management."[111] The proportion of farmland given over to organically grown crops now exceeds that in the United States[112] but is still far below many European countries.[113] Domestic organic produce is sold in all but the smallest supermarkets, as well as in specialist chains like Santa Cruz (which also sells dietary supplements and "natural" produce not certified as organic). Tens of thousands of families buy organic food and other fair-trade or eco-friendly products through the Homemakers' Union Consumers Co-op, a leading social enterprise.

More than half of Santa Cruz's ninety-seven branches are in Greater Taipei, as are all four branches of Green & Safe.[114] The density of organic-food outlets in Taipei is a reflection of the capital's higher income and education levels, but also due to the fact that many people elsewhere can get pesticide-free vegetables from their own or their relatives' land. This preference for informally sourced produce is one reason why many organic farmers struggle to find buyers for their crops. Liao Cheng-chou, a lecturer for the Taiwan Environmental Information Association, says practitioners of nature-friendly farming need help selling their crops, rather than additional instruction in agricultural techniques. He regards farmers' markets as essential channels, as in such places consumers can meet farmers, hear their stories, and properly understand both how they grow food and why their approach is gentler on the environment.[115]

One such venue in Taipei is 248 Agronomy Market, founded by social activist Yang Ju-men. Protesting the impact WTO membership was having on Taiwan's farmers, in 2003–2004 Yang placed seventeen small bombs at various locations around Taipei, mixing rice in with the explosives to underline his point. No one was hurt, and he surrendered once he felt his message had been heard. After more than three years in jail, Yang received a presidential pardon. He told the April 2013 issue of *CommonWealth* that he had come to realize that the country's agricultural sector can only be protected if people's attitudes and behavior change, and now he is trying to effect such change.

Among the regulars at HOPE Weekend Farmer's Market is Hsieh Shu-hsuan from Hsinchu. Hsieh sometimes struggles to sell what she grows, even though her daughter promotes her oranges, lettuces, and cabbages on social media and has designed posters that explain why pesticide-free crops often look tatty.[116] The preference many local consumers show for perfect-looking fruits and vegetables is recognized by Liao as a problem for the farmers he works with. Although he summarizes government support for what he is doing as "non-existent," the authorities do seem to be trying to remedy this particular problem through education: one current high school English textbook includes a lesson that emphasizes that how healthy or delicious something is bears no relation to how attractive it looks. (Another lesson addresses the issue of food waste.)

Liao recommends the Footprints in the Field Farmers' Market held each Saturday near Taipei's South Gate. Some vendors, he points out, drive more than two hundred miles to attend—and not in the expectation of making a profit, but rather "to share their joy and the results of their hard work." The market gets its name from the animal and bird footprints that are common on organic farmland, but seldom seen where artificial pesticides and fertilizers are sprayed. Many participants have received official recognition in the form of the Green Conservation Label, the country's first wildlife-centric certification system. According to a report posted on the COA's website on October 20, 2015, 186 farmers joined the scheme in its first three years.

Tse-Xin Organic Agriculture Foundation (TOAF), the organization that co-administers the Green Conservation Label, founded the island-wide Leezen chain of organic-produce stores. TOAF has also been guiding high-altitude farmers inside Taroko National Park as they transition to sustainable agriculture. Visitors can now see rows of pesticide-free cabbages, mustard greens, turnips, and tomatoes. The project, which began in 2010, includes help with marketing as well as growing.[117]

TOAF is a Buddhist organization, and throughout the country, Buddhism has long been a major driving force behind both environmentalism and vegetarianism. Liao is also a Buddhist, but he attributes his passion for nature-friendly agriculture not to his religion but to a desire to protect ecosystems for the sake of animals and insects as well as humans, while benefiting farmers and expressing *gǎn-ēn* (a sense of gratitude for nature's gifts). Allowing your land to die, he says, would show disrespect to the ancestors who farmed and passed it on. Liao has worked closely with Atayal indigenous communities, and he is proud to have received an Atayal name, Teymu Watan.

The COA recognizes the USDA's National Organic Program (NOP) as equivalent to domestic standards, even though the former—unlike the latter—tolerates trace amounts of chemicals in certain circumstances. However, so much paperwork must be completed before food from overseas can be sold in Taiwan as "organic" that some importers instead label their products "natural."[118] They are not the only ones who find the current rules frustrating. According to Liao, some farmers simply cannot afford the NT$200,000 (US$6,858) it costs to complete the organic certification process.

Hsieh is not pursuing certification, saying her principal motivation is *găn-ēn*. She draws on her Hakka heritage to preserve what she cannot sell in the form of jams and pickles. She turns ginger that is past its prime into a snack by stir-frying it with juice from sugarcane she has grown herself but cannot sell because the canes are "too short, too thin, and too ugly."

One younger farmer's devotion to traditional, sustainable agriculture was the subject of a *Taipei Times* article on March 6, 2017. Kao I-hsin acquired a water buffalo from a farmer who was too old to look after it and began using it to plow fields. He hopes to preserve what he calls "water buffalo culture," which includes maintaining the animal's health through herbal remedies that only a handful of elderly folk still remember.

Some organic farmers have benefited from a growing demand for djulis (the Paiwan name for *Chenopodium formosanum*, a native cereal also known as red quinoa). Its proponents claim it has weight-loss and anti-cancer properties. Gram for gram, it has almost as much protein as beef and far more dietary fiber and iron than sweet potatoes.[119]

Ljuwa, an indigenous farmer nicknamed "Mr. Djulis," has played a major role in reviving this crop. After learning about quinoa's properties, and that the quinoa consumed in Taiwan was imported from South America, he started cultivating djulis seeds his grandmother had saved. Thanks to his village's remote location, meeting organic standards was not difficult. However, he and the forty-plus neighboring farmers he now works with have faced several other difficulties. For instance, djulis is usually planted in October, but rain at the beginning of spring means the pseudo-cereal is often wet when it is time for harvesting. This problem has been solved by buying a large-capacity drying machine, but it cost the villagers more than NT$2 million (about (US$69,000).[120]

Ljuwa's determination and persistence have brought a degree of fame, as well as some economic success. Within Taiwan, he is often asked to speak at entrepreneurship events, and in 2017 he traveled to the United States to receive a gold medal at the Invention and New Product Exposition in Pittsburgh.

6

❖ ❖

Supplying the Consumer

Taipei's Markets

"There's food everywhere!" say the tourists who just got back from Taiwan, referring not merely to the restaurants and night markets but also to the convenience stores, the supermarkets, and the mom-and-pop grocery stores. The farther you go from downtown Taipei, the more likely you are to see bamboo shoots or watermelons being sold on the roadside—very often by the farmer who grew them or one of his relatives.

Against a backdrop of anemic GDP growth and wage stagnation,[1] and during a period when global food prices were relatively stable, supermarket revenue grew 55.5 percent between 2009 and 2016. This was ahead of the 34.7 percent expansion recorded by the food-and-beverage services category, which includes restaurants and takeout tea shops. In the same period, sales at the country's convenience stores (which in total outsell supermarkets, but depend more on nonfood products such as cigarettes) rose 45.6 percent.[2] But these figures do not necessarily prove that Taiwanese are cooking at home more than before. In large part, they reflect a shift in buying habits that began in the 1970s.[3] Traditional markets—where record-keeping and taxation are far from comprehensive—have been gradually losing ground to large, well-lit retailers where prices are obvious and much of the fresh merchandise is refrigerated. One of these is Jasons Market Place, a high-end Singaporean grocery store full of imported produce with twenty-two locations in Taiwan. Among hypermarkets, the industry leader is French multinational Carrefour, with nearly one hundred stores.[4] Partnering with the Uni-President Group, which brought 7-Eleven to Taiwan, Carrefour has developed branches in urban centers rather than suburbs, because Taiwanese consumers are not yet used to shopping in out-of-town malls.[5]

Taipei City Market Administration Office (TCMAO), a branch of the city government, supervises more than one hundred markets, including some that specialize in flowers, semi-precious stones, and secondhand miscellanea, rather than food. Excluded from the official tally are farmers' markets organized by not-for-profit organizations and held on land borrowed from public-sector entities. Also going uncounted are several places in the suburbs where fruit and vegetable vendors gather habitually, without the benefit of facilities, and sometimes at risk of being fined. In these informal mini-markets, housewives and senior citizens buy greens from miniscule market gardens, soil-streaked carrots that were still in the ground when the sun rose, and other ultra-local produce.

One of the greatest concentrations of market activity in Taipei is in the old Wanhua District. An entire block on the south side of Fumin Road is given over to the city's main fish and seafood market and Taipei First Fruits and Vegetables Market. Taipei Second Fruits and Vegetables Market is located on another side of the city, beside Addiction Aquatic Development (see below).

Wholesale trade in seafood peaks in the hour before dawn, while the smaller retail area caters to shoppers until lunchtime. In the latter, as in markets throughout Taiwan, vendors remove viscera and roe by hand and use machines to scrape off fish scales. When seafood is auctioned, each lot is assigned a four-digit code that corresponds to one of 153 types of produce, 50 of which are sold both frozen and unfrozen.[6] No. 2181 is red tilefish, chosen by *CommonWealth* magazine as one of "Happy Taiwan's 60 Wonderful Ingredients"[7] and sourced from Taiwan by restaurant owners in Japan. No. 2563 is rabbitfish, known in Chinese as *chòudù yú* ("stinky stomach fish"). No. 3481 is frozen parrotfish. No. 4513 is three-spot swimming crab. No way to successfully farm the crucifix crab, the ridged swimming crab, or the three-spot swimming crab has yet been discovered, and most of those eaten in Taiwan are caught along the north coast using baited cages.[8]

By the time the capital's office workers clock in, business in the wholesale fruit and vegetable market has petered out. Market officials wheel the dozens of portable auction rostrums—stainless-steel trolleys, each equipped with a computer terminal and an LED screen on a pole to display lot details and prices—back to the storeroom. Buyers load up and leave; suppliers offer whatever they did not sell at knockdown prices to passers-by. Taiwanese have not been slow to embrace plastics, but here and in other markets, big baskets woven from bamboo slats are used to haul cabbage and watermelons.

The main part of the market is a hangar-like expanse without partitions, just white strips on the asphalt. Sugarcane vendors, who sell both the common "red" variety

(*Saccharum officinarum*) and the "black" (actually dark purple) wild variety (*Saccharum spontaneum*), have their own set of bays. Most fruits and vegetables arrive and leave in cardboard boxes marked with their place of origin. A lot of produce travels more than one hundred miles, or all the way across the Pacific. Depending on the season, one might see ginger from Nantou or common beans from Meinong in Kaohsiung. Nectarines and grapes from the United States and apples from Chile are sold alongside passion fruit from Puli and pineapples from Xingang in Chiayi.

Within a side building, two dozen stalls specialize in pickles, including Hakka-style preserved mustard greens and bamboo shoots of various sizes. A man who says he is thirty-two—and by no means the youngest stallholder here—explains that the fat brown, hemispherical disks kept in cold water are duck-blood curd, while the rectangular blocks are pig-blood curd.

A thriving general morning market fills the north side of Fumin Road and several nearby lanes. The unit of measurement here and in every market on the island is the catty (*jīn* in Mandarin, *kin* in Holo). In Taiwan, as in Japan, one catty is 600 grams (1.32 pounds).[9] Because most of Taipei's married women work, ready-to-eat items are almost as numerous as raw ingredients. Some of these are quite traditional—for example, *óaⁿ kóe*. The bulk of this savory pudding-type dish is pulped *indica* rice, to which a little lotus-root starch or corn flour has been added. Topped with sautéed mushrooms and small chunks of fried pork, it is steamed in a shallow bowl; the Holo and Mandarin names both mean "bowl pudding." Just before eating, it is flavored with garlic puree and *jiàngyóu gāo*.

A dumpling vendor here says he sells more than five thousand wontons and *jiǎozi* on an ordinary morning, more in the run-up to holidays and festivals. All are made by hand.[10] Compared to their counterparts in some other countries, Taiwanese vendors are not especially vocal. Yet two distinct sounds rise above the hubbub. One is the thump of cleavers hitting wood as chickens are dismembered. The traditional practice of keeping poultry alive until the moment of sale was halted several years ago. On May 18, 2013, the day after the ban on live poultry slaughtering at traditional markets took effect, *Taipei Times* quoted some vendors as complaining that sales had dropped by 30–40 percent. Chickens and ducks are now slaughtered at a centralized location under government supervision; the conditions in which they are cut up and bagged are far from operating-room clean, but this seems not to bother market regulars. Another part of the soundscape is the whine of shoppers' scooters as they weave between pedestrians and the trolleys used by informal vendors who do not own or rent a formal spot. The drive-through restaurant may be an American invention, but Taiwan can claim as its own the drive-through wet market.

Much of the heavy lifting in these places is done by women in their forties and fifties; the men smoke with abandon. TCMAO understands there is much room for improvement in terms of hygiene and appearance, and it has renovated more than a score of the capital's larger markets since the late 1990s. Several have been demolished and rebuilt from scratch. In others, the improvements have been as simple as adding stainless-steel partitions so shoppers are never splashed when meat is butchered.

Installing new floor drains and sewers reduces odors and pollution caused by the cutting of poultry and meat and makes it more difficult for rodents to get in.[11] The addition of elevators and much better bathrooms reflects TCMAO's hope, as their website puts it, to "meet the needs of an aging society for a safe shopping environment, yet preserve the human touch of the traditional market."

At traditional markets, married women continue to dominate the customer base. One study found that female consumers are nearly four times more likely than men to frequent traditional vegetable markets, while females who habitually shop at supermarkets outnumber males by 1.4:1. People without a living spouse—and those whose income or level of education is higher than average—are less inclined to get their fresh fruits and vegetables from traditional markets. Yet older people are significantly less likely to shop in a supermarket because the produce is perceived as being not quite so fresh, and "low prices are not associated with the supermarket concept in Taiwan."[12]

A 2008 poll found that while 84 percent of adults had shopped at a hypermarket, 82 percent still went to wet markets for fresh meat, vegetables, and fruit. Traditional markets have better-quality food, according to 43 percent, while 27 percent said there was a market nearer to their home than a hypermarket. The reluctance of many consumers to buy produce they cannot press and sniff has prompted some hypermarket chains to create "replica wet markets" in their meat and seafood sections.[13]

Younger consumers are thought to be more willing to buy frozen imported meat, rather than the fresh cuts preferred by the older generation. Currently, most pigs are slaughtered in the cities where their meat will be sold. Transporting them alive from the south, where most are raised, to Greater Taipei adds significantly to the expense of pork, as the pigs lose carcass weight during the trip. Each year, several thousand animals die during the journey; the stress of up to six hours on a truck ruins the meat of others. The COA has for decades been promoting the sale of chilled and frozen pork, but it has encountered resistance from farmers and others in the supply chain.[14]

There is a chance Taiwan's fresh-food markets will die out with their current customers, and TCMAO does not take the thousands who shop along Fumin Road each morning for granted. So more people, including tourists, have an opportunity to "experience the charm, hospitality and character of the capital's markets," the Taipei City Government has been sponsoring an annual traditional market festival since 2007. Around forty thousand people attended 2017's two-day festival, which featured tasting sessions and recipe sharing.[15] Prizes were awarded to thirteen vendors in four categories: ready-cooked foods; miscellaneous fresh foods; innovative marketing; and classic braised meat.

The drawbacks of traditional markets are well understood. Something can be done about the bad smells and dirty floors. Parking can also be made more convenient. The authors of one study say vendors should be encouraged to mark everything they sell with prices and to provide more information about the provenance of fresh items and the composition of ready-made foods. They recommend that market management committees use modern polling methods to understand consumers' actual needs. What is more, because those living nearby are an important source of custom, traditional markets should work hard to maintain good relations with the community and endeavor to win local loyalty by supporting festivals and other events.[16]

If the objective of a market renovation project is to attract an entirely new demographic, then Addiction Aquatic Development (AAD) has been a great success. Before part of Taipei Fish Market was transformed into AAD in 2012, very few young men in Taipei would have considered taking their girlfriends to a market on a date. Now a place where high-end seafood is both sold raw and served in restaurants (of which there are five), AAD attracts so many people that there are frequent complaints about waiting times and having to stand to eat. In late October 2017, it ranked fifty-third among nearly twelve thousand Taipei eateries reviewed on TripAdvisor. It would surely place higher if, as in many of the capital's food courts, customers were allowed to buy in one area and eat inside another, and if tourists did not gripe that credit cards are not accepted. (In that respect, AAD follows local market convention.)

Diners enjoy seafood at Addiction Aquatic Development in Taipei. *Steven Crook*

With its lobster-filled tanks and shelves full of premium sakes, AAD offers a satisfying walk-through experience. The interior exemplifies Japanese-influenced elegance. A striking difference between AAD and a typical market is the lighting. Instead of alternating between dank gloom and the glare of unshaded white light-bulbs, visitors enjoy the kind of soft (yet effective) illumination they would expect in the lobby of a boutique hotel.

BUILDING A FUTURE OUTSIDE THE MARKET

Founded by Jen Jen-chang, who relocated with his family to Taipei from Shang-hai in 1947, Hoshing Confectioneries was for many years a leading maker and vendor of traditional Shanghai-style *sōng gāo*—loose, fluffy cakes made from rice—as well as various Chinese confectionaries. Jen began by selling from a stall on Nanhai Road, near Taipei Botanical Garden. In 1951, he opened a store in nearby Nanmen Market. In 1975, the business passed to the second generation, led by Jen Tai-hsing. (The first character of his given name is the same as that in "Taiwan"; this is fairly common among children of mainlanders born on the island after 1949.) More than forty years later, a member of the third generation—Jen Tai-hsing's daughter, Jen Chia-lun, working with her husband, Cheng Kuang-yu—is transforming how this confectionary business presents itself and its products to the world. She recalls,

> When I was studying in London, a favorite pastime was visiting traditional markets. A key difference between the UK and Taiwan—and this fascinated me—is that in London and elsewhere in the UK, markets are filled with young people. They're places full of stories, and that's a great selling point. In Taiwanese culture, traditional markets are visited by old folks. The younger generation finds little of interest in them. This contrast really made me think, and inspired me to explore and research the two cultures further. Before this experience, I had no interest in or intention of taking over my family's business. My father was giving up hope that the business could be passed on to the third generation.[17]

Over the past decade or so, Taiwan has seen the emergence of a range of cultural-creative industries, nurtured by a government keen to reduce the economy's dependence on its shrinking manufacturing sector. After returning to Taipei in 2016, Jen Chia-lun and her husband began exploring the idea of running a "culture-creative" shop in conjunction with her father's. "Our ultimate goal is to attract young people to enjoy traditional markets. We wanted to combine our design knowledge and our UK experience," says Jen, who did graduate study in space and product design, while Cheng focused on narrative environment.

"At first, the plan was to open it at my father's shop in Nanmen Market, one of Taipei's oldest markets. But after observing and evaluating, we thought: 'Why not start where young people hang out?' We then decided to launch our 'culture-creative' confectioneries shop in Dadaocheng, a place full of history and stories. Dadaocheng attracts young people, and its personality coincides with our goals," says Jen.

In a country where tangible reminders of the world before the 1970s are scarce, nostalgia is a powerful force. Recognizing this, the couple branded their venture Hoshing 1947 and rented a historic single-story shop-house on Dihua Street, Dadaocheng's most traditional and charming thoroughfare.

Rather than simply sell the same items as her father and grandfather, Jen and Cheng have modified the recipes to better suit modern consumers. In an era when families are smaller and Taipei people eat far less rice than before, many people find Jen Tai-hsing's *sōng gāo* and *sū bǐng* (flaky pastries) too large. The couple accordingly reduced the size of these signature products by two-thirds and adjusted the sweetness to suit modern preferences, while staying as close as possible to the original texture and quality. Getting the percentages of rice flour and water just right took hundreds of attempts, they say, but the result is a range of bite-sized, deliciously moist and soft, Chinese traditional snacks.

Jen Chia-lun says that when it comes to flavors, "We constantly keep our eyes and minds open for seasonal ingredients, to keep young people interested." Among

The Hoshing 1947 store in Dadaocheng, Taipei.
Hoshing 1947

the most successful have been original-taste jujube paste and black rice with chest-nuts. The ponlai rice for the latter was supplied by another newcomer to Dihua Street. "We work closely with our neighbors. For example, we use fabrics from neighboring shops for our curtains, and the curtain poles also come from this street. We all benefit, as our aim is to make Dadaocheng a great historic place that appeals to all ages and walks of life," she explains.

Whereas the original Hoshing in Nanmen Market is simply a shop, Jen and Cheng wanted to create a place "where people can come in, sit down, and enjoy themselves." All the decorations and materials were produced in Taiwan, and the open kitchen Jen designed allows customers to see the cake-making and -steaming process. "It creates a sense of warmth. The temperature, the steam in the air. When people come here, they use all their senses," she says.

ALTERNATIVE SALES CHANNELS

When it comes to both general e-commerce[18] and online food shopping,[19] Taiwan is ahead of the global curve. Food manufacturers, among them Hoshing 1947, and retailers make considerable use of Facebook[20] and Line (a messaging app phenom-enally popular in Taiwan and Japan) to promote and sell their products. In summer 2017, a Facebook group dedicated to Taiwanese soy sauce featured ads not merely for different sauces but also for almond cookies, dried mushrooms, rice vermicelli, and camellia oil. The internet makes it possible for home-based artisanal food makers to reach beyond their neighbors and the nearest farmers' market. A typi-cal Facebook post reads, "A-luo-ha: Fourth-generation *lǔwèi* maker. Not sold in stores, available only via the internet. Minimum order for home delivery: NT$500 [US$17.22]."

Even companies that enjoy first-rate reputations and good access to mainstream retail systems make use of the internet. "Few supermarkets have enough shelf space to stock all of our products. Direct sales, online and through agents, are therefore important," says Brian Chuang of soy-sauce maker Wuan Chuang Food Industrial Co. Ltd.[21] Online marketing has played a major part in developing demand for Hsin Lai Yuan Food Co. Ltd.'s "white" soy sauce.[22] Online vendors meet the needs of tea fans outside the country who discover a taste for oolong while touring the island but struggle to find a satisfactory supplier when they return home.

Beverage businesses can use social media to boost interest in alcoholic drinks, but are not allowed to accept orders via the internet.[23] In spring 2016, the gov-ernment approved a draft law to permit the selling of alcohol online. But a few months later, the bill was withdrawn, apparently after objections by civic groups that campaign against drunk driving and domestic violence. Takao Beer boss

Alex Lu thinks lifting the ban "would really help those smaller brewers who lack sales channels."[24]

Lu says around 30 percent of Takao Beer's sales are through Carrefour hypermarkets. Agents and distributors, who have gotten the company's brews into approximately one thousand bars and restaurants around the country, account for another 50 percent. Direct sales from the company's two outlets in Kaohsiung, and from pop-up stores at cultural events and outdoor festivals, make up a tenth. Sales via Eslite contribute a further 3–5 percent of the total. This is surprising, considering that Eslite is a bookstore chain.

When Eslite was created in 1989, its focus was on high-brow subjects like art and architecture, rather than best sellers. Its gradual transformation into a "lifestyle emporium"[25] has seen the addition of a foods corner ("Eslite Flavor") to each branch. Here, craft beers from three Taiwanese brewers (plus a few from overseas) are sold alongside loose-leaf teas, djulis, dried fruits, soy sauce, and other premium items. Getting Eslite to stock his beers was very difficult, Lu says. He had to convince the bookstore of the quality of his products, that sales would justify the shelf space, and also that their appearance would fit in with the chain's design ethos and refined atmosphere.

One person who tried an entirely different approach to selling food is Kate Chiu, founder of Taipei's Naked Supermarket. Local media often described the store, which operated between 2015 and 2017, as an environmentalist effort to reduce food waste and packaging, because grains, nuts, spices, and other produce were sold via gravity bins and customers were encouraged to bring their own bags or containers. For Chiu, however, Naked Supermarket's central mission was to "celebrate the joy of cooking, and to make getting ingredients much more convenient."[26]

"Many people who start cooking after watching Jamie Oliver or Nigella Lawson on TV feel frustrated when trying to find ingredients that are common in Western countries but extremely hard to find in Taiwan, for example lentils and cumin," explains Chiu, who first used many of these foods while working in a French restaurant in Taipei. She was able to find some of them in herbal medicine stores, but "usually sold by the pack, when I needed only a teaspoon to boost the flavor in a dish. Then the rest of the pack sat on the top shelf in my kitchen for months or years, and went bad. This is a waste of food as well as money." When explaining the store's concept to customers, Chiu says she often compared it to the traditional *dăyóu* style of shopping.

Naked Supermarket focused on products from Europe, not bothering with ingredients that are easy to obtain locally, like adzuki beans or mung beans. "Many people came to us asking for grains, beans, and spices they've heard of, or seen on TV or in books. But the Taiwan market is rather small, and only a few suppliers import such ingredients. Some products are hard to obtain simply because the market for such ingredients is too small, and there's no profit to be made at all for suppliers or sellers. We were constantly asked for, but couldn't sell, poppy seeds. They're still not legal here, despite being a common ingredient in other countries."[27]

The supermarket's public kitchen was often used to demonstrate food-preparation techniques. "The recipes we introduced were ones we liked, and we didn't make any assumptions about the target audience when selecting recipes," says Chiu, adding that mulled wine and boeuf bourguignon were especially popular.

FROM TEMPLE FAIRS TO NIGHT MARKETS

Before Taiwan became an affluent society, gods' birthdays and religious parades were among the few occasions when ordinary people could take time out from the daily struggle to survive and enjoy themselves. Wherever there was a *miào huì* ("temple gathering" or "temple fair"), there would be vendors selling hot snacks such as sweet-potato congee.[28]

The connection between the spiritual life of Taiwanese people and their approach to food is nothing like the dietary prescriptions of Judaism, Islam, or Hinduism. Yet local religious culture has certainly been conducive to the growth of street food. Adherents of mainstream religion support and pray at a particular shrine near where they live or in their hometown. At the same time, there is a tradition of visiting affiliated temples. Many join these excursions more for a change of scenery than to engage in solemn, spiritual introspection. Offering incense does not take long. Once the visitor has shown proper reverence to the enshrined deities, there is plenty of time to explore the precinct, watch the performance troupes that add color and spectacle to many *miào huì*, and get something to eat from a peddler.

For at least a century—and probably much longer—some of the best places for street food have been near major temples. In 1920s Taipei, the neighborhood around Xia-Hai City God Temple and Yongle Market (these days best known for fabrics) was renowned for its food stalls. In the same decade, vendors near Wanhua's Longshan Temple were selling almond tofu, four-fruit soup (see chapter 3), and sweet, cold mung-bean soup.[29] The cylindrical savory rice cakes called *tǒngzǐ mǐgāo* sold there in that era were likely less embellished than modern interpretations, which incorporate oyster sauce, shrimp, and mushrooms, as well as pork (or pork floss), fried shallots, and soy sauce.

Several of the two dozen eateries clustered around Hsinchu's City God Temple serve the local specialties of rice vermicelli (*mǐfěn*) and pork meatballs (*gòng wán*). The former is often stir-fried with thinly sliced carrots and mushrooms, some greens, and a little pork. The latter come in a clear soup with chopped scallions and celery. The highly rated night market in Keelung, fifteen miles east of downtown Taipei, is known as Miaokow Night Bazaar; *miào kǒu* in Mandarin means "entrance to [Dianji] Temple." Some claim vendors have been a constant presence here since the shrine's founding in 1873. Others say the night market came into existence around the end of Japanese rule. There is a lot of seafood, as one would expect in a harbor city, and several visitors have been impressed by the crab *gēng*.

Dānzǐ miàn, a noodle dish associated with the southern city of Tainan but now available in many cities, first appeared in the nineteenth century. The modern version incorporates bean sprouts, cilantro, braised minced pork, garlic purée, and a dash of vinegar; a moment before serving, a single peeled shrimp is placed on top. The Chinese name describes how the pioneering vendor used a shoulder yoke to carry everything he needed to make the dish; supposedly he was a fisherman who needed another way to make money during the summer months when the sea was too rough for fishing. Because many non-Taiwanese first get to know *dānzǐ miàn* at Du Hsiao Yueh ("slack season" in Mandarin), a restaurant chain that has spread as far afield as Beijing, in English the delicacy is sometimes known as slack-season (or "passing the lean months") noodles. Ironically, slack-season noodles are now more often found inside air-conditioned eateries than at sidewalk stalls or night markets.

"Mongolian barbecue" is a postwar Taiwanese invention, inspired by stories of how Genghis Khan's soldiers used their swords and shields to slice and roast mutton and beef.[30] Like *dānzǐ miàn*, Mongolian barbecue is now restaurant fare rather than street food; strips of meat are pushed around a circular gas-heated griddle and then carried over to seated diners. In the late 1950s, by contrast, the east bank of the Tamsui River was crowded with stalls that advertised "Mongolian BBQ" in huge neon letters and cooked in the open air on overturned woks.[31]

Mobile vendors have been in decline since the 1960s, which is when after-dark bazaars really began to boom. Taipei folk of a certain age remember four or five distinct sounds from their childhoods. Those selling *jiàng cài* (the pickles made from cucumber or bamboo that older Taiwanese like to eat with rice gruel for breakfast) and *dòufu rǔ* rang bells to let people know they had arrived in the neighborhood; they traveled usually on carts equipped with something like a bookcase, so they could store and display several different kinds of pickles.

In the old days, ice-cream vendors blew bike horns, and roast sweet-potato peddlers used rotating bamboo rattlers. The *bào mǐ xiāng* (puffed rice or rice popcorn) makers had little need to announce themselves. The traditional machine, which some vendors still use, makes an explosive crack that can be heard a street or two away. After school, children would beg their mothers to give them a cup of rice and a few coins so they could enjoy both the spectacle of popcorn-making and the results. (Now, of course, you need not supply your own rice.) The men hawking *miàn chá*, who usually worked late in the evening and were often visually impaired, blew whistles. This now-seldom-seen treat is made by heating flour with a little sugar and some white sesame; it is served warm while it has a purée-like texture or as a powder accompanied by mung beans or Chinese mesona jelly.

The rapid growth of labor-intensive manufacturing allowed hundreds of thousands of country folk to swap life on a farm for a less monotonous urban existence. Because many of these migrants lived in poorly ventilated hovels without electric fans, let alone air-conditioning, in their free time they flocked to anyplace that was *rènào* (literally "hot and noisy," but meaning "bustling and festive"). What is more, these markets were good places to find cheap shoes and clothes, as well as grilled squid. In the 1970s, one scholar writes, "the high volume of returned orders caused night markets to become sales centers of cut orders and low-priced products. Today, night markets are still the place where export manufacturers sell goods whose quality makes them unsuitable for export."[32]

Taipei's best-known night markets are those at Shilin (where there have been daytime and evening markets for more than one hundred years) and Raohe Street, but more than a few individuals say the food is better, more traditional, and cheaper at Yansan and Nanjichang. The former is in Dadaocheng; the latter is in Wanhua, but some distance from the tourist hubs of Longshan Temple and Huaxi Street. In such places, unlicensed hawkers mingle with licensed vendors; to "insure" themselves against the risk of being ticketed, some of the former subscribe to a group that will pay their fine if they get caught.[33]

Just as many fresh-produce markets have been revamped, some night markets have tried to turn over a new leaf and reduce the amount of litter, grease, and smoke vendors and customers generate. When what was said to be north Taiwan's largest night market opened in summer 2017, the media focused not only on its size but also on design and operational features intended to reduce pollution and make the market a clean and pleasant place to visit. Each of the four-hundred-plus food businesses in Sing Ren Garden Night Market in Shulin will have to pass hygiene tests three times a week, provide filtered drinking water and eco-friendly utensils such as reusable chopsticks, and wrap takeaways in water-soluble plastic bags, *Taiwan News* reported on June 10, 2017. The drains beneath the market have been designed to separate oil from water. Every restroom has a baby-nursing room, and there is a children's playground. So the market can operate in all weathers, customers are sheltered from the rain and cooled by fans.

An earlier official effort to gather and impose order on food vendors was the creation of China Mall in 1961 on the eastern side of Zhonghua Road. By the late 1950s, the neighborhood was crowded by mainland Chinese refugees, many of whom operated stalls or shops. Responding to complaints about noise and dirt, the city leveled the shanties and slums and built eight modern market buildings.

According to a travel guide, by 1967 the mall housed 1,644 businesses.[34] Lu Yao-dong, a historian who was a teenager when he moved from his native Jiangsu to Taiwan, reminisced about the snacks he could find there, among them "iced plum juice and corn cake from Beijing, fried bread sticks and fried dough twists from Tianjin, spicy *chāoshŏu* dumplings from Sichuan, crossing-the-bridge noodles from Yunnan . . . and the Shandong baked wheat cake on which [the four Chinese characters meaning] 'Oppose Communism and Resist Russia' were printed."[35] But it was more than a place where mainlanders could preserve and enjoy the foodways of their home regions. The eateries here were frequented by all ethnic groups, and food scholar Yujen Chen regards the China Mall as a prime example of the "penetration and hybridization" of mainland cuisines throughout the island following World War II, "with mainland food gradually becoming part of the culinary map in Taiwan."

Taiwan has hundreds of thousands of citizens and permanent residents who were born in Southeast Asia; yet the culinary traditions of Thailand, Indonesia, and the Philippines are barely represented in local night markets. This is surprising, as eateries catering to the island's foreign workforce are not uncommon, and quite a few of the Vietnamese women who moved to Taiwan after marrying Taiwanese men now run restaurants. Innovations in food-stall cuisine seem to come from local vendors who look to Japan, Korea, or the West for ideas. Some night-market regulars are dismayed by such trends; others—among them the authors of this book—think an open-minded embrace of foreign influences is as Taiwanese as stinky tofu.[36]

Travel writers, and promotional materials issued by Taiwan's Tourism Bureau, give the impression that night markets are deeply embedded in the lives of the island's people. Yet there are some who never eat in these places. For a few citizens, it may be a class issue. Others dislike the crowds or the cooking smells. But for a significant number of night-market refuseniks, concerns about the safety of the ingredients is their main reason for avoiding cheap street food.

FOOD SCANDALS AND FOOD SAFETY

Consumers are often reminded to wash fruits and vegetables thoroughly, wherever they come from, because of the possibility of pesticide contamination.[37] At more than three hundred fifty locations around the country, including all major markets, specialists employed by local governments take samples for immediate analysis. They use a locally developed technology called Rapid Bioassay for Pesticide Residues (RBPR) and focus on produce (such as leafy vegetables) thought to be more susceptible to contamination or that comes from areas where high residue levels were previously detected. If a significant, yet acceptable, level of residue is found, the original shipper of the produce is issued a formal warning.

RBPR was devised because a lot of domestically grown food comes from farms that are too small to conduct their own testing. It can deliver results in about twenty minutes, meaning unsafe fruits or vegetables can be intercepted at the wholesale stage, before they are removed from the auction floor. In addition to being quick, RBPR is inexpensive, and not much training is required. However, it is less accurate compared to slower types of chemical analysis and cannot detect certain pesticides. It therefore supplements but does not replace more sophisticated methods.[38] Taiwan has shared the technology with several of its diplomatic allies, the government's International Cooperation and Development Fund announced on its website on February 22, 2017.

Misapplication of pesticides is not the only problem the authorities face. *Taiwan Business Topics* reported in February 2013 that a study had concluded that "unregistered and untested products—mostly smuggled in from China—accounted for more than 30% of the pesticides in use."

Despite the use of RBPR and other monitoring technologies, consumers of domestic produce still have good reason to be careful what they eat. Unscrupulous food businesses are nothing new: An Associated Press item published by the *Chicago Daily Tribune* on June 21, 1955, recounted that 250,000 bottles of soy sauce had been found to contain chemicals injurious to health. Officials ordered that every drop of the consignment be poured into the Tamsui River, perhaps without considering the consequences for those who lived downstream and ate locally caught fish.

Earlier this decade, a series of food-safety scandals shocked Taiwan's public. They are thought by some to have been a factor in the electorate's hammering of the KMT in 2014 and 2016.[39] *Taiwan Business Topics*, the American Chamber of Commerce in Taipei's monthly magazine, remarked:

> Taiwan's reputation as a gastronomic paradise is under threat. Beginning with plasticizer found in cold drinks, jams, and pastries, followed by tainted starch products and counterfeit olive oil made green with a chemical additive, and culminating in last year's horrific waste-oil scandal . . . the series of incidents has crushed consumer confidence in the safety of the food supply. The brazen malfeasance of prominent players . . . not to mention the inadequacies exposed in the government regulatory system, outraged the public as much as the gory details of tannery waste and diseased animal corpses mixed into food oil.[40]

The oil scandal led some consumers to instead cook with coconut oil. Others began making lard by hand, with a local newspaper reporting, "Sales of fatty cuts of pork, normally avoided by consumers, have grown markedly."[41]

While recognizing government efforts to put in place "rules and policies to enhance transparency and traceability in the food chain," *Taiwan Business Topics* noted that "for historical and cultural reasons, street food is almost entirely unregulated, a fact that has not diminished the popularity of night markets. Like owning a firearm in Nevada, it is considered the right of every Taiwanese person to set up a roadside stand to sell homemade *dòugān*."[42]

Since the scandals, the authorities have endeavored to register as many of the country's half-million-plus food providers as they can, and they have increased the number of food inspectors working for the Taiwan Food and Drug Administration.[43] Industry has also made some substantial investments. In summer 2017, I-Mei Foods Co. Ltd. began operating the private sector's first food radioactivity laboratory. In it, foods and their ingredients are tested to ensure compliance with international radionuclide limits.[44] Concern about the possibility of radioactive food entering the supply chain was obvious in late 2016, when public pressure forced Taipei to keep in place a ban on the importing of food produced in Japanese provinces affected by the Fukushima nuclear disaster.[45] I-Mei also announced that it was in the process of setting up a dioxin/polychlorinated biphenyl (PCB) trace pollutants laboratory.[46] All of these steps are sensible, but—the commotion notwithstanding—life-expectancy statistics suggest Taiwan has no truly exceptional, long-term food-safety problem. When it comes to smoking, drinking alcohol, and avoiding exercise, Taiwanese people are as guilty as the citizens of other developed countries. *Taiwan News* reported on September 29, 2016, that women enjoyed an average life expectancy of 83.62 years in 2015. For men, it was 77.01 years. Both numbers are higher than in the United States.

CONVENIENCE STORES: KINGS OF THE READY MEAL

Safety concerns have driven some consumers to favor imports over domestic produce, and they are one reason why certain people opt for a convenience-store ready meal rather than a freshly prepared *piāntong* (bento box). The former is a little more expensive but (consumers believe) is prepared in more hygienic conditions and less likely to include the cheapest possible ingredients.

Because many homes lack the means to reheat a prepackaged ready meal, and few have sizable freezers, more than 90 percent of the "TV dinners" consumed in Taiwan are sold by and microwaved at—and usually eaten at—7-Eleven or one of its competitors. Over the past decade, 7-Eleven and Family Mart have invested a lot in making their stores places where consumers are happy to linger. In addition to air-conditioning (which many cheap eateries lack) and both indoor and outdoor seating, customers can enjoy free Wi-Fi.[47] Furthermore, convenience stores are among the few places where you can get a hot meal after midnight.[48]

The range of food options is quite broad. Chinese/Taiwanese classics like Mapo tofu and pork chop on rice are sold alongside spaghetti, Thai- and Japanese-style curries, and cold noodles with sesame paste. Between 2011 and 2016, total sales by weight of chilled ready meals grew by 30 percent; they currently outsell frozen ready meals by more than 18:1.[49] Even faster growth, albeit from a very small base, has been recorded for prepared salads. Euromonitor International explains why in its report on the market for ready meals: "[Salads] are not typically part of the local diet, however, there has been a growing interest in light meals with fresh ingredients. Where once an uncooked meal would have been very unappetizing for many consumers, they have become attractive, especially in summer months and to aid weight management."[50]

Compared to conventional bento, mass-produced ready meals offer greater consistency and transparency. The labeling on 7-Eleven meals includes the number of calories and expiry date, as well as every ingredient—useful information for those managing allergies or trying to lose weight. Convenience stores are also popular places to pick up breakfast (often meat- or tuna-filled onigiri, known to Mandarin speakers as *fàntuán*) and hot snacks at any time of day or night. The latter include stewed savory snacks, similar to Japanese *oden* but known locally as *guāndōng zhǔ*, and pork hot dogs. Taiwan's first 7-Eleven opened in 1979; according to the company's website, by September 2017 the chain had almost fifty-two hundred outlets, and together they sell a massive amount of soda, beer, bread, cookies, and ice cream. It would be fascinating to know what percentage of the calories consumed each day in Taiwan is supplied by the chain, but no estimate has been published.

Convenience stores will probably never encroach on one of the most important branches of the *piāntong* industry: the delivery of lunchboxes to offices and factories. Around eleven o'clock each weekday morning, the staff at many eateries are focused on packing and dispatching stacks of bento; walk-in customers trying to place an order are tolerated but made to feel like unwelcome distractions.

7

❖ ❖

Landmark Restaurants

When a couple enters a "proper" restaurant in Taiwan—not a hole in the wall—a staff member is likely to greet them by asking for confirmation that they want a table for two, then suggesting where they might like to sit. If three people come in together, the waiter will ask in Mandarin, "Are there three of you?" But if the party numbers four, he or she may say "three plus one?" rather than "four." In Mandarin, this number (pronounced *sì*) sounds uncomfortably similar to the word for "death" (*sǐ*).

Once seated, the bill of fare is perused and orders are placed. To the annoyance of some foodies, many establishments offer a choice of meal sets, rather than an à la carte menu. In eateries where each entrée comes with a soup, a dessert, and a beverage, the customer may get to choose his or her drink but typically has no say in what precedes or follows the main course. Some European chefs who run restaurants in Taiwan are resigned to this way of doing things, saying it is what diners expect and are used to; others lament that it takes much of the joy out of going to a restaurant, because choosing and ordering builds anticipation.

Almost every other element in the dining experience is a variable. Customers may sit Japanese-style at a very low table, or on rickety plastic stools. It is by no means certain that they will use chopsticks. Twenty minutes, or two hours, might elapse between sitting down and walking out. When *shàng bān zú* ("go to work tribe," ordinary salaried men and women) eat after a long day at the office, they may pay more attention to their smartphone than to their dinner. In this chapter, we ignore the places where people go mainly to refuel—which is not to say that there is no wonderful cuisine to be enjoyed at food stands that operate under tarpaulins. The selection of restaurants in this chapter is not, therefore, an attempt to transect Greater Taipei's dining scene so much as a set of profiles to show where the city's inhabitants may go when they have time to properly indulge their love for food.

Taipei's restaurants have always been places where business and political deals are cemented, and information and gossip exchanged. During the Japanese colonial period, they also played a key role in the development of civil society by acting as venues for the dissemination of new trends and ideas. While researching Donghuifang—a leading banquet house of that era—one of the authors of this book made a discovery of personal significance. Katy Hui-wen Hung's family possesses a calligraphy scroll handwritten by Liang Qichao (1873–1929), a Chinese scholar and reformer, but exactly how it passed into their hands is long forgotten. Katy found out that in 1911, when Liang was in exile in Japan, he visited Taiwan and dined at Donghuifang in the company of local literati. At that time, Hung Yi-nan (Katy's great-grandfather) was head of Taipei's poetry society, and it was likely at Donghuifang that Liang presented him with the scroll to thank him for his hospitality and support.

One roadside eatery selling rice, noodle, and soup dishes operates between another offering beef, mutton, and fish steaks (right) and a cold-tea stand (left). *wagatsuma / Pixabay.com*

INDIGENOUS CUISINE: WULAI ATAYAL GRANDMA

Taiwan's Austronesian population has been on the island longer than any other ethnic group, but restaurants specializing in indigenous fare only appeared in the past quarter century. When aboriginal restaurateurs like Yabung Tally were growing up, many facets of Austronesian culture and lifestyles were disparaged. Only recently have aborigines dared (and been encouraged by the authorities and mainstream society) to express what makes them different from the Han majority.

According to Yujen Chen, the first restaurant in the capital to characterize itself as aboriginal opened in March 1994, near National Taiwan University. Chen points out that even though the restaurant's aspirations were cultural rather than financial, compromises had to be made: "Some dishes preferred by the aborigines were removed from the menu, such as the internal organs of flying squirrels, and a typical Amis dish, *silau*, which is salted meat with a particularly strong flavor. When some aboriginal dishes were criticized as 'too simple, too original' by consumers, the restaurant changed its cooking methods from steaming and boiling to stir-frying with seasoning that the Han are accustomed to." Chen goes on to note that even in southeastern Taiwan, where indigenous people are a very substantial minority, "the client base of aboriginal restaurants consists largely of other ethnic groups."[1]

One restaurant skillful at deviating from authenticity to better satisfy the public is Atayal Grandma, the best known of Wulai's indigenous eating places. While it does not go overboard in terms of aboriginal-themed decor, lacking the millet sprigs and muntjac skulls that adorn many indigenous restaurants, the eatery does meet Han expectations that foxtail millet and maqaw should feature prominently. Passers-by who want a taste of these exotic ingredients, but not a full meal, can enjoy one or both in the form of an ice cream.

A great many of the dishes on the menu are prefixed with the Chinese character for "mountain," indicating key ingredients are sourced from the hills. Flying squirrel is cooked in the Taiwanese three-cup manner. If that is not adventurous enough, there is *damamian* (see chapter 1). While indigenous people have a reputation for enthusiastic carnivory, Atayal Grandma tries to be vegetarian friendly. The meat-free version of the maqaw-flavored soup comes with bamboo shoots instead of chicken. Most of the vegetable dishes are stir-fried; a more salad-like option is *liángbàn* betel-nut flower. There are lots of mushrooms to be enjoyed, stir-fried or in soups. Steamed leaf wraps and *zhútǒng fàn* (see chapter 4) are popular takeout items.

Traditionally, the Atayal tribe used glutinous rice to brew alcohol, but since indigenous people are associated with millet wine, Atayal Grandma also sells yellowish millet wine. Maqaw honey tea is a sweet, fragrant tea enjoyed (hot or cold) by many customers.

TAIWANESE CUISINE: SHIN YEH AND LU SANG

Shin Yeh (the name means "flourishing leaves"), now entering its fifth decade, is one of the few Taiwan-based restaurant chains to have expanded beyond the island. It has branches in China and Singapore, and subsidiary brands devoted to Japanese shabu-shabu and buffet, but the core of its business is Taiwanese cuisine for a Taiwanese clientele.

Shin Yeh's website says that the founder's emphasis on "simple home-style Taiwanese dishes," instead of "high-end banquet dishes," at a time when many regarded mainland cuisines as classier than anything local, made the beginning period particularly challenging. Yet "the initial focus on simplicity and dedication to tradition later proved to be the winning strategy. . . . Madam Lee was hands-on in developing Taiwanese cooking into something that could be done in a restaurant setting."

The six branches (five in Taipei, one in Fujian) that focus on Taiwanese cuisine serve reinventions of *xiǎochī*, turning them into a fine-dining experience. The guabao buns are smaller than those hawkers use, because Shin Yeh recognizes that it is the quality of the protein, not the quantity of carbohydrates, that makes for a memorable *hó'kā ti*. The Taiwanese-American blogger behind *A Hungry Girl's Guide to Taipei*—who has been back to Shin Yeh repeatedly since 2006 and never wavered from "strongly recommend[ing]" its food—usually orders sweet-potato porridge and praises both the guabao and the spring rolls. While retaining old-time Taiwanese flavors, Shin Yeh has modified its cooking methods to suit modern preferences for food that is less oily and less salty.

Shin Yeh bills itself as Taiwanese. Lu Sang, on Yongkang Street, takes a further step down the localization path and specializes in delicacies from a single county, Yilan in the northeast. Rather than offer complimentary barley or black tea like many dining places, kumquat tea is provided, kumquats being one of the county's signature products. Like Shin Yeh, it is not too expensive for Taipei's middle class and sufficiently casual to attract all types.

One of Lu Sang's most popular menu items is an emblematic Yilan dish called *gāo zhā*. The second syllable can be translated as "dregs," and lets slip that this was originally a way to use up leftovers. Scraps were boiled up with some starch until they became a broth. This was left to cool and jellify, and then coated with flour and deep-fried. Lu Sang's version is much more refined, bringing together minced pork, chicken, and shrimp. Mixed with fish paste, these ingredients are cooked into a thick broth, then chilled. The jelly is cut into cubes, coated with a blend of cornstarch and tapioca flour, and then deep-fried and served piping hot.

JAPANESE INFLUENCES: MAZENDO AND KOKURAYA

When creating Mazendo, founder Sean A. Hsu drew heavily on his experiences studying for an MBA in Japan. In the first episode of *Around the World with Voyager*, broadcast in 2012 on The History Channel, Hsu told presenter Scott A. Woodward that among the things he learned there was a greater appreciation of perseverance and attention to detail. Also, he realized that the name of your restaurant may not mean much to passers-by, however large the sign. That is why Chinese script summarizing Mazendo's menu—"Noodles / Dumplings / Fried Rice"—is prominent on its storefronts, including the branch on Guangfu South Road, a neighborhood where the stores and fashions closely resemble those in Tokyo.

Mazendo's modern decor and attentive service may have been inspired by Japan, but the type of food it sells is typical of post-1945 Taipei. There are spicy noodle soups with beef, mutton, or pork; boiled and pan-fried dumplings; stir-fried vegetables; and *xiǎocài*, cold side dishes such as edamame. Many of the noodle dishes contain duck-blood curd. Knowing that not everyone wants to eat this ingredient, the staff take in their stride requests that it not be included. The restaurant makes a point of using only Wuan Chuang soy sauces (see chapter 2).

Hsu is also one of the backers of Kokuraya, a high-end Japanese-style restaurant that opened just around the corner from Mazendo's Guangfu South Road branch in early 2017. Kokuraya was developed in cooperation with Inakaan, a renowned eel restaurant that has been operating for more than one hundred years in Kyushu and takes its name from Inakaan's home city. Kokuraya's specialty is eel grilled over charcoal until the outer layer is crispy; many other places grill, steam, and grill again, so the texture is different. Eel liver can be had as a side dish.

"Our goal is to be as close as possible to the original in terms of taste and presentation," says Hsu.[2] One way the restaurant tries to achieve this is by using a new soy-sauce paste developed by Wuan Chuang to accompany eel meat. One hundred percent of the eels served in Kokuraya are sourced from Taiwanese eel farmers, several of whom have considerable experience supplying top-quality eels to Japanese customers.

To build excitement, before launching Kokuraya—before even finalizing a location—Hsu worked with a PR company and took thirteen Taiwanese reporters to Japan. There, they saw how eels were caught and farmed for Inakaan. Such largesse is very unusual in Taipei's restaurant scene. "Margins are low, so people in this industry are frugal. They don't want to spend money on things they can't see," says Hsu. Using a Chinese idiom to make his point, he adds, "But I believe 'use a longer line, and you'll catch a bigger fish.' We want people to come here because they're intrigued by our story."

Hsu dislikes "buy two, get one free" and similar deals often used to entice Taipei citizens to new restaurants. "I learned from my father [Hsu Chung-jen, the man often credited with making 7-Eleven convenience stores so successful in Taiwan] that giving away freebies and offering discounts gets people through the door, but it costs a lot and isn't sustainable," he says. "The key issue is how good your food tastes. You should be confident about your quality, and that you're ready."

FOODWAYS FROM THE MAINLAND: PENG'S GARDEN AND KAO-CHI

Taipei's most famous Hunanese restaurant was started by Peng Chang-kuei (1919–2016), known to some as the inventor of General Tso's Chicken, a dish often cited as an example of how Chinese dishes have been adapted to suit American palates. According to a December 2, 2016, obituary in the *Taiwan News*, Peng improvised General Tso's Chicken in 1952 while cooking for a US military delegation, and he came up with the name off the top of his head when an admiral asked what the deep-fried dish was called. Peng had been cooking for two full decades by then, having been apprenticed at an early age to a renowned Hunan chef.

Peng's attempts to cash in on American interest in Chinese food in the 1970s did not go well, even though ABC News featured him making his signature dish. By the mid-1980s, he had left New York and was back in Taipei, building the reputation of Peng's Garden. His contributions to the American food scene were not forgotten, however. The *New York Times* ran a substantial obituary, in which Peng was quoted as saying that his original version of General Tso's Chicken was "typically Hunanese—heavy, sour, hot and salty."[3] Few Taiwanese have heard of General Tso's Chicken, but those who know the story are intrigued by it. Peng's Garden still makes much of its founder's connection to the United States—even if, in one of the most memorable scenes in the 2014 documentary film *The Search for General Tso*, the chef reacts to photos of American versions of General Tso's Chicken by protesting that he cannot recognize what he is looking at.

By late 2017, Peng's Garden had four branches, seven banquet halls, and a newer brand called Xiang Ba Lao. Hunanese cooking has a reputation for being oily and spicy, and Xiang Ba Lao is designed to appeal to younger customers by promising less salt, less oil, and less starch, as well as affordable à la carte options and set meals. At all locations, General Tso's Chicken is on the menu. The meat is first marinated in soy sauce and cornstarch, then deep-fried until each piece becomes "dry on the outside, but tender within." The final stage is stir-frying the chicken with onions, ginger, garlic, a bit more soy sauce, sugar, vinegar, and dried peppers. The "Classic Dishes" section of the company's website reveals one difference between the Peng's Garden version and North American iterations: the restaurant uses the meat of native *tǔjī*, not broilers.

Kao-Chi's main branch on Yongkang Street is less than a hundred meters from Din Tai Fung's flagship outlet, and the former is often recommended to foodies unwilling to wait for a table at the latter, or who want someplace cheaper and less crowded. Kao-Chi serves dishes similar to its world-famous neighbor, founder Gao Si-mei having learned to make Shanghainese snacks during and after World War II.

Finding himself in Taipei in 1949, Gao set up a food stand. By 1969, he had a storefront, and the authenticity of his dishes led to an invitation to demonstrate the preparation of traditional Shanghainese snacks at the Presidential Office. By the mid-eighties, Kao-Chi had evolved into a real restaurant. There are now four branches, all in Taipei, and all serving signature dishes such as Shanghai-style fried pork buns, crispy radish pastries, and sautéed tofu skin with vegetables. Many regulars regard the sautéed crab with rice cake as an especially flavorsome delight. Perhaps the only way in which Kao-Chi may disappoint those used to Din Tai Fung is that the former's dumpling wraps are not quite so thin.

Given Din Tai Fung's international success, and the frequency with which non-Taiwanese speak in positive terms about Kao-Chi, the lack of English on the exterior of the latter's three-story flagship restaurant (or, for that matter, its website) is surprising. But the company takes good care of those who have been dining here for years. Setting aside the first floor for elderly customers who would rather not climb any stairs is surely also a smart business move, given how fast Taiwan's population is aging.

A RESTAURANT THAT SELLS STORIES: YUAN XIANG SHACHA HOT POT

The first generation of migrants from the Chazhou-Shantou region in China's Guangdong province to Taiwan made shacha (*shāchá jiàng*, see chapter 2) that was very similar to the sauces they and their parents had produced on the mainland. However, the second and third generations have tended to adopt local ingredients and methods, so much of the shacha made in Taiwan in recent decades (such as Bullhead Barbecue Sauce) tastes quite different. One of the few exceptions is Yuan Xiang Shacha Hot Pot, a restaurant where they continue to make their shacha from scratch.[4] To emphasize their provenance, on Yuan Xiang's storefront, the restaurant's name is flanked by the toponyms Guangdong and Shantou.

The story of Yuan Xiang starts in 1951, when Shantou native Wu Yuan-sheng (1912–1982) and his brother opened Qing Xiang Hot Pot, Taipei's first sha-cha hot-pot restaurant. The restaurant was located very near the Red House, a landmark in Ximending, then as now one of the capital's busiest shopping and entertainment areas. In 1966, members of the second generation started up Yuan Xiang Shacha Hot Pot, not far from the Red House on Emei Street. Thirty years ago, that restaurant moved to its current location on Xinyi Road, about two miles east of Ximending.

Like Kao-Chi, Yuan Xiang is now run by the third generation of the founding family. Bryan Wu has been in charge since 2005, and his brother is the chief shacha sauce maker. (Wu's uncle and aunt manage Qing Xiang and use the same shacha as Yuan Xiang.) Wu and his brother value the regulars who come for the old-time flavor and atmosphere. Rather than thoroughly revamp Yuan Xiang in the hope of attracting more trade, renovations and improvements have been subtle, so when customers walk in, they feel it is the same restaurant as thirty years ago. There are hundreds of hot-pot eateries in Taipei, and the capital's food scene changes fast, but Wu thinks Yuan Xiang's background and history give their restaurant an edge in the market.[5]

According to Wu, the two principles that ensure the quality of their shacha are the careful selection of ingredients and hygiene. The white sesame comes from a long-term business partner on Dihua Street; the ground peanut is also sourced from a supplier who has proved his reliability. Rather than rush the process, the sautéed garlic is thoroughly dried before it is used, to ensure that there is no mold. Other ingredients include fried shallots, dried flounder, dried shrimp, chili pepper, shredded coconut, about eight types of herbs and spices, soy sauce, and sugar. Dried shrimp replacing shrimp paste is one way in which Taiwanese shacha differs from Southeast Asian satay; Taiwanese find the smell of the latter too strong. Another difference is that satay lacks fried shallots.

Wu's approach to Yuan Xiang is conservative; yet, at the same time, he has been developing another brand to leverage his family's culinary history and expand their customer base. Since 2007, he has opened five branches of Old Shimen Shacha Hot-Pot around Taipei. The name invokes Ximending, where the family opened their very first shacha joint, but no branches are located there. In the flagship outlet on Zhongxiao East Road, amid thoroughly modern decor, photos and mementoes depict the three generations of the Wu family and their restaurants between the 1950s and the present day.

Meal sets and business lunches are available at Old Shimen, but not at Yuan Xiang. What is more, diners at the former can also order Sichuan-style *mălà* pots, laksa pots, and what are sometimes called "yin-yang" pots (allowing one table to enjoy two flavors). Another way in which Wu keeps favorite customers happy is by offering complimentary whisky. He learned from the principal of the high school he attended that men of a certain age sometimes like to drink whisky with dinner, and the custom has won him over. Beer has a wheaty fragrance that goes well with hot pot, he explains, but "nosing" pleasures to be had from whisky lift the fine-drinking/fine-dining experience to another level.

Wu says that, rather than put a lot of effort into marketing and promotion, his approach is to do comprehensive research, try to understand what young people want, and explore opportunities such as the opening of new shopping malls. If you open a new restaurant, he says, passers-by will soon see what is on offer and give it a try. Diners who enjoy themselves are the best form of promotion, of course, because they will tell their friends. Instead of approaching media and asking for coverage, Wu waits until they contact him and request an interview. But when it comes to social media, he is proactive, believing Facebook to be an invaluable tool for interacting with customers.[6]

A HAKKA OUTPOST IN THE CAPITAL: TUNG HAKKA CUISINE

Founded in 2003, and located not far from Addiction Aquatic Development (see chapter 6), this award-winning restaurant is named for a kind of tree that thrives in Hakka-majority areas in northwestern Taiwan. The tung oil tree (*Vernicia fordii*, sometimes called the kalo nut tree) has become an emblem of the Hakka people, and not merely because it grows on the hillsides where Hakka settlers struggled to establish themselves several generations ago. The more barren the soil, the more beautiful its white flowers; like Hakka people, the tree can do well even in the toughest of environments.

The restaurant aims for creative simplicity. On its website, it claims to "showcase innovative Hakka dishes without compromising traditional taste." While owner Zhan Qiao-fen's Hakka mother was running a noodle stall in Xindian, he was being raised by his grandmother (as Taiwan industrialized after the 1950s, it was very common for infants to be left with relatives in the countryside, while their parents built careers or businesses in the cities). The older woman both home-cooked traditional Hakka food and prepared feasts at festival times. When Zhan was in his final year at elementary school, his mother converted her stall into a proper restaurant. It enjoyed immediate success, and he often helped out after school. At that time, however, few non-Hakka had any concept of Hakka food, and only about a quarter of the items on the menu were Hakka; most were in fact Hunanese. Yet it was during this period that he gained both kitchen skills and a thorough knowledge of Hakka ingredients and food culture.

The food photos that Tung Hakka Cuisine posts on its website simultaneously confirm and refute Hakka culinary stereotypes. There are pig intestines, thick slabs of pork belly, and Hakka stir-fry. At the same time, there are lighter, more healthy-looking dishes like white jade vegetable fern and salted egg with bitter gourd.

Among restaurants that publish timelines charting their development, Tung Hakka Cuisine may be unique in listing hiccups alongside successes. In 2004, an attempt to convert a stir-fried vegetable fern dish into salad—using mayonnaise, ground peanuts, pork floss, and seaweed—was abandoned because diners tended to mix all the ingredients together, then find its appearance unattractive. The following year, amid a staff shortage, the restaurant introduced baked tapioca puddings, but daily dessert sales "did not reach a thousand [Taiwan] dollars," barely thirty US dollars. Yet the pudding proved a big hit with female customers in 2006, when sales "rose like an elevator."

That year saw two other breakthroughs. Not only did the kitchen staff perfect what is now acknowledged as their main signature dish (Stewed Taro, Sea Bass, Fish Ball, and Rice Noodles, using 100 percent rice noodles from Puli), but Tung Hakka Cuisine also collected the Hakka Affairs Council's national prize for Best Chef Team.[7]

Zhan told the June 28, 2014, issue of *China Times* that Warren Yang, the boss of Din Tai Fung (see chapter 3), is his business idol. He has expanded cautiously, adding one branch in New Taipei City and another in Taoyuan while maintaining two in the capital proper, at the same time hoping that he can export his brand "and gain international recognition."

CREATIVE WITHIN CONSTRAINTS: LOTUS POND HOUSE AND KUNMING ISLAMIC RESTAURANT

It is often said that you need not be a vegetarian, or even particularly health conscious, to rejoice in Taipei's vegetarian food. The cuisine at Lotus Pond House, which styles itself "six-star luxury, and offering the assurance of an established brand," has opened the eyes of many who associate plant-based diets with self-denial. Some say it is the best vegetarian restaurant in the capital, and, having won awards at the Taipei Gourmet Food Festival and from the central government's Tourism Bureau, it is certainly one of the most innovative—even if what it calls "a Continental-style buffet" does not look especially European.

Lotus Pond House's sashimi (made of konnyaku) is widely praised for its Q-ness, and its mock meats for tasting just like the real thing. The "eel" sushi and teriyaki "chicken" are made from soy. Lunch at Lotus Pond House is several times more expensive than in a run-of-the-mill eatery, but far from ruinous. What with the salad bar and various dim sum, each day close to a hundred different items are available. Because Lotus House Pond is vegetarian in the traditional Chinese sense, rather than vegan, the ice creams, cakes, and pastries are made with eggs and milk. Wood-ear drink is one of the beverage options, but organic *xìngrén* is prepared as a sweet soup rather than as breakfast-style "almond tea."

Vegetarian sashimi made of konnyaku at Lotus Pond House, Taipei.
Katy Hui-wen Hung

Established in 1990, and thus one of Taipei's oldest halal eating places, Kunming Islamic Restaurant serves Indian/Pakistani, Middle Eastern, Southeast Asian, and Yunnanese dishes, as well as vegetarian curries. Founder Yacoob Mah, a Burmese Muslim of Chinese descent, told the August 1, 2016 issue of *Excellence* magazine that he set up the restaurant because Muslim visitors and residents had so few meal options.

Over the past five years, the situation has gotten much better for observant Muslims. The number of halal-certified restaurants throughout the country was more than one hundred by the time *Focus Taiwan* reported their proliferation on March 10, 2017. Many of these food businesses are owned by non-Muslims who were swayed by government encouragement and subsidies. The authorities are doing this not so much for the benefit of the more than two hundred thousand guest workers from mainly Muslim Indonesia who live in Taiwan, or for the approximately sixty thousand ROC citizens who are Muslim, but rather for the Middle Eastern and Southeast Asian tourists they hope will soon come in droves.

RAW: ANDRÉ CHIANG SETS THE BAR HIGH

Other chefs, notably TV celebrity Ah-chi-shih (the only chef to have served three of the country's presidents), may be better known at home, but André Chiang is currently the Taiwanese kitchen maestro with the highest international profile. By late 2017, Chiang was overseeing six restaurants—Restaurant André (now closed) and three others in Singapore, Porte 12 in Paris, and RAW in Taipei. At RAW, diners relish eight-course set menus that emphasize seasonal produce.

Chiang explains the key difference between Restaurant André and RAW, which opened in 2014, in these words: "André was about André, but RAW is about Taiwan. I wanted everything to come from Taiwan, from head to toe. The wood we used to make the bar and waiting bench is from Taiwan. So is the artist who created it. So is the collateral that helped launch the restaurant."[8] The lighting of the dining area is intended both to add ambiance and to make it easier for guests who want to take photos of each dish before eating any part of it.

Given the rave reviews the restaurant has received, RAW should be a shoo-in for Michelin stars. But as soon as Michelin confirmed that it would publish a Taipei food guide in spring 2018, Chiang told reporters that he did not want RAW to be listed, explaining that he regards it as a training ground.[9]

RAW's thirty staff members are all Taiwanese. Their average age is around twenty-five, and few of them have significant overseas experience. (At Restaurant André, by contrast, up to eighteen nationalities were represented among its twenty-member staff.) "At RAW, we insist on using Taiwanese produce in every situation. Why? Because it will influence people to do the right thing. Many Taiwanese people still prefer Japanese rice to Taiwanese rice, or they buy imported fruit, even though Taiwan has such good produce," says Chiang. "We source a lot of products which few people realize Taiwan has," he adds, the Yilan caviar that RAW serves being one of the most surprising.

Every month, Chiang sits down with Chef Alain Huang to draw inspiration from what is newly available and what is in season: "At RAW, I'm still the first person to craft each idea, just like I was at Restaurant André." Perfecting a new dish can take months, or mere minutes, but he has yet to find a dish he cannot update into a modern version for RAW. "If I want to do it, I'll do it. I'll find a way," he says, because as soon as he has an idea, his experience suggests a hundred or more permutations to consider before he actually goes to work in the kitchen. He explains,

When opening RAW, I said our mission is to give a definition of what Taiwanese cuisine is today. Not grandma's flavors, not *lǔròu fàn*. Young people don't go to a night market to eat *lǔròu fàn*. I want to create something that belongs to now. There are so many influences nowadays when you look at street food. One example I always give is that, in Taiwanese cuisine, we use a lot of codfish, steamed or cooked in other ways. But Taiwan has no cod. It's all imported. We like cod, it's now rooted in our cuisine, we like it in different ways. So it belongs to us.

His take on baked potatoes (a twenty-first-century Taiwanese night-market snack) involves removing the innards, baking the skin only, and then using a soda siphon to whip the filling into a foamy mash. Not that the minimalist menus give much away when it comes to preparation methods. Many of the entries on the English version are a single word: "corn," "clam," "praline."

"No one had tried to do what we are doing at RAW, no one in the history of Taiwan's restaurants," he says. Yet he did not feel that he was taking a great risk. "I was confident. First of all, I'm Taiwanese. Spending so many years in France put me in a more neutral position to look at the market. Second, because young people look up to me, because I'm the first Taiwanese chef to attain an international profile, I feel I'm in a position of responsibility to give Taiwan what it really needs."

Chiang puts so much work into RAW in part because he wants Taiwan's local restaurant industry to up its game. "Here, the staff clean the kitchen four times a day. No other restaurant in Taiwan does that, but now we have one that belongs to Taiwan that does. The kids working here, someday they'll work in other restaurants, and they'll say 'that's how we do it.' Setting that benchmark, that standard, is very important." He has set another kind of precedent by halting sales of bottled mineral waters at RAW for environmental reasons. Diners are now offered the choice of filtered still or carbonated water.

"If you ask me, 'What is the Taiwanese way?' I would say 'temperature.' Temperature in many ways. The temperature of the food we eat. Temperature in relationships, in the colors we use. For Taiwanese, I think that's in our DNA. We don't necessarily need the best ingredients or the very best service. It took me many years to realize the uniqueness of this," says Chiang. Others have used the Mandarin term *rénqíngwèi* ("warmth and hospitality between people") to express similar ideas.

Chiang does not believe in educating his customers. "You live with your consumers. You should provide them with better options, but never educate them." Yet he is always willing to respond to customers who have criticisms to make, and he encourages his kitchen staff to do the same. At RAW, the kitchen staff serve the customers. "Who knows the dish better than the person who cooks it? They're ready to answer any questions the customer may have."

8

❖ ❖

Tipples and Teas

There is no tradition of matching particular dishes with alcoholic or nonalco-
holic drinks, so Taiwanese cuisine has no classic pairings like Chardonnay and
lobster or paella with a red Rioja. Complimentary black or barley tea is provided
in many restaurants; set meals invariably include a cold tea or a soda. The cheaper
the eatery, the sweeter the tea—likely more to mask its ordinariness than to satisfy
customer preferences. A lot of alcohol is drunk in Taiwan's karaoke parlors, but
only a small minority habitually orders alcohol when eating out. Some older men
like to drink whisky (neat or with ice, seldom with soda) when enjoying a banquet,
a mode of consumption probably learned from the Japanese.

Restaurateurs who want to sell significant amounts of alcohol "need to push it,"
says Dereke Bruce, who has been running European restaurants and delicatessens in
Taichung since 1993. "Taiwan is a tea-drinking country, for sure, but if you tell your
customers that drinking wine is very much part of the Italian food experience, for instance, lots of locals will buy a glass," the chef explains.[1] Bruce says that, compared
to when he worked in Taipei in the late 1980s, people in the capital now drink a lot
more wine when eating out, but the habit has yet to catch on elsewhere in Taiwan.
Also, markups are about half of what they would be in his native New Zealand.

F&B industry veteran Tom Chen has also noticed a shift in consumption patterns
in favor of red wines, in part because of its apparent health benefits. He says doc-
tors were among the first Taiwanese to regularly enjoy imported grape wines, and
that—among older people, at least—they are opinion leaders.[2] Since the Japanese

149

era, the medical profession has been Taiwan's most prestigious; what physicians say and do carries weight. Even so, few F&B businesses outside major hotels in big cities have wine lists. The Taiwan chapter of the Association de la Sommellerie Internationale was established in 2010 and has almost 150 members, but the majority are part-timers, hobbyists, or living in other countries.

In terms of around-the-clock availability, Taiwan is a drinker's paradise. Every convenience store sells a range of beers and spirits, and often a few wines. Whatever the law might say, hole-in-the-wall eateries that want to keep a refrigerator filled with cold beer for their customers face no practical impediments. Because there are no open-container laws, people can drink alcohol almost anywhere they like, though doing so is considered low class. Countervailing this accessibility are the enforcement of strict drunk-driving laws[3] and the scientific fact that millions of Taiwanese lack the gene required to properly metabolize alcohol.[4]

People very often eat without drinking alcohol, but very few drinks are imbibed without some kind of solid food. In the countryside, few females over the age of fifty drink. But when the menfolk gather in the courtyard for a few glasses of kaoliang or whisky, the host's wife is expected to bring out some hot (preferably salty or spicy) food—or at least some cold *xià jiǔ cài* appetizers (see chapter 9) like peanuts.

Beer-houses were especially popular places to eat and drink in the 1980s and 1990s. Unlike gastropubs, such establishments are seldom accused of being pretentious. Patrons sit on benches at long wooden tables, like in a German beer hall, and order *kuài chǎo* ("quick stir-fried") or *rè chǎo* ("hot stir-fried") dishes to wash down with lager. Many beer-house staples have strong flavors, for the same reason that bars in the United States provide complimentary peanuts or pretzels. (In Taiwan, they may offer dried salted broad beans.) Because beer-house food is cooked and served so fast, nothing arrives on the table overcooked. Alongside old favorites like kung pao chicken and pineapple shrimp balls, a typical menu might list clams stir-fried with garlic and basil, three-cup chicken, and three-cup King Oyster mushrooms. There is a darker side to the history of three-cup dishes: Before Taiwan became affluent, people would not waste any meat, even that of a chicken that had sickened and died; some said doing so would invite divine punishment. Generous amounts of rice wine, sesame oil, and soy sauce could disguise the condition of such meat, and applying a high heat would kill any bacteria.[5]

THE CAFFEINE INUNDATION

Soon after they began to settle in Taiwan, Han people discovered the island's indigenous wild-tea trees. These varieties faded from mainstream memory—even though researchers used them to create new hybrids, among them a highly success-ful black tea[6]—until the recent surge of interest in everything local. In the past few years, minute quantities of what is called *shān chá* ("mountain tea") or *yěshēng chá* ("wild tea") have been sold, either online or directly to tourists visiting the districts where they grow.

Tea was one of Taiwan's most important exports during the final third of the nineteenth century, and one of the people often credited with developing the local tea industry was British merchant John Dodd. He first visited Taiwan in 1860 and settled in Tamsui in 1864. By 1869, he was shipping tea to New York. In 1895—by which time Dodd had left the island, his fortune well and truly made—nearly ten thousand tons of Formosan oolong was being exported each year, and sixty-four thousand acres were devoted to tea cultivation.[7]

Black and oolong varieties were introduced to north Taiwan from Fujian at the beginning of the nineteenth century, but few farmers grew them in commercial quantities. Recognizing that certain locations in Greater Taipei such as Muzha and Sanxia were ideal for tea production, Dodd encouraged farmers to switch from indigo cultivation, and he loaned money so they could invest in tea seedlings from Anxi,[8] the county in Fujian dubbed "the tea capital of China." The Japanese colonial authorities saw the potential for even greater exports. At the 1900 Paris Exposition Universelle, they sponsored a booth to display oolong and pouchong tea from Taiwan, as well as the snacks often eaten when tea was drunk.[9]

Coffee has been grown in Taiwan since Dodd's era, but few locals regularly drank the beverage before the 1980s. The island's first coffee growers were British entrepreneurs. In the late nineteenth century, Tait & Co—a firm that specialized in camphor, opium, and tea—imported seeds from the Philippines and oversaw their planting at four locations in Greater Taipei. This attempt to develop a viable cash crop failed, but by World War I agricultural improvement efforts sponsored by the colonial authorities had resulted in beans good enough for shipment to the Home Islands.[10]

Taiwan's best known coffee-growing areas are now Gukeng in Yunlin County and Dongshan in Tainan, while two remote indigenous communities have man-aged to rebuild colonial-era reputations for quality arabica. Despite severe ty-phoon damage, around thirty tons per year—about a seventh of the country's miniscule coffee crop—comes from Dewen in Pingtung County, according to the website of San Formosan, a Taipei-based company that sells Taiwanese (and only Taiwanese) coffees. The coffee heritage of Laiji in Greater Alishan was so deeply buried that only after exposure to the drink in big cities did one local woman real-ize that, growing wild near her village, were coffee trees planted three generations earlier. Rather than sell the beans outside the community, she siphon-brews what she gathers for tourists.[11]

The combined annual production of these places does not meet even 1 percent of domestic demand. Per capita consumption close to tripled between 1990 and 2012, according to statista.com, and reached 122 cups in 2015.[12] Starbucks opened its first Taiwan stores in 1998.[13] Local chain 85°C Bakery Cafe, which launched six years later, now has four hundred branches in Taiwan and more than five hundred in China. It took just one decade earlier this century for the number of coffee shops to multiply from two hundred to twelve thousand[14]—yet businesses that serve coffee have been an established part of Taipei's entertainment scene since the 1930s.

During the colonial era, what Japanese speakers called *kafe* served Western-style meals with coffee. Some teahouses sold coffee as well as tea, and there were tearooms that offered snacks with coffee and music. Of course, in that era only a minority of Taiwanese had the opportunity or money to enjoy such places, but coffeehouses became important cultural loci. The owner of Bolero, founded in 1934, hung blank canvases on the walls, "for artist-customers to create paintings when moved to do so."[15] The financial and moral support he and other cafe owners offered artists is regarded by art historians as a key stage in the development of Taiwanese art.[16] After World War II, coffeehouses continued to be gathering places for the literati.[17]

Bolero was (and still is[18]) located in Dadaocheng, an old and thoroughly Taiwanese part of the city long associated with the tea trade. The appearance of coffee-serving establishments outside Taipei's Japanese-dominated neighborhoods shows how educated Taiwanese shared some of Japan's enthusiasm for Western-influenced lifestyles. Both the colonizers and the colonized viewed coffeehouses as symbols of modernity. At a time when few buildings had electricity, Taipei's coffeehouses used colorful lights to attract customers and electric fans to cool them. Rather than sit Japanese-style at very low tables, coffee drinkers reposed on Thonet-type chairs. In several establishments, however, the waitstaff uniform was a maid's white apron over a kimono.[19] But in one respect, these businesses were more similar to Japanese places of entertainment than European cafes: the clientele was almost exclusively male until sometime after World War II, and the role of waitresses was, in the words of Marc L. Moskowitz, "remarkably similar to women working in contemporary high-end hostess clubs."[20]

The number of coffee shops scarcely grew during the 1950s and 1960s, and not only because the mainlanders who dominated many parts of Taipei after 1949 preferred tea. With the import tariff for coffee set at 120 percent until 1968, the cost of a single cup was more than a full day's earnings for an average Taiwanese.[21] For many people, McDonald's was the first place where they could afford to sit and drink a hot pick-me-up. Mr. Brown, a local brand inspired by Japan's canned coffees, launched in 1982; varieties now include espresso, cappuccino, and macadamia nut. Cans of Mr. Brown are sold everywhere, piping hot or icy cold depending on the season. Other companies have entered the ready-to-drink market, but the first-mover still accounts for most of the quarter billion cans of coffee sold in the country each year[22]—and their profits underwrote the building of the country's first whisky distillery (see below).

Some early adopters were more concerned with being seen to drink coffee the right way than with finding the best java in their part of town. According to Moskowitz, local reporting in the 1980s stressed "the proper etiquette of coffee drinking." In the following decade, "the discussion shifted to how to discern between good- and bad-tasting coffee beans, and the particular differences between different kinds of blends . . . familiarizing one's self with the quality of the coffee itself [became] a marker of sophistication."[23] More recently, coffee vendors have noted a surge in those taking their morning jolt black[24] or with milk instead of cream.[25]

Coffee merchants are achieving quality as well as quantity. *USA Today* (on November 1, 2012) and the BBC website (on April 23, 2014) have both called Taipei one of the world's best cities for coffee drinkers. Taiwan has the talent as well as the enthusiasm, for sure. Kaohsiung-based Jacky Lai was named World Coffee Events' 2014 World Coffee Roasting Champion.[26] Berg Wu, winner of the 2016 World Barista Championship, gave up a career in engineering to concentrate on the Lobby of Simple Kaffa, his basement coffeehouse not far from the department stores on Taipei's Zhongxiao East Road.[27]

The passion for coffee shown by young Taiwanese like Lai and Wu has galvanized at least one tea lover.[28] The founder of Permanent Revolution of Tea aims to promote a tea-drinking culture that is, in the words of his company's website, "simple but fashionable, in line with modern life and aesthetic styles." This means sleek metal countertops, elegant yet informative packaging, and—to the delight of tea aficionados in a hurry—freshly brewed 100 percent Taiwanese premium infusions to go. Yet, after nearly a decade in business, the company has just three branches, and there has been no stampede of imitator-competitors. In the takeout market, those willing to fork over the better part of an hour's pay for a coffee seem to far outnumber those who want good tea.

But tea has not been relegated to a bit player. Per capita consumption has grown fivefold since 1980[29] and still exceeds that of coffee by a significant margin. However, domestic *Camellia sinensis var. sinensis* output peaked before World War II, and the 2015 tea harvest was one of the smallest ever at 15,879 tons. Nearly a third of that total was exported.[30] Taiwan grows black and green teas, but its global reputation rests on oolongs, which farmers wither under the sun, "bruise," and allow to partly oxidize. These leaves produce libations that Mary Lou Heiss and Robert J. Heiss call "distinctly Taiwanese in nature; only a few sips are necessary to appreciate these spectacular teas that uniquely express the terroir and tea-making style of Taiwan. . . . [They] are some of the world's most aromatic, expressive, expensive, and rare teas. Taiwan oolongs include a larger span of leaf styles and oxidation levels than their Chinese oolong cousins, giving tea enthusiasts more delicious choices to explore."[31]

The Heisses say that oolongs grown at altitudes above six thousand feet "possess sweet, refreshing, vivacious flavors and persistent, vegetal aromas."[32] Some attribute these characteristics to the moist, oceanic air currents that blow over plantations no more than twenty-five miles from the sea, thereby slowing growth.[33]

Officially, for every ton of Taiwanese tea sipped by the island's connoisseurs while they crack watermelon seeds and nibble peanut cookies, three tons of imported tea are guzzled. Much of the latter is packaged in factories, sold in supermarkets, and drunk cold between meals. Most of the rest ends up in the thousands of tea kiosks that are a unique feature of urban Taiwan. The key appeal of such businesses is that each beverage is made to order in a cocktail shaker, with the customer specifying how much or how little sugar or ice he wants. A tiny amount of tea finds its way into kitchens, where chefs use it to create such dishes as tempura made with fresh tea leaves and beef flavored with pu'er tea.

The menu at Chingshin, a prominent kiosk chain, includes Taiwanese oolong and Ceylon black tea. Winter-melon tea is a popular non-caffeine choice in summertime; traditional Chinese medicinal theory claims that it helps the body deal with hot weather. According to the bilingual menu on its website, in wintertime Chingshin sells hot longan and ginger teas. Among the milky options is a mung-bean smoothie, plus teas flavored with jelly made from Chinese mesona (*Platostoma palustre*, a distant relative of mint long known to Atayal and Paiwan aborigines, frequently translated as "grass jelly"), coconut jelly, or chewy tapioca "pearls." The last of these, black balls sucked up through a thick straw, are the distinguishing ingredient in the internationally known, Taiwan-invented refreshment called pearl milk tea or bubble milk tea. Pearl milk tea is a direct translation of *zhēnzhū nǎichá*. Another common name for the same drink, *bōbà nǎichá*, is seldom rendered in English; *bōbà* is actually slang for large female breasts.

PROBLEMS IN TEA PARADISE

Wang Duan-kai is a sixth-generation descendant of the founder of Geow Yong Tea Hong, a tea trading enterprise that did not open a Taipei branch until 1957, its 115th year of doing business. Geow Yong's roots are in Lukang, a famously conservative town in central Taiwan, but in 2012 a Taipei City Government publication praised Wang for bringing "new life and new ideas to the venerable old business." Moving from Dadaocheng to a more central location on Changchun Road, Geow Yong reopened "in a more chic and stylish space that attractively complements the elegant packaging and designer tea implements. [Wang aims] to bring a more youthful and metropolitan spirit to the tea-culture experience."[34]

Unfortunately, one of Wang's fresh ideas ran afoul of the law. In 2014, he and several other tea company owners, as well as an importer, were indicted for smuggling tea from China and selling it as authentic Taiwan-grown tea. Wang and the others were found guilty in March 2017,[35] but Geow Yong was still in business at the time of this writing.

One response to the problem of authenticity has been the creation of a traceability system by the COA's Tea Research and Extension Station, which aims to ensure that teas originate from the labeled terroir. However, the system is, in the words of an industry insider, "far from being popular, since participation is voluntary, the management and definition of the specific terroirs is left in the hands of individual farmers' associations, and the system goes against the usual practices in the trade."[36]

The issue of "creative blending" of local teas and imported teas is "not marginal," he says, adding:

> The biggest stumbling block is the local consumer itself. Taiwanese consumers tend to resist any form of price increase on traditional food items like tea. This creates a lot of pressure on the distribution chain, despite obvious increases in production costs. To meet this requirement, anybody in the distribution chain can and will blend in cheaper teas from other areas of Taiwan or abroad. It is important to say that this phenomenon is not just something that happens at the distribution stage. In fact, among the biggest buyers of imported teas are tea producers themselves! Very often, tea shops and vendors are unknowing victims of this practice. There seems to be a tacit acceptance of this practice by all, including consumers. As long as the tea tastes good and they feel they're getting a good deal, nobody complains. It needs to be said that one reason why this isn't so uncommon now is that the imported teas are good [the prize-winning Vietnamese tea bought by the Nantou grower who got into trouble proves this point[37]], and very often made by Taiwanese established abroad. I get the feeling many players now see this as a necessary evil if they're to stay in business.

The industry faces other challenges, according to the same informant. "At the grower-producer level, there is very little enthusiasm for the younger generation to pick up the family trade. Despite the recent bump caused by bubble tea and ready-to-drink products, tea is losing ground, especially with younger people. In a country where the tea industry is driven nearly exclusively by local demand, this creates an impression of standstill for many," he says. "I seem to see much more enthusiasm about Taiwanese teas coming from foreign buyers and enthusiasts. Unfortunately, the small quantity they purchase can do very little to change this dynamic and rekindle a lost sense of belonging and pride for the tea people of this island. Yet, while Taiwan's tea sector is gaining an international reputation for murky practices, the truth is and will always be: Taiwan remains a true treasure island when it comes to the teas it produces!"

FROM MONOPOLY TO MULTIPLICITY: BEER

The entity now known as Taiwan Tobacco & Liquor Corporation (TTL) has brewed most of the beer drunk throughout Taiwan's history. Its ancestor, set up by Japan in 1901, held island-wide monopoly rights over the manufacture and sale of tobacco, salt, opium, camphor, and alcohol; all profits accrued to the colonial administration.[38] The light and dark brews labeled Takasago Beer (Takasago being Japan's name for the highlands of Taiwan in the sixteenth and seventeenth centuries) were renamed Taiwan Beer in 1946. This German-American-style amber lager reached its current form in the 1960s when TTL's predecessor began using ponlai rice as an adjunct.[39]

Heavily carbonated and very slightly sweet, standard Taiwan Beer—the English word "classic" now appears on the emblematic white-and-blue cans—is 4.5 percent alcohol. The second most popular local brew is Taiwan Gold Medal Beer. Slightly stronger, and named because it has received several Monde Selection awards, Gold Medal gets the nod from many Western drinkers. Both go well with stir-fried and spicy dishes.

Since TTL was stripped of its monopoly advantage, big-brewery imports—notably Heineken, Budweiser, and Japan's Kirin Ichiban—have made major inroads. Taiwan Beer's shrinking market share (from nearly 80 percent in 2009 to 63 percent in 2015[40]) is not the result of complacency on TTL's part, however. The corporation sponsors a semi-professional basketball team (another is supported by and named for Kinmen Kaoliang Liquor Inc.) and has hired some of the country's biggest pop stars and soap opera actors as brand ambassadors. Several new beers have been launched since 2008. Production of Strong Black (a 7 percent alcohol amber/red lager) ceased within a year of its debut, but the Taiwan Weissbier (a German Hefeweizen-type brew) and a range of fruit-enhanced beers have found a niche. The last of these are around 2.8 percent alcohol; flavors include mango, pineapple, and grape. The most common complaint about 18 Days, a premium bottled "draft" beer that should be drunk no more than eighteen days after production, is that it can be hard to find.

Sadly for brewers, demand for beer is not huge. At 6.6 US gallons per adult per year, per capita beer consumption is less than a quarter of that in the United States. Nonetheless, craft beer makers have proliferated; more than twenty-five were said to be operating on the island at the beginning of 2017.[41]

Some think the situation is unsustainable, however. "It's a bubble. There are too many companies, and most of them don't brew their own beer. They use contract breweries," says Alex Lu, founder and boss of Takao Beer. "We don't have the same kind of craft beer culture in Taiwan as in many Western countries, and unfortunately no one is trying to build it," laments Lu. He complains that many of his competitors, rather than trying to educate the public and build long-term interest in craft beers and microbrews, simply try to steal market share from industry leaders such as his company.[42]

Lu founded Takao Beer in 2014. After phenomenal growth in 2017, the company was among the country's top three private-sector brewers. Lu attributes some of the growth to offering consumers a greater range of options, adding six types of beer to the original blonde ale. That attracts those who like to collect bottles, which he reckons is a meaningful number of buyers. Most Takao Beer drinkers are under thirty-five, says Lu, who was born in 1990: "The younger generation like things that are new, unique, or crafted."

Craft beers made by Kaohsiung-based Takao Beer.
Takao Beer

Lu is a Taipei native, but he chose to establish Takao Beer in the southern metropolis of Kaohsiung. Takao was the city's name until 1920, and Lu explains, "We wanted a thoroughly local name, as local support and local pride are very powerful assets." But, like most brewers on the island, he imports every ingredient except water.

Government policies have hampered the development of Taiwan's beer industry. Local brewers were disadvantaged because around the time that the government abolished its alcohol monopoly, it allowed huge international brands to establish footholds in the local beer market before liberalizing the manufacturing side, Lu says. In most parts of Taiwan, breweries can only legally operate in designated industrial zones.[43] In those cities and counties, therefore, opening a downtown brewpub is impossible. This is senseless from a food-safety as well as a business perspective. As Lu points out, beer is best consumed when it is fresh, and travel is the stage at which it is most likely to spoil. What is more, he says, neither banks nor venture capitalists seem willing to lend money to craft beer companies, even when—as in Takao Beer's case—they can show full order books.

Taiwan's handful of grape and fruit wineries encounter similar barriers. One of very few able to produce alcoholic beverages from fruit grown on-site and water drawn from its own spring is Cang Jiu Winery, located at the top of a wooded valley in Yilan County. Cang Jiu makes red and white grape wines, a kumquat wine, and a 52 percent alcohol liquor distilled from five types of grain. The valley's unspoiled environment and rich wildlife attract tourists, but the owner has to deal with a problem few winemakers have faced: a population of wild pigs that like to butt his kumquat trees, to make ripe fruit fall to the ground, so violently that the trees are sometimes toppled.[44] Another success story is Shu-Sheng Leisure Domaine in Taichung. Run by a family that grew grapes for TTL between the early 1950s and the late 1990s—and was then paid to tear up most of the vines as Taiwan prepared to enter the WTO—the winery has since 2014 won international awards for its fortified white wine and vino rosso.[45]

STRONGER STUFF

No intoxicant is more Japanese than sake, but the colonizers were forced to depend on shipments from the Home Islands until 1914. Only after the installation of refrigerated manufacturing facilities at the brand-new Taihoku Brewery (Taihoku being Taipei's Japanese name) was local production possible.[46] The brewery's trackside location, a mile east of Taipei Main Railway Station, offered not only convenient transportation but also access to water deemed suitable for making sake. The complex was shuttered in 1987, but part has been preserved and repurposed as Huashan

1914 Creative Park. What was called Jianguo Brewery between 1975 and 2007 was set up in 1919 on a separate site a few minutes' away, and it continues to function as a TTL facility under the name Taipei Brewery.

Another dozen years passed before local rice began to replace wine grain imported from Japan.[47] These days, Taiwan's main sake manufacturing site is the TTL facility in Taoyuan, half an hour from the capital. Sakes sold under the Yuchun ("jade spring") brand range in strength from 13.5 to 15 percent, and most are made from ponlai rice. Name notwithstanding, no part of the taro plant goes into the premium Taro Fragrance Sake, its special aroma being a property of Taoyuan 3, the twenty-first-century rice cultivar from which it is made.[48]

The characteristics of another recent variant, Yi-chuan Fragrant Rice, inspired one of the country's most go-getting farmers' cooperatives to try its hand at sake production. Wufeng District Farmers Association in Greater Taichung engaged a Japanese expert, sent technicians to the homeland of sake for training, and established a brewery in 2007.[49] Recognizing the importance of water quality to the process, the water used for washing and soaking the starch-rich grain cores is trucked in from a spring more than an hour's drive inland.[50] By 2012, Wufeng's Chuwu ("early mist") sakes were winning prizes in Europe and sold alongside the district's other value-added agricultural products, such as pumpkin and okra chips and rice rolls flavored with *kasu* (lees left over from sake production).

If Taiwanese sakes mark Japan's influence, the country's rice-fermented *huángjiǔ* ("yellow wine") brands perpetuate even older drinking and cooking habits. Shaohsing Chiew, TTL's version of China's famous Shaoxing Wine, is made from glutinous rice, ponlai rice, and wheat; the alcohol content ranges from 14 to 17.5 percent. Few Taiwanese nowadays drink Shaohsing Chiew, but home-cooking enthusiasts find it useful for everything from dressing hard-boiled eggs (the wine peps up a sauce made from angelica root, astragalus, and red dates) to replacing conventional rice wine in mushroom and chicken soup.

TTL also sells spirits more familiar to Americans and Europeans—including gin, rum, and vodka—but this market segment is dominated by whiskies,[51] all of which were imported until recently. After decades of blending and bottling foreign whiskies, TTL began distilling Jade Supremacy Taiwan Whisky at its Nantou Winery in 2008.[52] However, the country's oldest whisky maker belongs to the private sector. King Car Kavalan Distillery, on the other side of the mountains south of Taipei, has made astonishing progress since the first bottle of Kavalan whisky was released in late 2008.

The King Car Group began as a maker of aerosol pesticides and other household cleaning products, but it is best known for Mr. Brown canned coffees. Established with equipment and know-how imported from Scotland, the distillery uses Scottish and Finnish malt, plus yeast from France and South Africa. Kavalan now has a capacity of nine million liters (2.4 million US gallons) per year, making it one of the world's largest single malt distilleries.[53]

Kavalan bottles do not carry age statements; because of Taiwan's climate, whisky matures more quickly there than it does in Scotland. Also, the so-called "angel's share"—the proportion lost through evaporation as the whisky matures— is up to 15 percent, several times higher than in Scotland. The warehouse is not temperature-controlled and gets as warm as 104°F in summer.[54]

The distillery's expansion and its pricing strategy (few Kavalan expressions cost less than US$100, and some are more than US$400) make sense in light of the prizes and accolades its single malts have won every year since 2010. In the 2015 World Whiskies Awards, the Kavalan Solist Vinho Barrique Single Cask Strength was awarded the "World's Best Single Malt" and the "Best Asian Single Malt" prizes.[55]

Whisky's popularity is a recent phenomenon. During the 1960s, a cheap spirit with a high ethanol content, widely known by its Holo-language name of *thài pėh chiú*, sold well. Made from rice or sweet potatoes, it was packaged in large jars and sometimes sold by the glass at dry goods stores. Farmhands were among those who carried their own cups, so they could enjoy a snifter at the end of the workday.[56] Being what economists call an "inferior good," production ceased in the 1970s, when rising living standards meant ordinary folk could afford rice wine.

Over the past half century, the strong alcoholic beverage most often drunk in Taiwan is probably kaoliang. The English name of this smooth, clear spirit comes from the Mandarin word for sorghum (*gāoliang*), one of two grains from which the drink is made. (The other is wheat.) Kaoliang has been made in China for at least six hundred years, but the tradition did not get a foothold in Taiwan until after 1949, and then only because of the standoff between Mao's Communists and Chiang's Nationalists. KMT forces on Kinmen, a frontline island within shelling distance of the Chinese mainland, encouraged local farmers to grow sorghum, apparently because it grows tall enough for soldiers to hide in.[57] The farmers exchanged their sorghum crop for sacks of rice, and the former was handed over to the distillery that evolved into Kinmen Kaoliang Liquor Inc. The company now produces about two hundred thousand bottles per day of a drink sometimes compared to tequila because of its spicy aroma. Because it is owned by the local government, profits are shared in the form of free milk for the island's school children and other community programs.[58]

TTL makes a kaoliang called Yushan, in honor of the country's highest mountain. In 2017, Yushan kaoliang aged for six years was named the world's best baijiu at the San Francisco World Spirits Competition.[59] (Baijiu, a transliteration of the Mandarin words for "white alcohol," is a category of clear liquors made from rice, wheat, barley, sorghum, or other grains.) The previous year, the award went to the 58 percent Kinmen Kaoliang Liquor.[60] The alcohol content of other Taiwanese kaoliangs ranges from 38 to 63 percent, and a small amount finds its way into food. Some restaurants on Kinmen serve raw crab in a kaoliang-sauce, and in Greater Taipei a few food stalls hawk kaoliang-flavored sausages.

Kinmen Kaoliang Liquor Inc.'s website advises drinking the spirit straight, ice-cold in summer, or gently heated in winter. But that is not all kaoliang is good for. Cocktails caught on a while ago; on September 25, 2006, in time for Mid-Autumn Festival, *Apple Daily* told its readers how to make kaoliang-based versions of Blue Ocean and other mixed drinks, as well as alcohol-infused sorbets.

A few folk hoard bottles of bee pupae steeped in kaoliang, believing that a small glass of this concoction swallowed every evening can ameliorate rheumatism, gout, and memory decline.[61] If this is not adventurous enough, there is always snake wine. The April 1964 issue of the government-run English-language magazine *Free China Review* (since renamed *Taiwan Review*) informed its readers, "The brewing method is to soak a whole poisonous snake, skin, bone and all, in two gallons of kaoliang wine. The vessel is tightly sealed, then buried deeply underground. After a year, the snake will have completely dissolved and the white kaoliang is deep yellow. This wine is believed efficacious in curing rheumatism and ailments of the eye."

ABORIGINAL ALCOHOL

No meal in a tourist-oriented indigenous eatery is complete without a shot glass of cloudy, mildly alcoholic *xiǎomǐjiǔ* ("foxtail millet wine"). However, the tipple nowadays served to outsiders is not made the traditional way, in which human saliva took the place of yeast.

Reverend Georgius Candidius, a Dutch missionary during the VOC period, witnessed aboriginal women heating millet paste, chewing it, and then spitting the paste into a pot where it was left to mature. The wine was ready to drink after two months, he noted, but the longer it was kept, the better it tasted.[62] Two centuries later, a Dutch doctor described similar methods, but with rice rather than millet as the key ingredient.

> The preparation of this beverage . . . is as follows: one slowly cooks some rice and leaves it to swell, and then that is beaten into a dough. An old woman who prepares this beverage takes some of this rice gruel, chews on it and spits it into an earthen bowl, [continuing] until the contents of the bowl weighs about a pound. She then mixes the chewed portion with the rest of the rice dough. This mixture is then covered with water, put in a jar, and left to ferment for twelve months. During that time the fluid mass transforms into a strong, pleasant and fizzing beverage, reaching its utmost maturity after 20 to 30 years. When consuming this treat, one first pours off the liquid, and then eats the rest with a spoon.[63]

According to some versions of history, a Japanese policeman's refusal to accept a cup of home-brewed millet wine from a Seediq tribesman on the grounds that it was unsanitary was one of the sparks that ignited the Wushe Incident, the most serious aboriginal uprising of the colonial period.[64] (In the distant past, the Japanese themselves not only brewed a form of sake using the saliva of virgins but also incorporated the chewing and spitting into Shinto religious festivals.)[65]

Edward C. Taintor's report on his 1869 visit to Taiwan includes translated extracts from *Komalan Ting Chih*, a multivolume description of the northeast compiled between 1831 and 1852 by Han scholars teaching in what is now Yilan. They recorded:

When [the indigenes] have gathered in their crops they set apart enough for a year's supply of food, and make the rest into wine, of which they are very fond. . . . Their wine is made from glutinous rice. Each person takes a handful of rice in his mouth, and masticates it until soft. It is then put into an earthen jar, and by the next day it has fermented, so that by adding water, wine is produced. They consider sour wines the best.[66]

By contrast, modern *xiǎomǐjiǔ* is usually as sweet as a dessert wine. One winemaker, at least, has devoted herself to reviving the original taste, if not the ancient method. Ceng Chan Yu-cin spent twenty years working as a fruit and vegetable wholesaler in Taipei before calling it quits and moving back to Maolin in the south's mountainous interior. There, she felt saddened, yet motivated, when she realized that the traditional millet wine her fellow Rukai used to share on social occasions seemed unobtainable, and the art of making it virtually forgotten. By trial and error, and using snippets of knowledge picked up from women of her mother's generation (among the Rukai, as in other tribes, winemaking is a female responsibility), she discovered a way to re-create the millet wine of her youth. Pre-boiled millet cooked with raw, unhusked djulis is left exposed for a few hours, so mold can establish itself; then it is placed in a ceramic jar and covered with spring water. After a week, more water is added and the mix is stirred. A month later, the wine is ready. It is neither cloudy nor sugary, but clear with a yellowish tinge.[67]

When indigenous people drink with friends, they sometimes fill a jug with Red Label Rice Wine (occasionally *xiǎomǐjiǔ*), milk, and Mr. Brown coffee (or espresso). Drunk like a punch, the taste of this combination is not too far from Baileys Irish Cream. Some like to add a slug of Whisbih and/or coconut milk.

Whisbih and its competitor, Paolyta B, are energy drinks that are extremely popular with blue-collar workers. Because they contain medicinal ingredients, by law both should be sold only by licensed pharmacies. In reality, they are available at hundreds of betel-nut stands and mom-and-pop grocery stores; on April 27, 2016, *Apple Daily* reported that Taiwan's Food and Drug Administration had in the first quarter of that year levied fines on sixty-four businesses for illegally sell-ing the drinks. At the same time, the authorities reminded the public that, because both Whisbih and Paolyta B contain more alcohol than strong beer (as well as large amounts of caffeine), no more than a small beaker should be consumed each day, and a cup or two before driving could result in a drunk-driving penalty.

Fruit wines and different types of *xiǎomǐjiǔ* for sale in Wulai, Greater Taipei.
Katy Hui-wen Hung

WELLNESS IN A CUP: JUICES AND SMOOTHIES

Unless they are at a hotel buffet or a fast-food restaurant, few Taiwanese drink juice with their breakfast. The most popular early-morning drinks are cold black tea, often with sugar and milk added, and soy milk. Nonetheless, places selling takeout juices are almost as commonplace as tea kiosks. Vendors who squeeze oranges or crush sugarcane on the backs of small trucks are also quite common, but some consumers avoid these operations, as well as night-market juice peddlers, because they worry about the cleanliness of the machinery and the purity of the ice cubes. In middle-class households, especially those with children, juicers are becoming standard kitchen equipment.

Water quality is less of a concern inside department-store food courts, and there has been a proliferation of higher-end juice bars in the past five years. Tomato juice is drunk in far greater amounts than a decade or two ago. "White sugarcane juice," with bitter melon, guava, lemon, or milk, is a newish option. Health concerns are likely a major reason why fewer people than before seem to be drinking sugar-heavy papaya smoothies, a beverage that has been around since the 1960s.

The fad for wood-ear drinks has spread beyond Taipei. In small towns, it is now not unusual to see market vendors selling bottles of the drink (made by boiling thin slices of wood-ear mushrooms until the liquid is mostly reduced), often with goji berries added. The entrepreneurs who in 2014 launched 8more (slogan: "eat more, fit more") claim on the company's website to be the country's first white wood-ear specialists. Rather than use dried wood-ear from China, not knowing whether it has been bleached or drenched with preservatives, they source from organic farmers closer to home. The range of flavors advertised on the company's Facebook page in October 2017 included almond, apple, cashew with buckwheat, honey, and sesame with barley, but their products are far more expensive than the no-brand alternatives sold in markets: a 900 milliliter (1.9 US pints) bottle costs almost US$8, more than many Taiwanese earn in an hour.

9

❖ ❖

Teaching, Sharing, and Learning Taiwanese Cuisine

Julia Child often said that, after French cuisine, her second-favorite style of cooking was Chinese.[1] The woman dubbed "the Julia Child of Chinese cooking,"
Taipei's Fu Pei-mei (1931–2004), passed away a month after Child, at the end of a
pathbreaking career as an author, cooking instructor, and TV personality.

Like Child, Fu did not learn how to cook until she got married. But according
to historian Michelle King, whose interest in Fu has taken the form of scholarly
articles and conference papers, "there the resemblance ends: where Child sought
to introduce American audiences to the unfamiliar tastes and traditions of French
cuisine, Fu was demonstrating Chinese cooking to a new generation of postwar
housewives in Taiwan, who needed her expertise and guidance in the kitchen."[2]

Fu was born in a part of mainland China then under Japanese control, and she
attended a Japanese-language school. Her proficiency in Japanese helped her land
a job in a trading company after she arrived in Taipei as a nineteen-year-old and
made it possible for her to demonstrate cooking techniques on Japanese TV in the
late 1970s and early 1980s.

Wed at the age of twenty, Fu started to learn proper cooking skills a few years
later. Traditionally, a married woman should devote herself to her husband and
his parents, hence the Holo proverb *put hàu sim-pū saⁿ tǹg sio ū hàu cha bó ˙kiáⁿ
iô kòe kiô* ("even an unfilial daughter-in-law will cook you three hot meals, but a
filial daughter will 'cross the bridge' [get married and not prepare meals for her
own parents]").

Fu's case was somewhat different: Her mother and parents-in-law, trapped on the Chinese mainland after 1949, did not all reach Taiwan until 1962. Instead, it was her husband who put pressure on her. He expected her to provide food for the friends he invited over to play mahjong, but he complained frequently about the dishes she prepared.

> At the time, there were not many ways for a grown woman without nearby friends and family to learn how to cook, since there were no cooking schools or cookbooks readily available. Eventually, Fu paid a handful of restaurant chefs to come to her home for private cooking lessons. Over the course of two years, Fu cycled through the cuisines of Jiangsu, Zhejiang, Sichuan, Hunan and Guangdong provinces. Gradually, Fu, a northerner, developed enough skill to recreate elegant dishes of the southern Jiang-Zhe region . . . such as braised eel with chestnuts, pork with fermented tofu, or braised pork chin.[3]

Soon, the mahjong players were asking Fu to teach their own wives how to cook, thus starting her on the path that came to define her life. In 1962, the year Taiwan's first television station was launched, she made her TV debut. Her cooking show was at first weekly, but it later became a daily program. By the time she retired in 2002, she had demonstrated four thousand dishes.

Unlike Child, Fu saw a home cook's role as bringing gustatory happiness to her husband and children. The press praised her for balancing family life, which included devotion to her in-laws, with tremendous career success. "Fu Pei-mei's status as a wife and mother within an intergenerational family was not incidental or an obstacle to her career, but rather the cornerstone of her professional and personal identity," writes King.

In times past, most girls learned to cook peasant dishes from their mothers and grandmothers, while members of the gentry had servants to cook for them. But from the 1950s onward, and in Taipei more than anywhere else on the island, there was an explosion in the number of nuclear families. As King puts it, "College-educated women in postwar Taiwan found themselves suddenly faced with the social expectation after marriage of needing to feed their husbands and children, yet having no clue as to how to go about it."[4]

By providing the guidance they sought, Fu became a household name. These days, much about her appears quaint. Because of demographic and cultural changes, her core constituency—homemakers eager to cook delicacies true to the great culinary traditions of China—hardly exists. Nonetheless, Fu's daughter and daughter-in-law are among those who have been working hard to preserve and promote her legacy.

CARRYING THE TORCH:
ANGELA CHENG, TERESA LIN, AND PENNY PAN

Angela Cheng (born 1952) is Fu Pei-mei's oldest child. After an acting career, she spent the 1990s co-presenting her mother's cooking programs. With Teresa Lin, who is married to Fu's only son, Cheng coauthored the 2009 cookbook *Family Favorite Dishes*. Five years later, Lin came out with *Happy Yuezi Meals: 65 Nourishing Courses*, a specialist collection of recipes designed not only to restore the strength of a new mother during her month of postpartum confinement (see chapter 4) but also to lift her spirits and help her regain her pre-pregnancy figure.

One of Cheng's most important contributions has been to bring her mother's cookbooks back into circulation. By the beginning of this millennium, all three volumes of *Pei-mei's Chinese Cookbooks* (originally published in 1969, 1974, and 1979) were out of print, despite a steady trickle of orders for these landmark bilingual recipe books. According to Cheng, in 1967 her mother was the first cookbook writer to employ abbreviations that are now commonplace: a lowercase *t* for teaspoon, and an uppercase *T* for tablespoon.[5]

After various delays, thoroughly revised new editions were issued in 2004 and 2005. Some of the original recipes were modified or replaced by ones more attuned to current health concerns. There is less salt, fat, and sugar. For instance, Fu's Shandong Chicken was an entire bird deep-fried in a liter of oil, while Cheng's version uses chicken drumsticks shallow-fried in three teaspoons of oil.

Cheng does not use any MSG in her cooking, so there is no mention of MSG in the new editions. Moreover, because families have gotten much smaller, doing big dishes—like Shandong Chicken with a whole broiler—is often impractical. Rather than cooking for a large, extended family, the new recipes anticipate two to four people around the dinner table.

A decade after Fu's death, another revision-and-repackaging project reached bookstores. *Mother's Dishes: Fu Pei-mei's Family Recipes* features eighty-two of Fu's recipes organized into five chapters, accompanied by Cheng's comments and superb photographs. Given its title, it is no surprise that Cheng says this book is especially close to her heart. Asked which of her mother's recipes both encapsulate her legacy and are likely to appeal to North American palates, she nominates Deep-Fried Whole Fish with Sweet-Sour Sauce; fried dumplings (with a filling of pork, shrimp, black mushroom, and cabbage); chicken salad, Shandong style; and Ma-po's Bean Curd (see Cheng's version of the recipe in chapter 10). Cheng rightly points out that the last of this quartet, the classic also called Mapo tofu, is often made with beef in China. Only in Taiwan, where part of the population never eats beef, did pork become the standard protein.

Cheng, who freely admits she has not had a great deal of contact with local cooking styles (her husband is of Shanghainese origin), characterizes Taiwanese cuisine as lacking in big, elaborate dishes (*dà cài*). Rather, she sees it as a combination of home cooking (*jiācháng cài*) and the cooked snacks found in night markets up and down the island (*xiǎochī*). Not that she or her mother have been dismissive of Taiwan's culinary traditions: the new edition of *Pei-mei's Chinese Cookbook, Volume III* has a chapter dedicated to Taiwanese food. And Chef Lin Ming-tsan (see chapter 4) remembers Fu, who was then over sixty, coming to observe his father preparing for a banquet. Declining the chair he offered her, she stood engrossed all day, endlessly watching and taking notes, making the most of the opportunity to learn about bando cuisine.[6]

Fu's books reached a wide audience in North America, but during the 1970s she was not the only Taiwan-based cookery writer sharing her expertise with English-language readers far from the island. Su-Huei Huang's *Chinese Snacks*—issued by the US publishing arm of Wei Chuan Corp., one of Taiwan's largest food companies—went through multiple editions. The same author wrote several other books that Wei Chuan put out in English or bilingual editions, among them *Chinese One Dish Meals* and *Creative Chinese Oven Cooking*.

Rather than simply continue to write about cuisine, veteran food journalist Penny Pan seeks to elevate food culture and culinary education by various means. Pan is executive director of the Fu Pei-mei Dietary Culture and Education Foundation, and these days she devotes much of her time to Yamicook, the culinary institute she cofounded in 2010.[7]

Yamicook employs both Taiwanese and non-Taiwanese instructors and offers classes in several different areas, among them Taiwanese, Chinese, and Italian cuisines as well as baking and pastry making. There can be no doubting the caliber of the sixty-plus people who teach here, among whom are such established figures as Angela Cheng and Lin Ming-tsan. One reason why both are happy to pass on their knowledge to students at Yamicook is that neither have children willing to continue their families' culinary traditions. Transmitting this knowledge is perhaps the school's greatest contribution.

MINGCHIN CHIU AND LOHAS

Taiwan is a highly wired nation, and many people seek recipes online rather than in books. One of the most popular websites is iCook (https://icook.tw). By November 2017, it had compiled more than 150,000 pages of recipes and food preparation tips, organized according to national and regional cuisines, plus dozens of subcategories like "curries," "stomach-warming dishes," and "popular desserts." Users can also search by ingredient, there being 547 entries for asparagus and 186 for quinoa, but just 12 for powdered lotus root.

Alongside the national passion for food, there is a parallel appetite for food stories. The founder of Astoria Confectionary and Café, a member of the family that continues to run I-Mei, and RAW's André Chiang are among those who have penned books sharing their experiences and explicating their approach to business. A particularly compelling storyteller is Mingchin Chiu, author of *The Dry Goods Legend of Nan Chi Hang*. This 2015 book is more than a memoir of life in Hsinchu's largest dry goods store, and nostalgia is not the only reason why people want to hear what Chiu has to say.

Her opinions about healthy eating and caring for one's body are based on her massive experience and knowledge of dry ingredients. Now in her late seventies—but looking radiant, active, and far younger, despite several bouts of ill health—she is an inspiring proponent of a "LOHAS" eating philosophy. The acronym LOHAS ("Lifestyles of Health and Sustainability") is widely employed in Taiwan to sell everything from furniture to vacations; there is some overlap with the ideals of the global slow food/slow city movement.

Chiu has demonstrated numerous *yǎngshēng* ("wellness") dishes on TV, and many of her recipes have been published in *United Daily News*, a major Chinese-language newspaper. Her emphasis on original flavors, combined without additives, has gained her a following. *The Dry Goods Legend of Nan Chi Hang* includes twelve healthy recipes. Chiu not only explains how to prepare each item but also provides storage tips and advice for culinary innovators. But even those who have no intention of cooking will find her recollections of life in the store during its heyday between the 1930s and the 1990s quite fascinating.

After 1949, Nan Chi Hang was especially popular with wives of ROC Air Force officers stationed in Hsinchu. Many of them came to ask about side dishes served in the two restaurants her mother managed; this was a good opportunity for Chiu or other family members to turn a conversation about ingredients into a sale. Back then, she recalls, soy sauce was delivered to the store in barrels and sold by volume; customers had to bring their own containers.[8]

As well as mushrooms, sea cucumbers, and dried tendon, Nan Chi Hang was famous for the century eggs that Chiu and her two sisters prepared by hand. On their wedding days, the sisters were reluctant to let anyone see their fingers because repeatedly working with the solution that turns the egg whites dark brown and the yolks a greenish gray had stained their fingernails an unattractive yellow-brown.[9]

Chiu's father made a kind of fish sauce that was superb for flavoring and could also serve as a salt substitute. "Do you know how many fish are needed to make fish sauce? You need a pond about the size of a swimming pool, and it's filled with dead fish. The smell is unbelievably repulsive. I can still smell it today. As the dead fish ferment, [what comes out] has to be filtered again and again to produce premium fish sauce. . . . However, the process was too stinky, and people living nearby protested. My father had to stop production," she recalls.

Because of the prestige and importance of their store, and their extensive business network, Chiu's family was well known in the community, and visitors often came to their home for a drink and a chat. Using skills she had begun accumulating even before attending elementary school, Chiu would quickly put together a platter of *xià jiǔ cài* ("appetizers for wine"). The Taiwanese equivalent of tapas, these often included boiled pig's uterus, braised chicken's feet, sweet potatoes that had been boiled or steamed, and mullet roe. Chiu, like many of her generation, regards sweet potatoes as nobly encapsulating the spirit of Taiwan. She first wiped the blocks of roe with kaoliang liquor to get rid of the fishy odor and then marinated them in a miso-and-sugar mix for at least three days. Small cubes of roe were served on toothpicks, each with a small slice of daikon and some leek.

For visitors, Chiu often also prepared black firm tofu (*wū dòugān*)—flavored with sesame oil, soy sauce, black vinegar, and ginger puree—or her signature Chinese chives and taro bun (see Chiu's recipe in chapter 10). Her impressive creativity extends to making candied fruits, such as cherry tomatoes stuffed with sour plums that had been marinated in the juice of whole kumquats for at least three days. According to Chiu—who enjoys a reliable supply of fresh produce from organic and non-organic farms run by her acquaintances and business contacts—putting similar ingredients into a blender and mixing them with ice cream or yogurt makes for a delicious summertime treat.[10]

YABUNG TALLY: A TIAN MAMA SUCCESS STORY

Aware that WTO membership was about to put great pressure on the agricultural sector, in 2001 the Taiwan Council of Agriculture (COA) launched its Tian Mama (Mother Tian) initiative. The Chinese character *tián* means "field," and it is also a fairly common surname in Taiwan. The program aims to help women in farming communities monetize their cooking skills and knowledge of local produce by opening restaurants or shops selling homemade delicacies.

According to an April 16, 2008, report on the COA's website, with the help made available through Tian Mama, women can

> transform and improve themselves in order to provide employment opportunities.
> . . . The women use locally produced food materials from farming or fishing to cook
> diversified, delicious and locally unique cuisine. Working in concert with recreational
> farms, they form a supply-chain in local villages so that women can work and earn
> extra income . . . with experts in fields such as food hygiene, nutrition, process and

marketing, these women have developed a variety of delicious new health foods based on the ideas of low fat, low salt, low sugar, and high fiber (the so-called "3 Lows and 1 High"). They also cooperate with local farmers' associations to boost local tourism while making fine foods.

Acknowledging that "women in villages usually suffer from lower levels of confidence" and that many need to learn about branding and management, Tian Mama courses and workshops go way beyond nutrition, food hygiene, and dish decoration. The same COA report claimed the program had thus far created twenty-four hundred jobs. Another COA webpage cites Chen Wu Mei-yu, an Atayal aboriginal woman also known by her indigenous name, Yabung Tally, as one of Tian Mama's earliest and greatest successes.[11]

Yabung Tally remembers going out to gather snails as a child and her mother growing basil—both frequently appeared on the family's dinner table. But she herself knew little about cooking until she married; she then learned from and was inspired by her mother-in-law. Much later, challenged by the notion that real indigenous food is barely palatable, being hard to chew and lacking in variety, Yabung Tally began to apply some of what she had learned through Tian Mama.

Dishes served at LaWa DaiAn, including chicken with tana (bottom left) and sweet-potato French fries with tempura and a maqaw–white pepper powder (top right).
Katy Hui-wen Hung

She is credited as having invented much of the "indigenous cuisine" enjoyed today and has received government awards for her ingenious approach to angelica leaves, black nightshade, and pigeon peas. Her novel use of fresh or frozen "wet" maqaw in several dishes (and traditional sun-dried maqaw in seasonings and sauces) not only built a restaurant business that continues to thrive, and that she is gradually turning over to her son and daughter-in-law, but also attracted a stream of chefs and entrepreneurs eager to learn from her.[12]

Named LaWa DaiAn, in honor of Yabung Tally's mother-in-law, the restaurant in Yilan County's Datong Township expanded from two tables to twenty in the space of five years. Its fame has spread beyond Taiwan, and those hoping to dine there on a weekend usually need to book a month in advance.

Yabung Tally's creativity is obvious from the ways she employs maqaw, tana, and millet. Her signature maqaw sauce—used as dip for, among other things, juicy cold poached chicken—is made by bringing ground dried maqaw, tomato purée, ginger, rock sugar, and soy-sauce paste to the boil. The concoction is then chilled before lemon juice is added. Many people speak highly of the sweet-potato French fries and the tempura made with chop suey greens; both are seasoned with a powder that combines ground white pepper and maqaw. There is no salt in either the sauce or the powder, with maqaw taking its place. Millet and goji berries are used in LaiWa DaiAn's Chinese-yam soup, and possibly no other restaurant in the world serves guabao with grilled wild-boar meat (rather than braised, farmed pork) and tana-flavored buns.

TEACHING TAIWANESE CUISINE TO NON-TAIWANESE

Ivy Chen has been teaching cooking in Taipei since 1997. "I know how to introduce the uniqueness and vibrant character of Taiwanese food, and I'm very experienced at combining local and global produce and food trends," says the Tainan native, who defines Taiwanese cuisine as "a base of fresh and healthy food, with influences and ingredients from the Netherlands and other places, as well as China and Japan."[13]

Chen learned her cooking techniques and knowledge from chefs, local farmers, and others, and by studying and experimenting on her own. She says that, as she has gained more experience, the distinguishing features of Taiwanese cuisine have become more obvious to her: "We use more fresh herbs and spices, such as basil, coriander leaves, and shallots. Besides, Taiwan makes unique black-bean soy sauces, and we use lots of black sesame oil in our cooking."

According to Chen, some dishes in Taiwan share the same name as a well-known Chinese dish, but "the ingredients, flavors, and presentation are all different." In her experience, kung pao chicken in Sichuan is "far greasier [than in Taiwan], with a lot more chili oil."

Approximately five thousand people from more than seventy countries and regions have attended Chen's classes so far, and among them have been chefs and restaurateurs. "Some came especially to learn clear but flavorful broths, or for wok and dough techniques." Students from different countries are eager to learn different dishes, she has noticed, but *xiǎolóng tāngbāo*, pot stickers, and beef noodle soup are among the most popular, she says.

Given the growing popularity of guabao in the West, it is not surprising that Chen says it tends to be her Western students, not those from Asia, who ask her to teach them how to make guabao (Chen's guabao recipe is in chapter 10). "The most difficult part of making guabao is the bun, and my Western students tend to do this better than my Asian students, maybe because they've experience making pies or bread. Their kneading and rolling techniques are better," she says.

I never suggest to my students that they buy buns from a shop instead of making their own, as guabao buns are actually easier to prepare than *bāozi*. Also, not everyone lives near an Asian supermarket, and if they learn this skill, they can apply it to other recipes. I teach every dish from scratch, for example, for dumplings and baos, I teach my students how to make dough and fillings, and also how to meet special dietary requirements. Fish preparation, and cooking fish the Taiwanese way, is probably the most difficult thing for my Western students to learn.

Chen's cooking classes usually last three or four hours, during which students learn how to make—and then enjoy eating—three dishes. Occasionally, she will meet her students outside and spend an hour in a traditional market buying ingredients with them before getting down to work in the kitchen. She also conducts food-culture tours in the capital, typically starting at an afternoon outdoor market, then proceeding to a night market for snacks. For tourists with stamina, she extends this to an eatery where they can enjoy stir-fried beer-house food with cold beer.

Chen also likes to bring visitors to the Longshan Temple neighborhood in Wanhua area, to see the ups-and-downs of an historic area, and the century-old herbal alley packed with stores that specialize in wild herbs for people's health. While there, they can sample some of the neighborhood's special treats, such as pepper pork buns (*hújiāo bǐng*, baked in a tandoor-type oven) and herbal tea (*qīngcǎo chá*).

Calvin Tu pitches the small group classes he teaches at GOTUCOOK in Tamsui as a travel experience. "There's nothing better than learning about a local culture by tasting and experiencing the food. Even better is experiencing this food culture by learning how to cook local cuisine yourself," says the chef.[14]

Trained at Le Cordon Bleu and TAFE South Australia in Adelaide, where he specialized in modern Western and Asian cuisine, Tu worked as a chef in Australia until returning to Taiwan in 2011. At GOTUCOOK, he sets his prices so the classes are affordable for young travelers passing through Taiwan, and he endeavors to teach (in English and Chinese) in a way that is "as hands-on as possible, with plenty of one-on-one time for questions and answers."

"I do this to connect with people," says Tu, who first learned to cook and appreciate food from his mother. "Food gets people together, but food is also memory. I've been sensitive to flavors since I was a child, and good food flavors make for good memories. Sharing good memories with people who have the same interests and passions is delightful."

In a typical class, Tu's students may learn how to prepare beef-shank noodle soup with tomatoes and carrots, Taiwanese-style pickled cabbage, and a platter of *lǔwèi*. Asked which Taiwanese dishes he most recommends to Western gourmets, he names *lǔwèi*, three-cup chicken, and shredded chicken with gravy on white rice. The magic ingredient in the last one, he says, is deep-fried scallions. Tu helps Westerners understand Taiwanese food by relating local dishes to items that they are familiar with. For instance, he introduces *ròuzào fàn* as "pork Bolognese sauce on rice."

Tu has found that certain local foodways are more difficult for Westerners to accept than others. Americans, he points out, think pork *gēng* looks a bit like porridge, which they consider a breakfast food. Also, few of them find the concept of savory porridge appealing. A similar mental barrier stands between some people and the iconic oyster omelet. Not only do they think that egg dishes should be served for breakfast, rather than after dark, but they also find the lumpy texture off-putting. Most have eaten tofu; yet they are caught off guard by the use of fermented black soybeans (*dòuchǐ*) as a condiment.

"In general, I think Taiwanese are pretty adventurous when it comes to food," Tu remarks. He teaches culinary skills and restaurant management part-time in local vocational high schools, and he concludes that young people's interest in non-Taiwanese cuisines is not driven by any particular fascination with Western culture: "They can accept different flavors, and they're ready to explore, not just Western, but also Southeast Asian cuisines. The key thing is taste, not geography."

ANDRÉ CHIANG: TAIWAN'S FIRST CULINARY SUPERSTAR

Thanks to his 2013 autobiography, *Original Intentions*, and his achievements overseas, André Chiang is greatly admired by many Taiwanese. Born in Taipei in 1976, Chiang spent many years in France, rising to head chef at the three-Michelin-star Le Jardin des Sens. Between 2010 and early 2018, his Restaurant André in Singapore was variously lauded as the best place to eat in the city-state and (in 2017 by the World's 50 Best Restaurants) among the finest fifteen on the planet. In 2016, it was awarded two stars in Michelin's inaugural 2016 Singapore guide.

Chef André Chiang
Wang De-fan

When Restaurant André opened, it had more Taiwanese staffers than any other nationality. But for the final few years, Chiang was the only Taiwanese person working there, a fact that bothered him, and a reason why he made a bombshell announcement in October 2017 that he would soon be closing Restaurant André. In a statement on the restaurant's website, he said, "Returning to where I was born 40 years ago has always been my dream. Passing on everything I have to the next generation in Taiwan and China is my duty, and providing young chefs a better education and culinary culture is an urgent priority for me."

Chiang attributes his determination, work ethic, and gratitude to his mother. When Chiang was thirteen, she was offered a job running a Chinese restaurant in Japan. There, he often helped his mother, learning many kitchen skills. In Singapore, he was always keen to give his compatriots a chance, and his reputation in Taiwan was undoubtedly a reason why some hoped to work with him at Restaurant André. "We had more Taiwanese applicants than any other nationality, but none of them passed the probationary period to become permanent staff," he explains. He thinks this is because most lacked sufficient training. "In many cases, they were jumping straight from culinary school to one of the best restaurants in Asia. The difference is huge, and they couldn't bridge the gap." In general, he says, the applicants he got from other countries were not making such a huge leap.[15]

He agrees that the problem may also lie with the way many young people approach their careers. Leaders in many industries have complained that Taiwan's young people are too ready to admit defeat and switch jobs. During the probationary period, new arrivals at Restaurant André were expected to work fourteen to sixteen hours a day, while demonstrating their team spirit and commitment to the industry.

At RAW, Chiang interviews every applicant for every position for ten to fifteen minutes, because "some people don't have impressive CVs, but if they quickly understand my questions, I may well give them a chance." At the same time, he attaches considerable weight to the questions the applicants have for him. He also looks for consistency, pointing out that five years working for McDonald's may well be better than working at a string of hotels. He likes applicants who have had different life experiences, recalling one who had previously worked in a laboratory, suggesting a methodical and detail-focused personality. Yet he does not expect everyone to have the same strengths. Likening a restaurant to a sports team, he says, "You need some who are very energetic, some who are very organized, and some who are very creative."

Once a person is hired, "I try to make him or her a specialist, instead of training them to be a super-versatile chef who can do everything." He moves them around until their talent is apparent; then he gives them intensive training in those fields. "That way, they'll know, 'this is what I'm good at.' That boosts their confidence.

"I tell young people to spend time on everything they do. Spend time understanding a product. Spend time having a cup of coffee. Spend time reading the newspaper," urges Chiang. "These days, many things are so shallow. It's easy to get bored after three weeks' preparing mashed potatoes, but you won't know how different potatoes create different textures. You need to practice it 1,000 times; then you'll understand.

"Why are there so few Taiwanese at an international level in this industry? Many young guys have changed jobs so often. With a CV like that, you won't get anywhere internationally. You need a solid foundation. You need a specialty if you want to work on a global platform," he says.

Chiang is not alone when he picks holes in common attitudes to culinary work. An Italian executive chef and hospitality consultant based in Taipei since 2013 says that in the kitchens she has experienced in Taiwan, local staff are often taught only to make the dish they are expected to serve, and not given proper overall knowledge of the food. In her opinion, because there is a general lack of training and interest, relatively few people working in kitchens have a clear concept of what makes a good chef. The majority of those who go to culinary school do so because they do not like academic subjects, she thinks. She also gets the impression that few of them are proud of their jobs. At the same time, she is careful not to generalize. She has met culinary talents who work hard to become successful and well respected—but she remains dismayed that, in a country which loves and is proud of its cuisine, culinary careers are nowhere near as glamorous or respected as they are in Italy.

Yet Chiang believes that the general attitude to careers in the kitchen "is so much better now than ten years ago," and he thinks that he can take some credit for this. Now, when young people tell their mothers and fathers they want to become chefs, they can point to his success. And perhaps fewer Taiwanese parents (who have far more influence over their children's career plans than their Western counterparts) will be like old Mr. Zhu in Ang Lee's 1994 movie *Eat Drink Man Woman*. Himself a renowned chef in Taipei, Mr. Zhu listens uncomfortably as one of his former colleagues praises the cooking talents of his middle daughter, who cuts in angrily, "Until you banished me from the kitchen." The father's riposte reflects the low esteem in which food careers have traditionally been held: "Until you learned to do something serious with your life!" Mr. Zhu's colleague sides with the father, telling the daughter, "You owe it all to your father for throwing you out of our smelly kitchen and keeping you on the right path."[16]

Chiang thinks the Taiwanese students now entering culinary schools are more motivated and more ambitious than previously, and the percentage of female students has grown a lot in the past few years. "In Restaurant André, in the kitchen, we had more girls than boys. That is very rare in this industry, worldwide. In RAW, a quarter of the kitchen staff is female—higher than most kitchens in Taiwan."

Chiang believes that even if he had stayed in Taiwan, he would have achieved a similar degree of success: "It's about what you want to do, and what you want to achieve. Growing up in Taiwan, I intensively read international magazines and books." As a teenager, he taught himself to read recipes in French. "It's down to your drive. A lot of people think you need to go to Paris and learn at Le Cordon Bleu, but I don't believe that. You need a good teacher, of course."

He expects the country to produce other internationally successful chefs. "Physically you can be restricted, but your mind can be free." He does agree with one common complaint—that the local education system kills the creativity of many. But not everyone, he stresses. "The information you choose to put in your brain" is crucial, Chiang says. "One thing I really want to do is teach creativity, teaching color, teaching seasoning, flavor combinations, and senses. It's something that doesn't exist in culinary schools in Taiwan. They train you to be a cook, not a chef. How to cook something is just 20 percent of the process. The first 80 percent is how you compose the idea, and bring it to reality."

10

Signature Dishes and Recipes

The recipes here include dishes that are widely available in Taiwan, plus some items that are seen less often. This selection reflects Chinese, Japanese, and Austronesian influences on Taiwanese cuisine and balances innovations with old-time flavors. Some can stand alone as meals or snacks, but at least one—Ma-po's Bean Curd—is what gourmands call a *jīngdiǎn xiàfàn cài*, a "go-with-rice classic" that is unimaginable without a bowl of steamed white ponlai.

STEAMED WHOLE FISH WITH MAQAW, GINGER, SHREDDED CARROT, CHILI, AND SCALLIONS

Steamed fish with maqaw is found in almost every indigenous restaurant in north Taiwan, especially since Yabung Tally pioneered the use of fresh and frozen maqaw (see chapters 1 and 9). This recipe draws on Katy Hui-wen Hung's experiences with Atayal maqaw-harvesters and home cooks, and Lin Ming-tsan's Five-Willows Steamed Red Snapper (see chapter 4). Maqaw peppercorns are seldom available outside Taiwan, but according to food writer Marlena Spieler—who has cooked with some maqaw given to her by Katy Hui-wen Hung—fresh green peppercorns mixed with toasted Szechuan peppercorns should be a good substitute.

179

Ingredients for Four Servings

1 whole white-fleshed fish (grouper is ideal)
Shredded carrot, shredded chili pepper, and scallions to preference
1 two-inch piece fresh ginger, sliced
1 cup rice cooking wine (ideally Taiwanese Red Label for its subtle sweetness;
    otherwise Japanese sake for a sweeter taste, or Chinese rice cooking wine)
¼ cup light soy sauce
½ or 1 tablespoon maqaw peppercorns, crushed or ground

Method

1. Rinse gutted fish well, dry with paper towel, and score the fish with two slashes
   on each side. Presoak (but do not cook, to retain crunchiness) carrot, chili, and
   scallions in cold boiled water. Place the fish on a dish large and deep enough to
   accommodate the fish and liquid ingredients but will fit in your steamer. Lay ginger on fish, add rice wine and soy sauce, sprinkle maqaw on the fish, then steam.
2. Transfer fish to a serving platter; add presoaked ingredients on top. Pour liquid from dish on which the fish was steamed over the plated fish and serve
   immediately.

BRAISED BEEF SOUP
Shared by Sean A. Hsu (owner of Mazendo restaurants
and avid home cook; see chapter 7)

Served with various types of noodles, this is a truly Taiwanese signature dish. The
addition of soybean paste to the soup is a singular element, and the quality of the
paste is critical. To create a sweeter taste, this recipe uses cherry tomatoes instead
of the more commonly used chopped large plum tomatoes. In professional kitchens
in Taiwan, chicken stock is an important ingredient used liberally to enhance flavor. Few home cooks go to the trouble of boiling up chicken stock, of course, and
this recipe can be made with other kinds of stock.

Ingredients for Four to Six Servings

24 ounces beef brisket
½ onion, diced
1 carrot, diced bite size

2 thick slices peeled fresh ginger

20 cherry tomatoes, puréed

½ tablespoon soybean paste

½ tablespoon sweet bean paste

5 fluid ounces chicken stock

13½ fluid ounces water

1 tablespoon vegetable or peanut oil

1–1½ fluid ounces dark soy sauce, or soy-sauce paste for viscosity (taste and add as you go)

For spice pouch: 1 teaspoon cumin, ½ teaspoon cinnamon, ¼ teaspoon star anise

Method

1. Heat a little oil in a frying pan to medium-high and add the beef. When beef is browned and caramelized on all sides, take out and set aside. Reduce heat and add more oil if required. Add the diced onions and stir-fry until browned and caramelized.
2. Put all ingredients except the spice pouch into a pot over high heat and bring it to a boil. Turn to low and simmer for at least 2½ hours. Add spice pouch in the last hour of the cooking. Taste and add more soy sauce or soy-sauce paste in the last hour of the cooking as needed.

OLD-TIME FLAVOR SQUID AND WHELK
WITH GARLIC HOT POT
Shared by Lin Ming-tsan (banquet master; see chapter 4)

Among the men who frequented "liquor houses" (drinking establishments that also provided good food and entertainment) in their pre-1980s heyday, there can be very few who never tried this dish. According to Mingchin Chiu's book, *The Dry Goods Legend of Nan Chi Hang*, at that time squid and whelk with garlic hot pot was both a comfort food and a symbol of status.

This is another of Lin's *tshiú-lōo-tshài* signature dishes. "The more it's cooked, the more flavorful the soup," he says. At the same time, Lin instructs (and this makes his version different from that of many other chefs) that half the scallion greens should not be added until just two minutes before the pot is removed from the heat and served. This is done to retain their crunchiness and freshness and to create different layers of texture among the greens.

   Like his father before him, Lin always uses Top Shell brand canned whelks for
this dish, because the marinade they come in creates the soup's distinctive sweetness. He says that he has never considered using another brand. To achieve an
authentic old-time taste, lard should be used. In northern versions of this dish, pork
is often used. In the south, shiitake mushrooms and bamboo shoots are preferred.

Ingredients for Six Servings

1 large dried squid
6 cups soy oil (or more if needed) for deep frying
¾ ounce dried shiitake mushrooms, broken into chunks about the size of whelks
3 ounces pork belly and 3 ounces pork spare ribs cut into bite-size pieces,
    seasoned with ground white pepper
1 tablespoon soy oil for stir-frying
2 garlic cloves, crushed
14 ounces big scallion, cut into 2-inch sections, separating white and green parts
1 tablespoon lard
7 ounces Chinese celery, cut into 2-inch sections
5 cups chicken stock
1 can (10 ounces) whelks
½ cup canned whelk marinade
½ teaspoon salt
¼ teaspoon ground white pepper
Sesame oil to taste

Method

1. Skin the squid and score it on the inside (so it curls). Cut into 2-inch-long strips;
   the tentacles should be cut in halves or equal sections. Soak overnight in water
   with a pinch of salt. (Fresh squid can be used if preferred; one advantage of
   dried squid is that the soaked water can be added to the stock for flavoring.)
2. Heat oil to 320°F, and lightly brown the dried mushrooms, squid, and pork.
   Remove, drain, and set aside.
3. Stir-fry in oil the garlic and half the scallion whites, until tender. Remove and
   set aside.
4. In the hot pot, sauté in lard half of the scallion greens and celery, adding chicken
   stock to 70 percent full.
5. Add the mushrooms, squid, pork, and cooked scallion whites to the pot. Add
   in the remaining scallion whites and whelks. Cook over high heat until boiled;
   reduce heat to simmer for about another 10 minutes. Add chicken stock and
   whelk marinade as and when needed.

6. Add in the remaining half of the scallion greens 2 minutes before removing from heat. Add sesame oil as needed. Serve immediately.

MA-PO'S BEAN CURD
Shared by Angela Cheng (Fu Pei-mei's daughter; see chapter 9)

Angela Cheng says this dish (also known as Mapo tofu) is perhaps the one she cherishes most of all as a memory of her late mother. This recipe is presented in the form in which it appears in Fu's books, using the terms green onion, rather than scallion; brown peppercorn, instead of Sichuan peppercorn (*huā jiāo*); hot red pepper oil, not hot chili oil; and T and t for tablespoon and teaspoon, respectively. This Sichuanese specialty is made with a kind of hot soybean paste similar to that thought to have been instrumental in the emergence of Taiwanese beef noodles.

Ingredients for Four to Six Servings

8 two-inch cubes bean curd (tofu)
4 ounces ground pork (or beef)
1 t chopped garlic
1 T hot soybean paste
2 T soy sauce
¼ t salt
1 C soup stock
2 t cornstarch paste
2 T chopped green onion
1 t sesame oil
½ t brown peppercorn powder

Method

1. Discard hard edges of the bean curd. Cut bean curd into half-inch cubes and boil in hot water for about 10 seconds. Remove and drain.
2. Heat 2 T oil to stir-fry the ground meat, then add garlic, hot soybean paste, soy sauce, salt, and bean curd, mix slightly then add stock and boil for 3 minutes.
3. Thicken with cornstarch paste, then sprinkle with chopped green onion and sesame oil. Place on plate and sprinkle with brown peppercorn powder and serve.

Note: The dish should be cooked to be very spicy, salty, and piping hot. Hot red pepper oil may be added if you like it even hotter.

TAIWANESE STICKY RICE
Shared by Lin Ming-tsan

What is known in Mandarin as *yóufàn* ("oily rice") has a long history. In addition to being given as a present to friends and family when a baby reaches the age of one month, there is a custom of offering it to female deities who guard children from misfortune. Taipei's most famous sticky-rice supplier is Linhefa Glutinous Oil Rice Store on Dihua Street. Set up in 1894 and now run by a fourth-generation descendant of the founder, its sticky rice is in strong demand year-round, but even more so just before major folk-religion festivals. Both the recipe here and Linhefa's signature product offer a taste that the older generation warms to, but Chef Lin's is perhaps more buttery, and he is more generous when it comes to the ratio of non-rice ingredients to rice. Whereas Lin's recipe is more gingery, the store's *yóufàn* is less sticky and less spicy than Lin Ming-tsan's. As with several other dishes, Chef Lin believes lard is essential here to re-create the old-time flavor. Nevertheless, this recipe works well with different oils.

Ingredients for Six to Eight Servings

2 cups ponlai rice
½–1 tablespoon lard
1 tablespoon black sesame oil
1 ounce old ginger, finely chopped
2 tablespoons dried shrimp
4–5 dried shiitake mushrooms, soaked in cold water for about 30 minutes until
   softened all the way through, de-stemmed and sliced
5½ ounces sliced pork tenderloin
1 tablespoon light soy sauce
½ cup mushroom marinade
1 teaspoon sugar
1–2 tablespoons fried shallot flakes
¼ teaspoon white pepper
MSG to taste

Method

1. To cook the rice, rinse it and soak it for 2–3 hours, then drain. Place a piece of cheesecloth in the bottom of the steamer basket, add rice, and flatten out

using the back of a spatula. Steam for 30 minutes over high heat until cooked, then remove.

2. Heat lard in a large wok; sauté black sesame oil and ginger; add dried shrimp, mushrooms, and pork, then soy sauce; and stir. Add in mushroom marinade and sugar, mixing evenly, and simmer for about 10 minutes. Turn off heat and remove solids, leaving juice in the wok.

3. Place the steamed rice in a large container or wok. Mix in the solid ingredients, fried shallot, and season with white pepper and MSG. Stir by holding a spatula horizontally to avoid breaking the rice, slowly adding the juice from the wok. Stir evenly and thoroughly. Serve immediately.

GUABAO
Shared by Ivy Chen (cookery teacher; see chapter 9)

The guabao, or Taiwanese hamburger, can be eaten for breakfast (although some people find it too heavy), as a late-night snack, or at any time between. As explained in chapter 3, it has gained a following in some Western countries, but in Taiwan it fails to generate as much excitement as several other street foods.

Ingredients for Eight Steamed Buns

½ tablespoon active dry yeast
5 fluid ounces tepid water
10 ounces plain sifted flour
1 tablespoon sugar
Pinch of salt
1 tablespoon vegetable oil (more oil is needed for brushing the cut buns)

Ingredients for Braised Pork Slices

21 ounces pork belly, sliced about ½-inch thick and 3 inches wide
3 cups water
⅓ cup soy sauce
2 tablespoons rice wine
1½ tablespoons sugar
2 pieces of star anise or dried mandarin skin
1 stick of cinnamon (optional)

Ingredients for Pickled Mustard Greens

1 garlic, chopped
1 stalk of pickled mustard green, finely chopped
2 tablespoons soy sauce
1 tablespoon sugar

Garnish

½ cup sugared ground peanut (some people may prefer sugar-free ground peanut,
    but sugared ground peanut is more authentic)
2 stalks cilantro (coriander), chopped

Method for Buns

1. Dissolve dry yeast in tepid water for 3–4 minutes. Mix flour with sugar, salt,
   and oil in a large bowl. Leave a hole in the middle, then pour in the yeast water.
   Bring together the flour and knead the mixture into a dough. Cover with wet
   cloth, and allow to rest until it has doubled in size (40–60 minutes, depending
   on room temperature).
2. Divide dough equally into 8 portions. Roll into balls, then flatten into neat ovals
   at 7–8 mm thick. Lightly grease half of one side of each oval with oil. Fold each
   over itself with the greased side inside. Line the bottoms of steam baskets with
   wax paper or lightly greased baking paper; then position the buns in the baskets.
   Let the buns rest in a warm place for no more than 30 minutes until the buns
   rise another 50 percent.
3. Add 3–4 inches of water inside a pot or pan and set the steam baskets over it.
   Turn up the heat and bring water to a boil so you can see steam emerge from the
   baskets. Steam buns for another 12–13 minutes. Then keep the baskets over the
   pan for another 2–3 minutes before removing.

Method for the Pork and Greens

1. Simmer pork in water for 5 minutes, then remove and rinse. Mix in all the spices
   and ingredients, simmer for 40 minutes until the meat is tender.
2. Separately, sauté garlic in 2 tablespoons of hot oil; then add mustard greens for
   1 minute over low heat. Add soy sauce and sugar, and water if necessary. Stir-
   fry at low to medium heat for 8–10 minutes.
3. Assemble the buns by topping the pork belly with pickled mustard greens and
   garnish with peanut powder and cilantro.

CHINESE CHIVES AND TARO BUN
Shared by Mingchin Chiu

One of Chiu's *tshiú-lōo-tshài*, this 1950s snack has an auspicious name: in Mandarin, the first syllable of chive (*jiǔ cài*) is a homophone for everlasting (*jiǔ*), while *bāo* ("wrap") suggests bonding and togetherness. Some modern palates find the way in which the chives flavor the taro rather challenging, but this is a good example of "salty-sweet" Taiwanese flavor—rather like the old-style wedding cakes that were filled with minced fatty pork, winter melon, raisins, and mildly salted egg yolk, then coated with white sesame. According to Chiu, a popular modern simplification is to wrap the filling in wonton sheets to create crispy deep-fried parcels that many people find delicious.

Ingredients

21 ounces taro, peeled, washed, sliced
1 tablespoon light brown sugar
1 tablespoon sweet-potato flour
½ tablespoon lard or as needed
1 teaspoon chopped shiitake mushroom
1 tablespoon ground pork
1 tablespoon finely chopped dried shrimp
1 teaspoon fried shallot
Salt as needed
1 teaspoon vegetarian mushroom oyster sauce
7 ounces Chinese chives, chopped
½ tablespoon of vegetable oil or as needed

Method

1. Steam sliced taro until done, remove, and stir in sugar while warm. Rubbing until powdery, add sweet-potato flour, a little lard as needed, then knead into strips and cut into equal pieces.
2. Heat lard and sauté the mushroom, dried shrimp, pork, and shallot, adding salt as needed. Turn heat to high and add vegetarian mushroom oyster sauce. Turn off heat, stir and mix in chives, remove filling into a container, and set aside.
3. Press taro pieces into disks, add in cooked fillings, wrap and knead into a ball, and then press down flat.
4. Add a little oil; shallow-fry until golden brown.

STUFFED CABBAGE "CAKE" WITH GRAVY
Shared by C. K. Luo (Hakka resident of Hsinchu County)

This is a southern Taiwan Hakka dish traditionally made with pork, but turkey is an acceptable replacement. During the cooler months, cabbages are sometimes overabundant, and this recipe makes good use of them. This Hakka specialty is likewise usually served with rice.

Stuffed cabbage dishes can be found all over the world, and Japanese stuffed cabbage rolls began to appear on Taiwanese dinner tables during the colonial period. For coauthor Katy Hui-wen Hung, they were a comfort food often cooked by her mother, who was born and raised in Tokyo. Nowadays, they appear in convenience stores as something that can be added to a bowl of *guāndōngzhǔ*. This is a light, soy-flavored broth filled with various items including daikon and processed fishcakes, inspired by Japanese *oden*.

Ingredients for Four Servings

12 ounces ground pork
½ tablespoon finely chopped ginger
4–5 cabbage leaves
1 cup finely chopped Taiwanese cucumber pickled in sweet soy brine
1 tablespoon pickle brine
1 tablespoon rice wine
1 teaspoon light soy sauce
¼ teaspoon ground white pepper
1 teaspoon corn flour
½ teaspoon dashi (bonito) granules (optional)
Pinch of salt (or to taste)
1 tea egg or 2 salted duck egg yolks (optional)

For Gravy

1 teaspoon light soy sauce
1 teaspoon corn flour
Few drops of sesame oil
1 cup of water (adjust to preference)
Pinch of salt (or to taste)

Garnish

2 stalks coriander, chopped

Method for Making the "Cake"

1. Mix pork and ginger in a bowl and set aside. Core and separate leaves from the cabbage, choose 4–5 of the largest and nicest outer leaves, wash and cook in boiling water for 5 minutes. Drain, rinse with cold water, pat dry, and set aside.
2. Gently mix the pork and ginger with pickled cucumber, pickle brine, rice wine, corn flour, white pepper, soy sauce, dashi granules, and salt in a bowl.
3. Lay cabbage leaves in a small, round tin/dish, overlapping at the bottom and hanging over the side long and wide enough to wrap the meat mix. Put in half the meat mix, leaving a hole in the middle for the tea egg or duck eggs (if using); cover the egg(s) with the rest of the meat mix. Fold the overhanging cabbage leaves over the meat mixture to make a neat round parcel. Steam for about 45 minutes.

Method for Making the Gravy

Collect the juice from the steamed "cake." Mix corn flour and one cup of water (adjust to preference) to make a paste. Add the paste, soy sauce, and sesame oil to the juice and cook over medium heat. Salt to taste. Bring to boil and remove. Pour gravy over the "cake" and garnish with coriander. Serve immediately.

"POPCORN-STYLE" SALTY-CRISPY CHICKEN
WITH DIPS AND PICKLES
Shared by Zoe Jaian (Dadaocheng native and keen home cook)

Born on Dihua street to a chef father and a mother who ran a food stall between 1965 and 2007, Jaian and her siblings grew up helping their mother during school holidays, while also picking up food knowledge from their "zone pro site" father. She remembers handling shark's fin for preparing Buddha Jumps Over the Wall and recalls how it can stink. Her familiarity with *xiǎochī* includes this recipe for salty-crispy chicken (*yánsūjī*); like many night-market versions, it gets its sticky Q texture from sweet-potato starch. She believes dips and pickles are required to complement this very Taiwanese snack. The pickles negate the grease of the chicken, complementing it in the way that crunchy pickled cabbage goes perfectly with Taiwanese-style stinky tofu.

1. Ingredients for around 40 Pieces Salty-Crispy Chicken

21 ounces boneless, skinless chicken breast, cut into pieces 1 by 2 inches
1 cup sweet-potato starch
1 cup long-grain white rice flour
6 or more cups soy (or vegetable) oil
1 bunch of Thai basil leaves

Marinade

1 teaspoon light soy sauce
½ teaspoon five-spice powder
½ teaspoon cinnamon
¼ teaspoon ground white pepper
⅙ teaspoon ground black pepper
3 teaspoons cornstarch
1½ tablespoons rice wine
4 teaspoons white sugar
2 teaspoons salt
1½ tablespoons each of scallion, ginger, garlic, all finely chopped
1 medium-size egg

Method

1. Create the marinade and marinate the chicken pieces for at least 2 hours, preferably overnight.
2. Mix the sweet-potato starch and rice flour and coat the chicken.
3. Heat the soy or vegetable oil to 320°F. Deep-fry chicken until golden brown. About 20 seconds before ready, drop in basil leaves and deep-fry until darkened and crispy. Remove all, drain, and serve immediately.

2. Dip Ingredients

Standard Dip

2 cups soy paste
2 cups tomato ketchup
1 cup garlic puree
1 cup water
½ cup white sugar
2 teaspoons salt
1 teaspoon sesame oil

Add all the ingredients minus the sesame oil to a saucepan over medium-high heat, stir and bring to a boil. Add sesame oil, mix well, remove from heat and cool. Serve or store in jars refrigerated.

Sweet-and-Sour Dip

2 cups light soy sauce
2 cups tomato ketchup
1 cup garlic puree
1 cup rice vinegar
1 cup white sugar
2 teaspoons salt
6 tablespoons cold water
2 tablespoons cornstarch

Method

Add all the ingredients except water and cornstarch to a saucepan over medium-high heat, stir and bring to a boil. Mix the cornstarch and water to make a paste. Slowly add the paste to the saucepan to create desired thickness, and bring to boil; when thickened, remove from heat and cool. Serve or store in jar refrigerated.

3. Pickled Daikon Ingredients

1⅓ pounds daikon, peeled and cut into ¼ inch slices
1 ounce salt
1 ounce white sugar
1 ounce rice vinegar
2 thin slices ginger
1 red chili pepper, seeds removed and cut into small pieces

Method

Mix radish and salt in a container and cover in cold boiled water. Cover the container and refrigerate overnight. Pour away half the liquid; add in and mix well all seasonings with daikon and the remaining liquid. Cover and refrigerate for at least 3 hours before serving.

Tip: Drops of lemon juice add acidity if preferred.

The same recipe can be used for cabbage, or small (such as Persian) cucumbers with minor adjustments: adding drops of sesame oil and drops of rice vinegar, preferably just before serving, to avoid discoloring of cucumbers.

PINEAPPLE CAKE
Shared by Calvin Tu (chef and cookery teacher; see chapter 9)

According to Calvin Tu, bakers began adding powdered cheese to pineapple cake no more than ten years ago, but this counterintuitive practice has really caught on. "Pastries nowadays are much sweeter than when I was a kid, and cheese seems to balance the sweetness," he says. Packets of powdered cheese specifically for pineapple-cake making can be found in bakery-supplies stores and ordered online. Baking a pineapple cake is one of the options he offers to people taking his classes.

Ingredients for 12 Cakes

3½ ounces unsalted butter

1 ounce powdered sugar

1 small egg

1 ounce powdered milk

⅓ ounce powdered cheese (Tu suggests very fine Parmesan powder)

5 ounces cake flour

8½ ounces pineapple jam (any fruit jam will do, but it needs to be thick and dry
    enough to shape into a ball)

Method

1. Mix the butter and powdered sugar in a mixing bowl. Once it is a creamy and fluffy mixture, add the egg and mix well until blended fully with the butter.
2. Add the powdered milk and cheese, and use a spatula to fold the mixture into the butter mixture. After folding in, add the flour and fold in again. (Do not use a high-speed mixer—only a spatula—during this step to fold in mixtures.) Let the dough rest for 20 minutes at room temperature.
3. Roll the rested dough into a loaf and divide into 12 (1 ounce each) pieces. Divide the jam into 12 equal portions.
4. Roll dough pieces into balls and flatten in your palm; then add a portion of the filling into center of the flattened dough. Close the dough around the filling, rolling it into a ball to be placed in the mold.
5. Flatten the filled dough balls into a mold; to allow for expansion, the balls should not occupy more than four-fifths of the mold by depth.
6. Place mold shapes in a fan oven preheated to 340°F. Bake for 20–25 minutes. Remove from oven; turn cakes upside down and bake bottom side for 5 more minutes. Remove from oven and allow to cool before serving.

ARTISAN Q TAIWANESE NOUGAT
Shared by Morgan Liao (baker and caterer)

Morgan Liao, a trained pastry chef, operates a catering business in Taipei and teaches cooking and baking. Liao grew up in a military dependents' village and says she has always enjoyed doing things in kitchens. She came late to her current career, however. Intrigued by TV cooking and baking shows, she took a bakery course in Europe before becoming a food professional.

In this recipe, Liao puts a modern twist on the traditional confectionery known in Taiwan as *niú gá táng*. Nougat is said to have reached Taiwan via Shanghai. In the past decade, Liao says, Taiwanese who search for baking ideas online have embraced marshmallow-based nougat. Not only is it quick to make, and delightfully Q, but it also has a softer texture and contains less sugar than standard nougat. Being less sticky, it is kinder on your teeth, and it can be flavored with nuts, dried fruits, or even tea. Milk nougat made commercially in Taiwan tends to be made from maltose, trehalose, egg white, butter, milk powder, and salt. Liao's recipe, by contrast, has no egg white, granulated sugar, or salt.

Ingredients for Milk Nougat

2 ounces marshmallow
½ ounce butter
1¾ ounces powdered milk
1.4 ounces almonds
1 ounce cranberries

Ingredients for Cocoa Nougat

2 ounces marshmallow
½ ounce butter
1.4 ounces powdered milk
⅕ ounce cocoa powder
1.4 ounces almonds
1 ounce cranberries

Ingredients for Matcha Nougat

2 ounces marshmallow
½ ounce butter

1¾ ounces powdered milk
⅕ ounce matcha
1.4 ounces almonds
1 ounce cranberries

Method

1. Melt butter, add marshmallow, melt, and stir. Mix until creamy.
2. Add milk powder and cocoa or matcha; stir until the mixture is a non-sticky ball. Add almonds and cranberries, and then divide into 15 pieces.

The whole process takes around 20 minutes. For neater cutting, wait an hour or more for the nougat to cool.

Notes

INTRODUCTION

1. Wikipedia, "Taipei."
2. Crook, *Taiwan*, 3.
3. Handwerk, "Polynesians Descended from Taiwanese."
4. Diamond, "Linguistics: Taiwan's Gift to the World."
5. Shepherd, *Statecraft*, 49.
6. Shepherd, *Statecraft*, 50.
7. Shepherd, *Statecraft*, 91.
8. Shepherd, *Statecraft*, 386.
9. Weaver, "Dadaocheng," 15.
10. Fujii, "Formation of Taiwanese Identity."
11. Taipei City Government, "Demographic Overview."
12. Jiang et al., "An Estimation of the Out-Migration."
13. Li, *The Evolution of Policy behind Taiwan's Development Success*, 68–71.
14. Phillips, "About Me."
15. Shunk, "5 Reasons Why Taipei Is the Best Food City in the World."
16. Bowles, "How Taiwan Became the Hottest Food Destination on Earth."

CHAPTER 1

1. Wall Text, National Museum of Prehistory, Taitung.
2. *Taiwan Today*, "Study Confirms Earlier Human Activity in Taiwan."
3. Tsang, "Recent Discoveries at the Tapenkeng Culture Sites in Taiwan," 64.

4. Li, "First Farmers and Their Cultural Adaptation in Prehistoric Taiwan," 612–30.

5. Tsang, "Recent Discoveries at the Tapenkeng Culture Sites," 63.

6. Ibid.

7. Anderson, *Food and Environment in Early and Medieval China*, 23.

8. Kuang-ti Li, email message to Steven Crook, July 14, 2017.

9. Shepherd, *Statecraft*, 100.

10. Tsang et al., "Broomcorn and Foxtail Millet Were Cultivated in Taiwan about 5,000 Years Ago."

11. Liu, "Taiwan Quinoa," 101–3.

12. Lee et al., "Diet and Subsistence Mode of Neolithic Yuanshan People in Taiwan," 18–27.

13. Chang and Stuiver, "Recent Advances in the Prehistoric Archaeology of Formosa," 540.

14. Lee et al., "Dietary Reconstruction of the Iron Age Population at the Fantzuyuan Site," 34–43.

15. Yushan National Park, "Bunun Tribe."

16. Taiwan Indigenous Culture Park, "Atayal Tribe."

17. Andrade, *How Taiwan Became Chinese*, 20.

18. Chen Di (1541–1617) was a scholar who accompanied an anti-pirate expedition to Taiwan in 1603. He described the island and its indigenous inhabitants in *An Account of the Eastern Barbarians*.

19. Shepherd, *Statecraft*, 29.

20. Li, Tsang, Chu, and Hsing, "Taiwan as an Austronesian Homeland."

21. Kuang-ti Li, email message to Steven Crook, July 20, 2017.

22. Hsu, "The History and Cultural Research of Taiwan Cuisine," 14.

23. Shepherd, *Statecraft*, 32.

24. Blussé, Everts, and Frech, *The Formosan Encounter*, 18.

25. Hsu, "The History and Cultural Research of Taiwan Cuisine," 18.

26. Jacobs, "A History of Pre-Invasion Taiwan," 11.

27. Andrade, *How Taiwan Became Chinese*, 20.

28. Shepherd, *Statecraft*, 8 and 35.

29. Overseas Community Affairs Council, "Roxburgh Sumac."

30. Wills, "The Seventeenth-Century Transformation," 88.

31. National Museum of Taiwan History, "Fishery."

32. Quoted by Teng, "Taiwan in the Chinese Imagination, 17th–19th Centuries."

33. Cauquelin, *Aborigines of Taiwan: The Puyuma*, 204–6.

34. Pei, "Hunting System of the Rukai Tribe in Taiwan," 19.

35. Ibid., 2.

36. Taitung County Government, "*Trichodesma calycosum*."

37. Yang, "Preliminary Study and Analysis of Aboriginal Dietary Culture," 357.

38. This delicacy was sampled at Wulai Atayal Grandmother, an indigenous restaurant in New Taipei, by Andrew Zimmern for his *Bizarre Foods* TV show, series 1, episode 11.

39. Hsu, "The History and Cultural Research of Taiwan Cuisine," 18.

40. Yang, "Preliminary Study and Analysis of Aboriginal Dietary Culture," 356.

41. Quoted in Cauquelin, *Aborigines of Taiwan*, 199–200. De Mailla, whose nationality is unrecorded, had been sent to map and report on Taiwan for the Chinese imperial court.

42. Hsu, "The History and Cultural Research of Taiwan Cuisine," 18.

43. Pickering, *Pioneering in Formosa*, 148.

44. Simoons, *Food in China*, 509.

45. Pickering, "Among the Savages of Central Formosa, 1866–1867," 31.

46. Pickering, *Pioneering in Formosa*, 161–62.

47. Taintor, *The Aborigines of Northern Formosa*, 15.

48. Thomson (1837–1921) was later the British royal family's official photographer. His images of Taiwan are preserved at the Wellcome Library in London.

49. Thomson, *The Straits of Malacca, Indo-China and China*, chapter 11.

50. Taylor, "A Ramble through Southern Formosa."

51. Mackay, *From Far Formosa*, 256 and 263.

52. Ibid., 82–83.

53. Chen, *Big Bowl, Big Spoon*, 58.

54. Mackay, *From Far Formosa*, 70.

55. Ibid., 213.

56. The laws that restrict hunting are complex, sporadically enforced, and beyond the scope of this book.

57. Lee, "Eating and Drinking Snake Still Popular Fare."

58. Ibid.

59. Crook, "Herping and other Nocturnal Adventures," 23.

60. Yang, "Going Back into a Future of Simplicity," 12.

61. Fisheries Research Institute, "Successful Breeding of Native Snails."

62. Purchon, *The Biology of the Mollusca*, 385.

63. Land Snails of Taiwan, "*Achatina fulica Bowdich*, 1822."

64. MataTaiwan.com, "Aboriginal Food Collection."

65. Pickering, *Pioneering in Formosa*, 109.

66. H. M. Cheng, email interview by Steven Crook, June 19, 2017.

67. MataTaiwan, "Amis, the People that Eat Frogs and . . . Tadpoles!"

68. Liu and Liu, "Disease and Mortality in the History of Taiwan," 248–60.

69. Roy, *Taiwan: A Political History*, 20–21.

70. Shepherd, *Statecraft*, 146-149.

71. Lee, "Legacy Unearthed in Tainan Science Park."

72. Crook and Hung, "Fungus among Us," 49.

73. Kuo, "Mullet Roe Brings Gold to Taiwan's Fishermen."

74. Chiu, Wu, and Chung, "Chinese Fishing Methods Damaging Taiwan's Seas."

75. National Taiwan University, "Ethnozoology of the Tsou, Taiwan: Fishing with Poison."

76. Steere, "Formosa."

77. Chang, "Farmland Ecology and Water Conservation."

78. Chen, Tsai, and Tzeng, "Freshwater Prawns of Taiwan."

79. Crook, "Balancing on the Brink," 16–18.

CHAPTER 2

1. Liu and Hou, "21% of Married Taiwanese Aged 35 and Above Live with Parents."

2. The phrase "Firewood, rice, oil, salt, [soy] sauce, vinegar, and tea are the seven necessities to begin a day" has been widely used since at least the twelfth century.

3. National Museum of Taiwan History, "Nom Nom Taiwan: The Story of Dietary Culture."

4. A fully restored (and impossibly spotless) traditional kitchen can be seen at Taipei's Lin An Tai Historical House and Museum (http://english.linantai.taipei).

5. Chiang and Schrecker, *Mrs. Chiang's Szechwan Cookbook*, xvii.

6. H. M. Cheng, email interview by Steven Crook, May 4, 2017.

7. Taipei Water Park, "Period of Taipei Water Source Site."

8. *Taipei Times*, "Lung Cancer Is Top Killer of Women."

9. Liang, "Cooking with Taiwanese Memory."

10. Huang, "Tatung Builds a Cross-Generation Rice Steamer."

11. Schirokauer, Brown, Lurie, and Gay, *Brief History of Chinese and Japanese Civilizations*, 597.

12. Shurtleff and Aoyagi, *History of Soybeans and Soyfoods in the Netherlands*, 5.

13. Chen, *Big Bowl, Big Spoon*, 108.

14. Brian Chuang, personal interview with Steven Crook and Katy Hui-wen Hung, Taipei, March 21, 2017.

15. Oscar Chung, "A Sauce for All," 34.

16. USDA Foreign Agricultural Service, "Taiwan Expands GE Regulations."

17. Chou, "GM Foods Banned from School Menus."

18. Sean A. Hsu, personal interview with Steven Crook and Katy Hui-wen Hung, Taipei, March 21, 2017.

19. Teng, "Soy Sauce: Fermenting for Four Generations," 77–81.

20. Shurtleff, Huang, and Aoyagi, *History of Soybeans and Soyfoods in China and Taiwan*, 2073.

21. Jodie Tsao, email interview with Steven Crook, September 19, 2017.

22. Shurtleff, Huang, and Aoyagi, *History of Soybeans and Soyfoods in China and Taiwan*, 1728.

23. Liu, "Advancing Peanut Oil's Local Legacy," 91.

24. Chang, "Camellia Oil: An Old Staple Morphs into a Superfood," 79.

25. Ibid., 83.

26. Yang, "Daughter Takes Over Bullhead Sauce."

27. Hong, "Black Vinegar or White Vinegar: Which Has Less Sodium?"

28. Lee, "New Life in Old Vats," 55–57.

29. Lee, "Mapping the Social Contexts of Taiwan Rice Wine in Cooking," 1.

30. Ibid., 1–2.

31. Chen, "Deadly Methanol Levels Found in Bootleg Wine."

32. Tsai, "A Century of Rice Wine Culture," 8–10.

33. Wan, *Home-Style Taiwanese Cooking*, 158.

34. *Taipei Times*, "Taiwan Faces Tough WTO Fight to Slash Rice Wine Tax."

35. Tsai, "A Century of Rice Wine Culture," 11.

36. Directorate General of Budget, Accounting and Statistics, 2013 and 2014 budget for TTL.

37. Lu et al., "Prevalence of Osteoporosis and Low Bone Mass."

CHAPTER 3

1. Tzeng, Kao, Yeh, and Pan, "Food Consumption Habits and Frequency among Taiwanese," 63.

2. Selya, *Development and Demographic Change in Taiwan*, 243.

3. Lee, "Disposable Utensil Bans Take Effect."

4. Wall text, "Nom Nom Taiwan—The Story of Dietary Culture," National Museum of Natural Science (January 20–September 4, 2016).

5. Hsiao, "Seventeen Tons of Chopsticks Found to Contain Toxins: FDA."

6. Robyn Eckhardt, email interview by Steven Crook, October 19, 2017.

7. Crook, "Ins and Outs of Taiwan Hot Pots."

8. Shurtleff and Aoyagi, *History of Soybeans and Soyfoods in the Netherlands*, 21.

9. Another important fertilizer for sugarcane was goose-bone dust: Shurtleff and Aoyagi, *Early History of Soybeans and Soyfoods*, 287.

10. Shurtleff and Aoyagi, *History of Soybean Crushing*, 1982.

11. Shurtleff, Huang, and Aoyagi, *History of Soybeans and Soyfoods in China and Taiwan*, 1727–28.

12. Ibid., 2166.

13. Ibid.

14. Huang Dah Mu Foods Co. Ltd., "Origins of Dougan."

15. Mikiko Ishii, email interview by Steven Crook, May 11, 2017.

16. In September 2017, the set menu at Shoun RyuGin, in the same building and co-owned by the same company as RAW (see chapter 7), was priced at US$237 per person, not including alcoholic drinks.

17. Wu, "Cultural Nostalgia and Global Imagination," 110.

18. Shinju (a pseudonym) writing in 1902 and quoted in Chen, "Embodying Nation in Food Consumption," 28.

19. Yukiko Sato, telephone interview by Katy Hui-wen Hung, June 27, 2017.

20. Wu, "Cultural Nostalgia and Global Imagination," 111.

21. Ibid., 112.

22. Ibid., 121.

23. Ibid., 122.

24. Sean A. Hsu, personal interview with Steven Crook and Katy Hui-wen Hung, Taipei, March 21, 2017.

25. Chen, "Curry Wafts over Taiwan."

26. Goossaert and Palmer, *The Religious Question in Modern China*, 284.

27. Chen, "Taiwan, Global Vegan Capital," 73.

28. Goossaert and Palmer, *The Religious Question in Modern China*, 283.

29. Mai Bach, personal interview with Steven Crook and Katy Hui-wen Hung, Taipei, March 21, 2017.

30. She still had more than twelve thousand followers as of May 9, 2017.

31. For the same reason—fear they may be used to make illegal drugs—poppy seeds are also outlawed.

32. Muchin Lee, email message to Steven Crook, March 5, 2017.

33. Such opinions are expressed in the forum at Animals Australia: http://www.animalsaustralia.org/.

34. Sun, "History of Beef," 38.

35. Ibid., 50.

36. Ibid., 51.

37. Ibid., 41.

38. Watanbe, "Meat-Eating Culture of Japan."

39. Sun, "History of Beef," 72.

40. Ibid., 77.

41. Ibid., 101–2.

42. Ibid., 159.

43. Ibid., 119.

44. It seems that no restaurants in Greater Taipei currently serve buffalo meat. However, it does appear on the menu at a few places in Hualien County.

45. Sun, "History of Beef," 137.

46. Tseng, "The Wu Yuan-Sheng Family," 64–65.

47. Sun, "History of Beef," 143–44.

48. Jordahl, "Taiwan Adopts Ractopamine MRLs for Beef, Not Pork."

49. Sun, "History of Beef," 152.

50. White, "Taiwan and Globalization," 167–68.

51. McDonald's, which opened its first branch in Taipei in 1984, had 413 outlets as of mid-2015. For its population, Taiwan has more than twice as many McDonald's outlets as South Korea, but fewer than Japan.

52. Sun, "History of Beef," 155.

53. Ibid., 156.

54. H. M. Cheng, email interview by Steven Crook, May 4, 2017.

55. The number of US soldiers stationed in Taiwan peaked at 19,000 in 1958, then varied between 4,000 and 10,000 until 1977. Additionally, tens of thousands of steak-eating US personnel went to Taiwan for R&R during the Vietnam War: Kane, "Global U.S. Troop Deployment, 1950–2003."

56. Hong, "Eat Up! The Origin of Japanese Ramen."

57. Chen, "Embodying Nation in Food Consumption," 153.

58. Teng, "Let's Get Sauced!" 85.

59. Su, "Gangshan Goat-Meat Eating Culture," 201–4.

60. Mackay, *From Far Formosa*, 78.

61. Chen, "Taiwan Dairy Cattle and Milk Culture," 28–29.

62. USDA Foreign Agricultural Service, *2016 Taiwan: Dairy and Products Annual*.

63. Pan et al., "Diet and Health Trends in Taiwan."

64. Ibid. 26.5 percent of respondents said lactose intolerance was the main reason they did not consume milk. Much higher lactose-intolerance rates have been reported for some other Asian populations.

65. USDA Foreign Agricultural Service, *2016 Taiwan: Dairy and Products Annual*.

66. Davidson, *The Island of Formosa*, 254–55.

67. Mackay, *From Far Formosa*, 276.

68. Pickering, "Among the Savages of Central Formosa," 31.

69. Tong, "Taiwan Bans the Consumption of Cat and Dog Meat."

70. H. M. Cheng, email interview by Steven Crook, May 4, 2017.

71. Tseng, "Taiwanese Cuisine in the Japanese Era."

72. Crook and Hung, "Getting a Handle on the Taiwanese 'Hamburger,'" 43.

73. Shapiro, "Din Tai Fung: Taiwan's Culinary Icon," 38.

74. Ibid., 37.

75. Sheridan, "Fast-Food Chains Thrive in Taiwan," 30–33.

76. Chen, "Embodying Nation in Food Consumption," 78.

77. Erway, *The Food of Taiwan*, 136.

78. Prentice, "Taiwan's Little Burma."

79. Visit to Huaxin Street by Steven Crook, March 21, 2017.

80. Lai, "Rise and Development of Hakka Cuisine."

81. Linda Lau Anusasananan, email interview by Katy Hui-wen Hung, January 30, 2017.

82. Yang, "Hakka and Hakka Food Culture," 363.

83. Ding, "Mountain Bitter Gourd."

84. *Epoch Times*, "Hakka Make a Towel."

85. Chang, "The Hakka Cuisine Competition 2016," 71–73.

86. Hakka Affairs Council, "Innovative Hakka Cuisine."

87. *Epoch Times*, "Thrifty Hakka Stir-Fry."

88. Sauer, "When Almonds Are Apricots."

89. Chang Chiung-fang, "SunnyHills Bakery: Modest Brilliance," 25–29.

90. Ibid., 25.

91. Chien and Xie, *Astoria Confectionary and Café*, 244–48.

92. Ibid., 248.

93. Fulco, "How Sweet It Is," 34.

94. Chien and Xie, *Astoria Confectionary and Café*, 241.

95. Cheung, "A Life Devoted to Political Freedom."

96. Kao and Lu, *A Baker Has a Dream: The I-Mei Story*, 121.

CHAPTER 4

1. Jordan, *Gods, Ghosts and Ancestors*, 27.

2. Ibid., xxi.

3. In 1937, the Japanese government launched the "Kominka Movement" to erase Han identity in Taiwan and promote loyalty to the emperor in Tokyo. More than one thousand shrines were demolished or repurposed; many effigies were hidden until the end of World War II. But compared to the anti-religion campaigns in Mao's China, the Japanese program was mild.

4. Taiwan Historica, *Dictionary of Taiwan Folk Artifacts*, Entry 002389.

5. Jordan, *Gods, Ghosts and Ancestors*, 59.

6. Fan, "Hsinpu's Fangliao Yimin Temple."

7. Taiwan Historica, *Dictionary of Taiwan Folk Artifacts*, Entry 002385.

8. Erway, *The Food of Taiwan*, 204.

9. Pan, "Hakka Rice Food."

10. Phillips, "For Double Ninth Festival, a Cake of Nine Layers."

11. Pan, *Atlas of Botanical Idioms*, 17.

12. Pan, *Formosa Plant Culture: 101 Taiwan Plant Species*, 54.

13. Museum of Hakka Tourism and Cuisine in New Taipei City, "Ciba."

14. Lien, *General History of Taiwan*, 465–68.

15. Pang Rice Dumplings, "What Is Commonly Used to Wrap Dumplings?"

16. Pan, "Hakka Rice Food."

17. Lien, *General History of Taiwan*, 465–68.

18. E. N. Anderson, *Everyone Eats: Understanding Food and Culture*, 120.

19. Executive Yuan, "Traditional Festivals."

20. Everington, "How to Celebrate Mid-Autumn Festival in Taiwan."

21. Lien, *General History of Taiwan*, 465–68.

22. Coolidge, "A Colorful Celebration of Life's Abundance."

23. Liao Cheng-chou, personal interview with Katy Hui-wen Hung, Taipei, February 15, 2017.

24. Ping Ming Health, "Warming and Cooling Characteristics of Common Foods."

25. National Palace Museum, "The Three Best Friends in Winter."

26. Tsao, *The Humble Life of Oyster Omelet*, 230.

27. Chen, "Embodying Nation in Food Consumption," 53.

28. Ibid., 54.

29. Ibid., 52–53.

30. Jordan, "The Popular Practice of Religion," 148.

31. Kaohsiung City Government, "Delivering Culinary Magic at Roadside Banquets."

32. Lin Ming-tsan, personal interview with Katy Hui-wen Hung, Taipei, February 20, 2017.

33. Chen, "Embodying Nation in Food Consumption," 88.

34. Ji, "Lin Ming-tsan."

35. Tsao, *The Humble Life of Oyster Omelet*, 114–17.

36. Chen, "Embodying Nation in Food Consumption," 69–71.

37. Reitaku School, "A Summary of Teng-hui Lee's Life."

38. Chen, "Embodying Nation in Food Consumption," 96.

39. Yan, "ROC Year 99 Taiwan Forever: State Banquets."

40. Chen, "Embodying Nation in Food Consumption," 97.

41. Ibid., 100.

42. Yan, "ROC Year 99 Taiwan Forever: State Banquets."

43. Andrews, "The 'Three Golden Opportunities,'" 18.

44. Tsao, *The Humble Life of Oyster Omelet*, 115.

CHAPTER 5

1. National Statistics (Taiwan), Survey of Family Income and Expenditure.

2. Liao Cheng-chou, personal interview with Katy Hui-wen Hung, Taipei, February 15, 2017.

3. Council of Agriculture, "'Light Up Taiwan's New Agriculture.'"

4. National Statistics (Taiwan), *2010 Agriculture, Forestry, Fishery and Animal Husbandry Census.*

5. USDA Foreign Agricultural Service, "Taiwan: Grain and Feed Annual."

6. International Trade Administration, US Department of Commerce, "Taiwan—Beef."

7. Mao and Chi, "Agricultural and Industrial Development in Taiwan."

8. Lee, "Overview of Food Security and Policy Directions in Taiwan."

9. Crook, *Keeping Up with the War God*, 49.

10. Executive Yuan (Taiwan), "Agriculture," in *ROC Yearbook 2016.*

11. Council of Agriculture, "Taiwan's Agricultural Genetic Modification."

12. Hsu, in *Americans and Chinese*, contrasts Han inheritance practices with those in Japan and suspects (page 302) that Japan's "one-son inheritance rule . . . materially helped the process of modernization" in that country by forcing non-inheritors to leave their villages, thereby accelerating urbanization and the creation of non-farming businesses.

13. National Statistics (Taiwan), *2010 Agriculture, Forestry, Fishery and Animal Husbandry Census.*

14. Ibid.

15. Dr. Dyno Keatinge, interviewed in Crook, "The World Vegetable Center Is in Tainan."

16. Yang and Han, "Policy Analysis of Implementation of 'Small Landlord Big Tenant' in Taiwan."

17. Sui, "Taiwan Transition: From City Life to the Countryside."

18. Shepherd, *Statecraft*, 57.

19. Ibid., 57–59.

20. Ibid., 85 and 87.

21. Ibid., 263 and 265.

22. Ibid., 138.

23. Ibid., 175.

24. Swinhoe, "Notes on the Island of Formosa," 9.

25. Shepherd, *Statecraft*, 156.

26. National Museum of Natural Science, "Agriculture in Taiwan (before 1945)."

27. Kuroda, "Empirical Investigation of the Rice Production Structure in Taiwan 1976–93."

28. Shepherd, *Statecraft*, 158.

29. Gemma, "The Rice Economy in Taiwan," 246.

30. University of Arkansas, "Per Capita Rice Consumption of Selected Countries."

31. Food and Fertilizer Technology Center for the Asian and Pacific Region, "Agriculture in Taiwan."

32. Ding, "Dryland Rice: East 1, 2 and 3 Cultivars," 11.

33. Y. I. C. Hsing, "Rice in Taiwan."

34. National Taiwan University, "Revival of the NTU Eikichi Iso Memorial House."

35. Council of Agriculture, "Agricultural Production."

36. Dalrymple, *Development and Spread of High-Yielding Rice Varieties*, 16.

37. Fell, "Migration through the Lens of Political Advertising," 129.

38. Barker, Herdt, and Rose, *The Rice Economy of Asia*, 57.

39. Ibid., 25.

40. These gastropods, introduced to Taiwan from Florida in the early 1980s by farmers who hoped to develop export businesses, are far from delicious and thus left alone by Taiwanese who collect and eat wild snails.

41. Papademetriou, "Rice Production in the Asia-Pacific Region."

42. Pereira and Guimaraes, "History of Rice in Latin America," 434.

43. Williams, "Sugar: The Sweetener in Taiwan's Development," 221.

44. Shepherd, *Statecraft*, 163.

45. Williams, "Sugar: The Sweetener in Taiwan's Development," 222.

46. At the same time, Taiwan ranked number three for bananas and canned pineapples, fourth for sweet potatoes, sixth for tea, tenth for rice and peanuts, and thirteenth for salt: Hsiao and Hsiao, *Economic Development of Taiwan*, 193.

47. Taiwan Sugar Corp., "Brief—Research & Development."

48. Jiang, "Tainan's History Informs Rich Food."

49. Hung, "From 'What to Eat?' to 'Delicious Food,'" 44.

50. Chen, "Embodying Nation in Food Consumption," 174.

51. Council of Agriculture, "Agricultural Production."

52. Ibid.

53. Pan, *Formosa Plant Culture*, 304.

54. Chang, "Nostalgic Imagination: The Sweet Potato in Taiwan," 1.

55. Ibid., 6.

56. Council of Agriculture, "Sweet Potato."

57. Ignacio Chang Chih-Ping of Taiwan Sweet Potato International Food Co., email message to Steven Crook, July 6, 2017.

58. Executive Yuan (Taiwan), "Agriculture," in *ROC Yearbook 2016*.

59. Council of Agriculture, "Mango—the Fruit from Taiwan."

60. The land area given over to the cultivation of betel nuts (areca nuts) is triple that on which bananas are grown, and the former is technically a berry. Japanese apricots are also known as Chinese plums.

61. Pan, *Formosa Plant Culture*, 301.

62. Ibid., 304.

63. *Taiwan Today*, "The Fruits of Foreign Trade."

64. World Bank Publications, *Exporting High-Value Food Commodities*, 103.

65. One source making this claim gives a figure of 297 pounds per capita per annum: International Business Publications, *Taiwan: Doing Business and Investing in Taiwan Guide Vol. 1*, 132. In 2010, the USDA Foreign Agricultural Service put annual fruit consumption in Taiwan at 286 pounds per person: "Taiwan—Fresh Deciduous Fruit Annual." However, some estimate annual per capita intake of bananas in Uganda, Rwanda, and Burundi at more than 480 pounds. Because they are starchy and not especially sweet, some Taiwanese do not think of bananas as "fruit" but as a filler between meals.

66. Tom Chen, personal interview with Katy Hui-wen Hung, Taipei, June 10, 2017.

67. Chang, Hsia, and Griffith, "The FMD Outbreak in the Taiwan Pig Industry."

68. Liu, "Hog Island," 7.

69. Tzeng and Low, "Animal Health Body to List Taiwan as FMD-Free."

70. Strak, "Taiwan's Challenging Future in Pig Farming."

71. Jennings, "In Taiwan, Leftover Food Scraps Help Farmers."

72. Pork Checkoff, "World Per Capita Pork Consumption."

73. Liu, "Hog Island," 91.

74. Most Taiwanese operations have fewer than five hundred hogs. In the United States, herds numbering under five thousand are considered small: Strak, "Taiwan's Challenging Future in Pig Farming."

75. Liu, "Hog Island," 8.

76. Ibid., 108.

77. Lin, "Behind the US Pork Protest."

78. Council of Agriculture, "Taiwan Black Hair Production and Marketing Strategic Alliance."

79. Cheng and Ju, "Legacies and Development of Taiwan Indigenous Black Pig Industry."

80. Huang, "Demand Strong and Prices High Around Mid-Autumn Festival."

81. The Poultry Site, "USDA International Egg and Poultry."

82. Chen, "Vicissitudes of Turkey Culture in Taiwan."

83. Pan et al., "Diet and Health Trends in Taiwan."

84. *Epoch Times*, "Origin of the Duck Gift."

85. Executive Yuan (Taiwan), *ROC Yearbook 2015*, 165.

86. Ibid., 166.

87. Kaohsiung Museum of Fisheries Civilization, "Chronicles."

88. Friend, "Meat Consumption Trends in Asia Pacific."

89. *Japan Times*, "Japan's Demand for Seafood Declines."

90. National Oceanic and Atmospheric Administration, "Americans Added Nearly 1 Pound of Seafood to Their Diet."

91. Chung, "Fishing for the Future," 5.

92. Liao and Liao, "An Economic Evaluation of Shrimp Farming Industry in Taiwan," 189–91.

93. Lee, "Taiwan Tilapia," 36.

94. Liao and Liao, "An Economic Evaluation of Shrimp Farming Industry in Taiwan," 195.

95. Chung, "Fishing for the Future," 4–5.

96. Chan, "Taiwan Tilapia Farmer Turns Poor Man's Fish into Gold."

97. Frank Tai, personal interview with Steven Crook and Katy Hui-wen Hung, Wufeng, October 13, 2016.

98. Miles and Chang, *Mushrooms*, 225.

99. Emery, "Taiwan's Mushroom Industry," 2.

100. Pan et al., "Diet and Health Trends in Taiwan."

101. Chu Rui-Jong, personal interview with Steven Crook and Katy Hui-wen Hung, Wufeng, October 13, 2016.

102. Typhoon Morakot in 2009, the deadliest typhoon to hit Taiwan in recent years, is thought to have felled more than three million trees.

103. Rainfall per square mile in Taiwan is about 2.6 times the world average, but precipitation per capita is less than one-eighth of the global average: Council of Agriculture, "History of Irrigation in Taiwan, Part 1."

104. Fang, "Status of PFAL in Taiwan," 40.

105. Fang, "Representative PFALs in Taiwan," 353.

106. Ibid., 351.

107. Chen, Yeh, and Liu, "Plant Weight Measurement System for Plant Factory," 8–16.

108. Canada lacked a federal certification system until June 2009.

109. Fahey, "Certification Now Required for Organic Food in Taiwan."

110. Hsieh, "Organic Farming for Sustainable Agriculture in Asia."

111. Ibid.

112. Executive Yuan, "New Agricultural Paradigm."

113. *Taipei Times*, "Organic Farming to Be Prioritized: COA."

114. Santa Cruz Organic Store, "Shops."

115. Liao Cheng-chou, personal interview with Katy Hui-wen Hung, Taipei, February 15, 2017.

116. Hsieh Shu-hsuan, in discussion with Katy Hui-wen Hung, Taipei, February 19, 2017.

117. Crook, "Enjoying Taroko Gorge's Fabled Beauty," 37.

118. International Trade Administration, US Department of Commerce, "Taiwan—Labeling/Marking Requirements."

119. Liang, "Red Quinoa Proved to Fight Cancer."

120. MataTaiwan, "Mr Quinoa from Tjuwabar."

CHAPTER 6

1. *China Post*, "Working Class Wages Stagnant for Average 2.3 Years: Survey."

2. Ministry of Economic Affairs (Taiwan), *Annual Report of Trade and Eating-Drinking Places Activity Surveys*.

3. Li and Houston, "Factors Affecting Consumer Preferences for Major Food Markets in Taiwan."

4. *China Post*, "Hypermarket Sales Could Hit New High in 2017."

5. Hitt, Ireland, and Hoskisson, *Strategic Management*, 78.

6. Visit to Taipei Seafood Wholesale Market by Steven Crook, August 29, 2017.

7. Chen, "Happy Taiwan's 60 Wonderful Ingredients: Red Tilefish."

8. Chung, "Crabs Up for Grabs," 24–26.

9. In Hong Kong, Singapore, and Malaysia, one catty is slightly more than 600 grams. In China, it is 500 grams.

10. Visit to Fumin Road by Steven Crook. August 29, 2017.

11. Liao, "Reconstruction of Huannan Market Starts Nov. 6."

12. Tsai, Wu, Wang, and Weng, "Selection between Traditional Market and Supermarket," 106–8.

13. Wu, "Hypermarkets Battle for Hearts and Minds."

14. Lin, "Behind the US Pork Protest."

15. Lin, "Taipei Traditional Markets to Reproduce Classic Good Tastes."

16. Tsai, Wu, Wang, and Weng, "Selection between Traditional Market and Supermarket," 164–65.

17. Jen Chia-lun, personal interview with Katy Hui-wen Hung, Taipei, June 6, 2017.

18. Mehra, "E-commerce in Taiwan."

19. The Nielsen Company, "More Than Half of Taiwan Consumers Are Willing to Buy Groceries Online."

20. Eighty-two percent of internet users in Taiwan have Facebook accounts, the highest percentage in the world: Fulco, "Facebook Still Dominates," 26.

21. Brian Chuang, personal interview with Steven Crook and Katy Hui-wen Hung, Taipei, March 21, 2017.

22. Teng, "Soy Sauce: Fermenting for Four Generations," 79.

23. Fulco, "Facebook Still Dominates," 26.

24. Alex Lu, personal interview with Steven Crook, Kaohsiung, September 6, 2017.

25. Lee, "Robert Wu Turned Eslite Bookshop into a Lifestyle Store."

26. Kate Chiu, email interview with Steven Crook, March 14, 2017.

27. In 2001, a Taipei bakery owner was convicted of illegally importing poppy seeds: Lin, "Court Convicts Bagel Shop Owner over Poppy Seeds."

28. Hsu, "The History and Cultural Research of Taiwan Cuisine," 63.

29. Ibid., 64.

30. Wikipedia, "Mongolian Barbecue."

31. H. M. Cheng, email interview with Steven Crook, May 4, 2017.

32. Tsai, "Culinary Tourism and Night Markets in Taiwan," 255.

33. Tseng, "Development of Hawkers in Taiwan."

34. Huang, *Journey in Taiwan: Vol. 1*, 45.

35. Translation based on a version by Chen, "Embodying Nation in Food Consumption," 77.

36. Hsu, "Taiwan's Night Markets Go Global."

37. Hsu, "Wash Your Fruits, Vegetables: FDA."

38. Food and Fertilizer Technology Center for the Asian and Pacific Region, "Rapid Bioassay of Pesticide Residues (RBPR)."

39. Stratfor Worldview, "Taiwan's Ruling Party Suffers after Elections."

40. Ferry, "How Safe Is Taiwan's Food?" 16.

41. Chen, "Coconut Oil and Lard Not Ideal Alternatives."

42. Ferry, "How Safe Is Taiwan's Food?" 17.

43. Ibid.

44. Liao, "I-Mei Foods Begins Operation of Radiation Laboratory."

45. Zhou, "Taiwan Keeps Ban on Food from Japanese Radiation Zones."

46. Liao, "I-Mei Foods Begins Operation of Radiation Laboratory."

47. Euromonitor International, "Ready Meals in Taiwan," 2.

48. Her, "Serving Quick Meals Around the Clock," 28.

49. Euromonitor International, "Ready Meals in Taiwan," 3.

50. Ibid., 1.

CHAPTER 7

1. Chen, "Embodying Nation in Food Consumption," 124–25.

2. Sean A. Hsu, personal interview with Steven Crook and Katy Hui-wen Hung, Taipei, March 21, 2017.

3. Grimes, "Peng Chang-kuei."

4. Tseng, "The Wu Yuan-Sheng Family," 58.

5. Ibid., 58–59.

6. Bryan Wu, personal interview with Katy Hui-wen Hung, Taipei, May 16, 2017.

7. Hakka Affairs Council, "Innovative Hakka Cuisine."

8. André Chiang, personal interview with Steven Crook and Katy Hui-wen Hung, Taipei, August 29, 2017.

9. *Japan Times*, "Michelin Guide Set to Boost Taipei's Foodie Creds."

CHAPTER 8

1. Dereke Bruce, telephone interview with Steven Crook, September 5, 2017.

2. Tom Chen, personal interview with Katy Hui-wen Hung, Taipei, June 10, 2017.

3. Chung, "Tough New Laws in Taiwan to Curb Drink-Driving."

4. Bolton, "Around Half of Taiwan's Population Lack a Gene."

5. Hung, "From 'What to Eat?' to 'Delicious Food,'" 61.

6. TaiwanTeaCrafts.com, "Going Wild for Shan Cha."

7. Taiwan Tea Corp., "History of Taiwanese Teas."

8. Digital Taiwan, "John Dodd, Lu Chunsheng, and the Age of Taiwanese Tea."

9. Chen, *Big Bowl, Big Spoon*, 20.

10. National Museum of History, *Early Taiwanese Coffee Culture*, 105–7.

11. Crook, "Bonding over Coffee."

12. Chen and Huang, "Taiwan Consumes 2.85 Billion Cups of Coffee in 2015."

13. Starbucks was introduced to the Taiwan market by Uni-President Group's President Chain Store Corp., which also runs Taiwan's 7-Eleven convenience stores as well as the island's Mister Donut and Cold Stone Creamery chains.

14. Quartly, "Taipei Coffee Culture," 32.

15. National Museum of History, *Early Taiwanese Coffee Culture*, 11.

16. Ibid., 93.

17. Moskowitz, "Drinking Modernity," 205.

18. Since 1976 there have been two Boleros a few doors apart on Minsheng West Road; the newer branch is managed by the younger brother of the manager of the original Bolero.

19. National Museum of History, *Early Taiwanese Coffee Culture*, 85 and 89.

20. Moskowitz, "Drinking Modernity," 203.

21. Ibid., 205.

22. Luxner, "Mr. Brown Coffee."

23. Moskowitz, "Drinking Modernity," 206.

24. Chen and Huang, "Taiwan Consumes 2.85 Billion Cups of Coffee in 2015."

25. Tom Chen, personal interview with Katy Hui-wen Hung, Taipei, June 10, 2017.

26. *Taiwan Today*, "Champion Roaster Takes Taiwan Coffee to Next Level."

27. Wu and Kuo, "Taiwanese Barista Named 2016 World Champion."

28. Ter, "Tea-sing Flavors," 37.

29. In the same period, Taiwan's population grew 30 percent: Crook, "Exploring the World of Taiwanese Tea," 26.

30. Executive Yuan (Taiwan), *ROC Yearbook 2016*, 153.

31. Heiss and Heiss, *The Tea Enthusiast's Handbook*, 110.

32. Ibid.

33. Crook, "Exploring the World of Taiwanese Tea," 26.

34. *Discover Taipei*, "Your Guide to Taipei's Heritage Tea Shops," 8.

35. *Liberty Times*, "Eight Tea Business-People Sentenced for Smuggling Chinese Tea."

36. Anonymous, personal interview by Steven Crook, July 21, 2017.

37. Wu and Low, "Vietnamese Tea Found Being Passed Off as Taiwanese."

38. The monopolies bureau was taken over by the KMT after World War II, stripped of its privileges in 2002, and restructured as a state-run enterprise the same year so Taiwan could join the WTO. Abolishing the salt monopoly led to the end in 2002 of domestic salt production, which had been continuous since at least 1664.

39. Weaver, "Post-Monopoly Prosperity," 43.

40. Ferry, "Craft Beer in Taiwan," 7.

41. Ibid., 6–7.

42. Alex Lu, personal interview with Steven Crook, Kaohsiung, September 6, 2017.

43. Ferry, "Craft Beer in Taiwan," 8.

44. Crook, "Yilan: Sights at the End of the Tunnel," 19.

45. Lee and Chung, "Taichung Wine Wins Gold Medal."

46. Huashan 1914 Creative Park, "History of Huashan."

47. Wu San-Lien Foundation for Taiwan Historical Materials, "Taiwan's Early Alcohol Bottle Labels."

48. Lin, "Meet Taiwan Sake in Taoyuan Brewery."

49. Wufeng Farmers' Association Distillery, "About."

50. Chen, "Wufeng Sake."

51. International Trade Administration, US Department of Commerce, "Taiwan—Wine and Spirits."

52. Weaver, "The Blossoming of the Taiwan Whisky Market," 49.

53. Emen, "Taiwan's Kavalan Whisky Distillery."

54. Crook, "Yilan: Sights at the End of the Tunnel," 19.

55. Kavalan Whisky, "Kavalan Celebrates World's Best Whisky Awards."
56. Tsai, "A Century of Rice Wine Culture," 12.
57. Shih, "Sorghum Liquor Helps Build Kinmen's Fortunes."
58. Seydewitz, "Kinmen Lives on Kaoliang," 28–30.
59. Wehring, "San Francisco World Spirits Competition 2017."
60. *Taipei Times*, "Kinmen Kaoliang Liquor Wins Global Awards for Baijiu."
61. *Gooread*, "Preparation and Function of Bee-Pupae Wine."
62. Digital Museum Project, "Pingpu Cultural Information Network."
63. Bechtinger, *Het eiland in de chineesche zee*, 15.
64. Wikipedia, "Warriors of the Rainbow: Seediq Bale."
65. Hoffman, "Kanpai! Sake through the Ages."
66. Taintor, *The Aborigines of Northern Formosa*, 33–34.
67. Peng, "A Good Drink."

CHAPTER 9

1. Woo, "Master Chef Brought Cuisine to the Masses."
2. King, "The Julia Child of Chinese Cooking."
3. Ibid.
4. Ibid.
5. Angela Cheng, personal interview with Katy Hui-wen Hung, Taipei, March 6, 2017.
6. Lin Ming-tsan, personal interview with Katy Hui-wen Hung, Taipei, February 20, 2017.
7. Visit to Yamicook by Katy Hui-wen Hung, February 6, 2017.
8. Mingchin Chiu, personal interview with Katy Hui-wen Hung, Taipei, February 22, 2017.
9. Chiu, *The Dry Goods Legend of Nan Chi Hang*, 89.
10. Mingchin Chiu, personal interview with Katy Hui-wen Hung, Taipei, February 22, 2017.
11. Council of Agriculture, "Tian Mama: A Short Story."
12. Sanxing District Farmers Association, *Outstanding Female Farmers Data Book*, 3–4.
13. Ivy Chen, email interview with Steven Crook, October 24, 2017.
14. Calvin Tu, personal interview with Katy Hui-wen Hung, Taipei, May 1, 2017.
15. André Chiang, personal interview with Steven Crook and Katy Hui-wen Hung, Taipei. August 29, 2017.
16. Translation by Allen, *Taipei: City of Displacements*, 62.

Bibliography

Allen, Joseph R. *Taipei: City of Displacements*. Taipei: SMC Publishing, 2012.

Anderson, E. N. *Food and Environment in Early and Medieval China*. Philadelphia: University of Pennsylvania Press, 2014.

———. *Everyone Eats: Understanding Food and Culture*. New York: New York University Press, 2005.

Andrade, Tonio. *How Taiwan Became Chinese*. New York: Columbia University Press, 2007.

Andrews, Lia. "The 'Three Golden Opportunities': Key Times Women Can Improve or Damage Their Health." *Journal of Chinese Medicine*, no. 103, October 2013.

Barker, Randolph, Robert W. Herdt, and Beth Rose. *The Rice Economy of Asia, Volume 2*. Los Banos, CA: International Rice Research Institute, 1985.

Bechtinger, Jos. *Het eiland in de chineesche zee*. Batavia, Dutch East Indies: Bruining et Wyt, 1871. Translation at http://www.reed.edu/Formosa/texts/Bechtinger1871.html (accessed October 4, 2017).

Blussé, Leonard, Natalie Everts, and Evelien Frech. *The Formosan Encounter: 1623–1635*. Taipei: Shung Ye Museum of Formosan Aborigines, 1999.

Bolton, Doug. "Around Half of Taiwan's Population Lack a Gene Required for Metabolizing Alcohol." *The Independent*, August 20, 2015. http://www.independent.co.uk/life-style/health-and-families/health-news/around-half-of-taiwans-population-lack-a-gene-required-for-metabolising-alcohol-10464725.html (accessed June 15, 2017).

Bowles, Tom Parker. "How Taiwan Became the Hottest Food Destination on Earth." *Esquire*, September 15, 2015. http://www.esquire.com/uk/food-drink /news/a8841/taiwan-food-guide/ (accessed January 16, 2018).

Cauquelin, Josiane. *Aborigines of Taiwan: The Puyuma: From Headhunting to the Modern World*. Abingdon, UK: Routledge, 2004.

Chan, Rachel. "Taiwan Tilapia Farmer Turns Poor Man's Fish into Gold." *Taiwan Today*, October 16, 2011. http://taiwantoday.tw/news.php?unit=6,23,45, 6,6&post=10535 (accessed May 26, 2017).

Chang Chiung-fang. "Camellia Oil: An Old Staple Morphs into a Superfood." *Taiwan Panorama*, August 2016.

———. "SunnyHills Bakery: Modest Brilliance." *Taiwan Panorama*, October 2016.

———. "The Hakka Cuisine Competition 2016." *Taiwan Panorama*, November 2016.

Chang Hui-Shung, Chung-Jen Hsia, and Garry Griffith. "The FMD Outbreak in the Taiwan Pig Industry and the Demand for Beef Imports into Taiwan." *Australasian Agribusiness Review* 14 (2006). http://www.agrifood.info/review/2006 /Chang_Hsia_Griffith.html (accessed April 20, 2017).

Chang Kwang-Chih and Minze Stuiver. "Recent Advances in the Prehistoric Archaeology of Formosa." *Proceedings of the National Academy of Sciences* (1966) 55: 3.

Chang, May Y. H. "Nostalgic Imagination: The Sweet Potato in Taiwan." Foundation of Chinese Dietary Culture. http://www.academia.edu/12520485/Nostalgic _Imagination_the_Sweet_Potato_in_Taiwan (accessed July 15, 2017).

Chang Wen-lian. "Farmland Ecology and Water Conservation." Department of Bioenvironmental Systems Engineering, National Taiwan University. http://hippo .bse.ntu.edu.tw/~wenlian/eco-eng/farm/farm-2.htm (accessed July 17, 2017).

Chen Cheng-wen and Frances Huang. "Taiwan Consumes 2.85 Billion Cups of Coffee in 2015." *Focus Taiwan*, October 10, 2016. http://focustaiwan.tw/news /aeco/201610100011.aspx (accessed June 16, 2017).

Chen, Ivan. "Taiwan, Global Vegan Capital: An Eco-Friendly Lifestyle." *Taiwan Panorama*, August 2017.

Chen Ko-han. "Wufeng Sake—Reinventing Japanese Tradition." *Taiwan News*, May 6, 2009. http://www.taiwannews.com.tw/en/news/940411 (accessed June 15, 2017).

Chen Liang-rong. "Happy Taiwan's 60 Wonderful Ingredients: Red Tilefish." *CommonWealth*, June 21, 2017. http://www.cw.com.tw/article/article.action?id= 5083058 (accessed August 30, 2017).

Chen, Melody. "Deadly Methanol Levels Found in Bootleg Wine." *Taipei Times*, December 6, 2002. http://www.taipeitimes.com/News/taiwan/archives /2002/12/06/0000186056 (accessed October 2, 2017).

Chen Rou-jin. "Curry Wafts over Taiwan." *China Times*, February 10, 2015. http://www.chinatimes.com/newspapers/20150210000894-260115 (accessed August 17, 2017).

Chen Rung-Tsung, Chu-Fa Tsai, and Wann-Nian Tzeng. "Freshwater Prawns of Taiwan with Special References to Their Biogeographical Origins and Dispersion Routes." *Journal of Crustacean Biology* 29, no. 2 (2009): 232–44.

Chen, Ted. "Coconut Oil and Lard Not Ideal Alternatives: Experts." *China Post*, October 28, 2013. http://www.chinapost.com.tw/taiwan/national/national-news/2013/10/28/392307/Coconut-oil.htm (accessed March 25, 2017).

Chen Wei-Tai, Yu-Hui F. Yeh, and Ting-Yu Liu. "An Automated and Continuous Plant Weight Measurement System for Plant Factory." In *Advances and Trends in Development of Plant Factories*, ed. Alejandro Isabel Luna-Maldonado, Juan Antonio Vidales-Contreras, and Humberto Rodríguez-Fuentes. Lausanne, Switzerland: Frontiers Media, 2017.

Chen Yuan-peng. "Vicissitudes of Turkey Culture in Taiwan." *Dong Hwa Journal of Humanities and Social Science Online*, December 2015. http://journal.ndhu.edu.tw/e_paper/e_paper_c.php?SID=128 (accessed September 6, 2017).

Chen Yujen. "Embodying Nation in Food Consumption: Changing Boundaries of 'Taiwanese Cuisine' (1895–2008)." PhD diss., University of Leiden, Netherlands, 2010.

———. *Big Bowl, Big Spoon: Are You Full?* Taipei: Unitas UDN Group, 2014.

———. "Taiwan Dairy Cattle and Milk Culture." *Taiwan Communication*, no. 83, September 2014.

Cheng Chun-chun and Yu-ten Ju. "Legacies and Development of Taiwan Indigenous Black Pig Industry in Liouduei Area in South Taiwan." *Taiwan Historical Research* 20, no. 4 (December 2013): 135–77.

Cheung, Han. "Taiwan in Time: A Life Devoted to Political Freedom." *Taipei Times*, August 2, 2015. http://www.taipeitimes.com/News/feat/archives/2015/08/02/2003624440/1 (accessed October 3, 2017).

Chiang Jung-feng and Ellen Schrecker. *Mrs. Chiang's Szechwan Cookbook*. Menlo Park, CA: Askmar Publishing, 2010.

Chien, Archibald, and Xie Zhu-fen. *Astoria Confectionary and Café*. Taoyuan: Ink Publishing, 2015.

China Post. "Working Class Wages Stagnant for Average 2.3 Years: Survey." February 10, 2017. http://www.chinapost.com.tw/taiwan/national/national-news/2017/02/10/491282/working-class.htm (accessed July 27, 2017).

———. "Hypermarket Sales Could Hit New High in 2017." May 30, 2017. http://www.chinapost.com.tw/taiwan/business/2017/05/30/498102/hypermarket-sales.htm (accessed September 4, 2017).

Chiu Chun-fu, Wu Cheng-feng, and Jake Chung. "Chinese Fishing Methods Damaging Taiwan's Seas." *Taipei Times*, November 27, 2016. http://www.taipei times.com/News/front/archives/2016/11/27/2003660074 (accessed September 18, 2017).

Chiu Mingchin. *The Dry Goods Legend of Nan Chi Hang*. Taipei: Linking Publishing, 2015.

Chou, Christine. "GM Foods Banned from School Menus." *China Post*, December 15, 2015. http://www.chinapost.com.tw/taiwan/national/national-news/2015 /12/15/453548/gm-foods.htm (accessed September 6, 2017).

Chung, Lawrence. "Tough New Laws in Taiwan to Curb Drink-Driving." *South China Morning Post*, June 25, 2013. http://www.scmp.com/news/china/article /1268153/tough-new-laws-taiwan-curb-drink-driving (accessed June 13, 2017).

Chung, Oscar. "Fishing for the Future." *Taiwan Review*, July 2009.

———. "A Sauce for All." *Taiwan Review*, January 2010.

———. "Crabs Up for Grabs." *Taiwan Review*, August 2013.

Coolidge, Tony. "A Colorful Celebration of Life's Abundance: Amis Harvest Festival." *Cultural Survival*, July 6, 2016. https://www.culturalsurvival.org/news /colorful-celebration-lifes-abundance-amis-harvest-festival (accessed October 5, 2017).

Council of Agriculture. "Taiwan Black Hair Production and Marketing Strategic Alliance." February 2001. http://www.coa.gov.tw/ws.php?id=4047 (accessed June 27, 2017).

———. "History of Irrigation in Taiwan, Part 1." 2006. http://doie.coa.gov.tw /english/about-history-part1.asp (accessed April 20, 2017).

———. "Agricultural Production." 2015. http://eng.coa.gov.tw/ws.php?id=2505 271 (accessed June 5, 2017).

———. "Taiwan's Agricultural Genetic Modification Technology Development Follows the Active R&D and Efficient Management Policy." February 9, 2015. http://eng.coa.gov.tw/theme_data.php?theme=eng_news&id=409&print=Y (accessed May 11, 2017).

———. "Mango—the Fruit from Taiwan that Earned Its International Reputation." August 22, 2015. http://eng.coa.gov.tw/ws.php?id=2503976 (accessed May 17, 2017).

———. "Tian Mama: A Short Story." July 2016. https://www.coa.gov.tw/ws.php ?id=2505152 (accessed October 17, 2017).

———. "'Light Up Taiwan's New Agriculture. Young Farmers Are the Winners' Creates Novel Future for Agriculture." October 20, 2016. http://eng.coa.gov.tw /ws.php?id=2505335 (accessed April 14, 2017).

———. "Sweet Potato." 2017. http://eng.coa.gov.tw/ws.php?id=9432 (accessed July 10, 2017).

Crook, Steven. *Keeping Up with the War God*. Brighton, UK: Yushan, 2001.

———. "Ins and Outs of Taiwan Hot Pots." *Taiwan Today*, November 26, 2010. http://taiwantoday.tw/news.php?unit=18,23,45,18&post=24427 (accessed August 28, 2017).

———. "Yilan: Sights at the End of the Tunnel." *Taiwan Business Topics*, June 2012.

———. "Balancing on the Brink." *Taiwan Review*, August 2013.

———. "Exploring the World of Taiwanese Tea." *Taiwan Business Topics*, July 2014.

———. "The World Vegetable Center Is in Tainan." Interview with Dr. Dyno Keatinge. *Taiwan Business Topics*, May 2015.

———. "Enjoying Taroko Gorge's Fabled Beauty." *Taiwan Business Topics*, July 2015.

———. "Bonding over Coffee: An American Inspired by Life of Taiwan." *Life of Taiwan*, November 10, 2016. http://lifeoftaiwan.com/travel/american-inspired -by-life-of-taiwan-tour/ (accessed May 14, 2017).

———. "Herping and Other Nocturnal Adventures in Taiwan's Forests." *Taiwan Business Topics*, July 2017.

———. *Taiwan: The Bradt Travel Guide*. Chalfont St Peter: Bradt Travel Guides, 2014.

Crook, Steven, and Katy Hui-wen Hung. "Fungus among Us." *Taiwan Business Topics*, January 2017.

———. "Getting a Handle on the Taiwanese 'Hamburger.'" *Taiwan Business Topics*, January 2017.

Dalrymple, Dana G. *Development and Spread of High-Yielding Rice Varieties in Developing Countries*. Washington, DC: USAID, 1986.

Davidson, James W. *The Island of Formosa, Past and Present*. New York: Macmillan, 1903.

Diamond, Jared M. "Linguistics: Taiwan's Gift to the World." *Nature*, February 17, 2000. https://www.nature.com/articles/35001685 (accessed January 9, 2017).

Digital Museum Project. "Pingpu Cultural Information Network." http://museum 02.digitalarchives.tw/dmp/2000/pingpu/education/Essay/essay-pepo/10.htm (accessed October 4, 2017).

Digital Taiwan. "John Dodd, Lu Chunsheng, and the Age of Taiwanese Tea." http:// culture.teldap.tw/culture/index.php?option%3Dcom_content%26id%3D2290 :john-todd-li-chunsheng-and-the-age-of-taiwanese-tea (accessed September 1, 2017).

Ding Da-fang. "Mountain Bitter Gourd." JoiiUp, December 14, 2015. https://www .joiiup.com/knowledge/content/295 (accessed October 3, 2017).

Ding Wen-yan. "Dryland Rice: East 1, 2 and 3 Cultivars." *Taitung Agricultural Issues*, March 2012, no. 79, 11. http://www.ttdares.gov.tw/htmlarea_file/web _articles/ttdares/4187/79-05.pdf (accessed September 5, 2017).

Directorate General of Budget, Accounting and Statistics (Taiwan). 2013 Budget Description: Tobacco and Wine.

———. 2014 Budget Description: Tobacco and Wine. Taipei.

Discover Taipei. "Your Guide to Taipei's Heritage Tea Shops." May–June 2012.

Du Hsiao Yueh Restaurant. "History of Du Hsiao Yueh." http://www.noodle1895 .com/site/index.html#!/about (accessed September 11, 2017).

Emen, Jake. "Taiwan's Kavalan Whisky Distillery: Up Close and Personal." *The Whiskey Wash*, July 19, 2016. https://thewhiskeywash.com/distillery-profiles /taiwan-kavalan-whisky-distillery/ (accessed September 15, 2017).

Emery, Robert F. "Taiwan's Mushroom Industry: A Study in Export Growth." Division of International Finance, Federal Reserve, February 2, 1965.

Epoch Times. "Hakka Make a Towel." September 28, 2008. http://www.epoch times.com/gb/9/9/28/n2671337.htm (accessed October 30, 2017).

———. "Thrifty Hakka Stir-Fry." January 18, 2011. http://www.epochtimes.com/ b5/11/1/15/n3143737.htm (accessed October 11, 2017).

———. "Origin of the Duck Gift." May 24, 2014. http://www.epochtimes.com/ b5/14/5/24/n4163354.htm (accessed May 18, 2017).

Erway, Cathy. *The Food of Taiwan: Recipes from the Beautiful Island.* Boston: Houghton Mifflin Harcourt, 2015.

Euromonitor International. "Ready Meals in Taiwan." *Ebook*, October 2016.

Everington, Keoni. "How to Celebrate Mid-Autumn Festival in Taiwan." *Focus Taiwan*, August 24, 2015. http://focustaiwan.tw/news/asoc/201509240016.aspx (accessed October 18, 2017).

Executive Yuan (Taiwan). *ROC Yearbook 2015.* Taipei, 2015.

———. *ROC Yearbook 2016.* Taipei, 2016.

———. "New Agricultural Paradigm to Support Sustainable Development." August 27, 2016. http://english.ey.gov.tw/News_Content2.aspx?n=8262ED7A2591 6ABF&s=2B236B068A17AA20 (accessed June 20, 2017).

———. "Traditional Festivals." March 29, 2017. http://www.ey.gov.tw/state/ News_Content3.aspx?n=6A1DF17EC68FF6D9&s=AA8FC7B656DC7B32 (accessed August 22, 2017).

Fahey, Michael R. "Certification Now Required for Organic Food in Taiwan." Winkler Partners, October 3, 2007. http://www.winklerpartners.com/?p=989 (accessed June 27, 2017).

Fan Ming-hwang. "Hsinpu's Fangliao Yimin Temple and Yimin Beliefs and Activities." Wu San-Lien Foundation for Taiwan Historical Materials, September 3, 2001. http://www.twcenter.org.tw/thematic_series/history_class/tw_window/ e02_20010903 (accessed August 19, 2017).

Fang, Wei. "Status of PFAL in Taiwan." In *Plant Factory: An Indoor Vertical Farming System for Efficient Quality Food Production*, ed. Toyoki Kozai, Genhua Niu, and Michiko Takagaki. Cambridge, MA: Academic Press, 2015.

———. "Representative PFALs in Taiwan." In *Plant Factory: An Indoor Vertical Farming System for Efficient Quality Food Production*, ed. Toyoki Kozai, Genhua Niu, and Michiko Takagaki. Cambridge, MA: Academic Press, 2015.

Fell, Dafydd. "Migration through the Lens of Political Advertising." In *Migration to and from Taiwan*, ed. Kuei-fen Chiu, Dafydd Fell, Lin Ping. Abingdon, UK: Routledge, 2014.

Ferry, Tim. "Craft Beer in Taiwan: A Passion, Not a Fashion." *Taiwan Business Topics*, January 2017.

———. "How Safe Is Taiwan's Food?" *Taiwan Business Topics*, February 2015.

Fisheries Research Institute. "Successful Breeding of Native Snails." http://www.tfrin.gov.tw/friweb/frienews/enews0077/h1.html (accessed June 21, 2017).

Food and Fertilizer Technology Center for the Asian and Pacific Region. "Agriculture in Taiwan." http://www.fftc.agnet.org/view.php?id=20110705103744_104108 (accessed April 23, 2017).

———. "Rapid Bioassay of Pesticide Residues (RBPR) on Fruits and Vegetables for Market Inspection." May 2010. http://www.fftc.agnet.org/activities.php?func=view&id=20111031154406 (accessed August 25, 2017).

Friend, Elizabeth. "Meat Consumption Trends in Asia Pacific and What They Mean for Food Service Strategy." Euromonitor International, August 25, 2015. https://blog.euromonitor.com/2015/08/meat-consumption-trends-in-asia-pacific-and-what-they-mean-for-foodservice-strategy.html (accessed May 25, 2017).

Fujii, Shozo. "The Formation of Taiwanese Identity and the Cultural Policy of Various Outside Regimes." In *Taiwan under Japanese Colonial Rule, 1895–1945: History, Culture, Memory*, ed. Binghui Liao and David De-wei Wang. New York: Columbia University Press, 2006.

Fulco, Matthew. "How Sweet It Is: Taipei Embraces Macarons." *Taiwan Business Topics*, January 2015.

———. "Facebook Still Dominates Taiwan's Social Media." *Taiwan Business Topics*, April 2017.

Gemma, M. "The Rice Economy in Taiwan: Demand and Supply Determinants and Prospects." In *Developments in the Asian Rice Economy*, ed. M. Sombilla, Mahabub Hossain, B. Hardy. Los Banos, CA: International Rice Research Institute, 2002.

Gooread. "Preparation and Function of Bee-Pupae Wine." August 20, 2017. http://www.gooread.com/article/20123546124/ (accessed October 2, 2017).

Goossaert, Vincent, and David A. Palmer, *The Religious Question in Modern China*. Chicago: University of Chicago Press, 2011.

Grimes, William. "Peng Chang-kuei, Chef behind General Tso's Chicken, Dies at 98." *New York Times*, December 2, 2016. https://www.nytimes.com/2016/12/02/world/asia/general-tso-chicken-peng-chang-kuei.html (accessed October 11, 2017).

Hakka Affairs Council. "Innovative Hakka Cuisine." September 22, 2016. http://web3.hakka.gov.tw/lp.asp?ctNode=2363&CtUnit=766&BaseDSD=24&mp=21 76&ps= (accessed October 6, 2017).

Handwerk, Brian. "Polynesians Descended from Taiwanese, Other East Asians." *National Geographic News*, January 17, 2008. https://news.nationalgeographic .com/news/2008/01/080117-polynesian-taiwan_2.html (accessed January 11, 2018).

Heiss, Mary Lou, and Robert J. Heiss. *The Tea Enthusiast's Handbook: A Guide to the World's Best Teas*. Berkeley, CA: Potter/TenSpeed/Harmony, 2012.

Her, Kelly. "Serving Quick Meals Around the Clock." *Taiwan Review*, August 2013.

Hitt, Michael R., Duane Ireland, and Robert Hoskisson. *Strategic Management: Competitiveness and Globalization, Cases*. Independence, KY: Cengage Learning, 2008.

Hoffman, Michael. "Kanpai! Sake through the Ages." *Japan Times*, October 12, 2013. https://www.japantimes.co.jp/life/2013/10/12/general/kanpai-sake -through-the-ages/#.Wdsd-DB-VPZ (accessed October 5, 2017).

Hong Yu-qi. "Black Vinegar or White Vinegar: Which Has Less Sodium?" *Business Weekly*, March 1, 2017. http://health.businessweekly.com.tw/AArticle.aspx? id=ARTL000083124 (accessed October 2, 2017).

Hong Zhi-wen. "Eat Up! The Origin of Japanese Ramen." *Apple Daily*, April 8, 2016. http://www.appledaily.com.tw/realtimenews/article/forum/20160408/834106/ (accessed May 22, 2017).

Hsiao Chu-an. "Seventeen Tons of Chopsticks Found to Contain Toxins: FDA." *China Post*, December 31, 2015. http://www.chinapost.com.tw/taiwan/national/ national-news/2015/12/31/454890/seventeen-tons.htm (accessed August 21, 2017).

Hsiao, Frank S. T., and Mei-Chu Wang Hsiao. *Economic Development of Taiwan: Early Experiences and the Pacific Trade Triangle*. Singapore: World Scientific, 2015.

Hsieh Sung-Ching. "Organic Farming for Sustainable Agriculture in Asia with Special Reference to Taiwan Experience." Food and Fertilizer Technology Center for the Asian and Pacific Region, September 1, 2005. http://www.fftc.agnet .org/library.php?func=view&id=20110801133519 (accessed June 27, 2017).

Hsing, Y. I. C. "Rice in Taiwan." In *Encyclopaedia of the History of Science, Technology, and Medicine in Non-Western Cultures*. Dordrecht: Springer Science and Business Media. https://www.researchgate.net/publication/302516270_Rice_in_ Taiwan (accessed April 23, 2017).

Hsu, Francis L. K. *Americans & Chinese: Passage to Differences*, third edition. Taipei: Bookman Books, 1981.

Hsu, Jenny W. "Taiwan's Night Markets Go Global." *Wall Street Journal*, June 20, 2014. https://blogs.wsj.com/chinarealtime/2014/06/20/taiwans-night-markets -go-global/ (accessed September 28, 2017).

Hsu, Stacy. "Wash Your Fruits, Vegetables: FDA." *Taipei Times*, June 27, 2014. http://www.taipeitimes.com/News/taiwan/archives/2014/06/27/2003593791 (accessed August 22, 2017).

Hsu Yu-Chun. "The History and Cultural Research of Taiwan Cuisine." Master's thesis, Tamkang University, Tamsui, 2013.

Huang Dah Mu Foods Co. Ltd. "Origins of Dougan." http://www.huangdahmu .com.tw/zh/company/3.html (accessed August 23, 2017).

Huang De-shi. *Journey in Taiwan: Vol. 1*. Taipei: Commercial Press, 1967.

Huang Pei-jin. "Demand Strong and Prices High around Mid-Autumn Festival." *Liberty Times*, August 31, 2017. http://news.ltn.com.tw/news/life/paper/1131291 (accessed September 12, 2017).

Huang Yi-jun. "Tatung Builds a Cross-Generation Rice Steamer." *CommonWealth*, April 13, 2011. http://www.cw.com.tw/article/article.action?id=5002077 (accessed July 24, 2017).

Huashan 1914 Creative Park. "History of Huashan." https://www.huashan1914 .com/w/huashan1914/History (accessed June 15, 2017).

Hung, Chiu-hsien. "From 'What to Eat?' to 'Delicious Food.'" In *Taiwanese Food History*, ed. May Y. H. Chang. Taipei: Foundation of Chinese Dietary Culture, 2013.

International Business Publications. *Taiwan: Doing Business and Investing in Taiwan Guide Vol. 1, Strategic and Practical Information*. Alexandria, VA: International Business Publications.

International Trade Administration, US Department of Commerce. "Taiwan—Labeling/Marking Requirements." June 6, 2017. https://www.export.gov/ article?id=Taiwan-Labeling-Marking-Requirements (accessed June 28, 2017).

———. "Taiwan—Beef." June 6, 2017. https://www.export.gov/article?id=Taiwan -Beef (accessed June 13, 2017).

———. "Taiwan—Wine and Spirits." June 14, 2017. https://www.export.gov/ article?id=Taiwan-Wine-and-Spirits (accessed June 16, 2017).

Jacobs, J. Bruce. "A History of Pre-Invasion Taiwan." *Taiwan Historical Research* 23 (2016).

Japan Times. "Japan's Demand for Seafood Declines, Especially among Young Generation: Report." May 20, 2016. https://japantoday.com/category/national/ japans-demand-for-seafood-declines-especially-among-young-generation-report (accessed May 25, 2017).

———. "Michelin Guide Set to Boost Taipei's Foodie Creds Even Further." November 16, 2017. https://www.japantimes.co.jp/news/2017/11/16/business/ michelin-guide-set-boost-taipeis-foodie-creds-even/#.WnvUD-d-VPY (accessed December 24, 2017).

Jennings, Ralph. "In Taiwan, Leftover Food Scraps Help Farmers Sustain Porky Appetites." *Guardian*, March 23, 2016. https://www.theguardian.com/sustainable-business/2016/mar/23/taiwan-food-waste-pork-production-farming-recycling-environment (accessed April 21, 2017).

Ji Yu-xuan. "Lin Ming-tsan: Do Your Favorite Work, and Life Will Be Happy." *China Times*. http://magazine.chinatimes.com/lifeplus/20151114003167-300507 (accessed July 24, 2017).

Jiang, Alex. "Tainan's History Informs Rich Food." *Taipei Times*, March 21, 2010. http://www.taipeitimes.com/News/taiwan/archives/2010/03/21/2003468569 (accessed August 29, 2017).

Jiang, Z., H. Mi, and Y. Zhang. "An Estimation of the Out-Migration from Mainland China to Taiwan: 1946–1949." *Chinese Journal of Population Science* 8, no. 4 (1996): 403–19.

Jordahl, Rick. "Taiwan Adopts Ractopamine MRLs for Beef, Not Pork." *Farm Journal*, July 26, 2012. http://www.porknetwork.com/pork-news/Taiwan-adopts-ractopamine-MRLs-for-beef-163922096.html (accessed April 27, 2017).

Jordan, David K. *Gods, Ghosts and Ancestors*. Taipei: Caves Books, 1985.

———. "The Popular Practice of Religion." In *Cultural Change in Postwar Taiwan*, ed. Stevan Harrell and Huang Chun-chieh. Taipei: SMC Publishing, 1994.

Kane, Tim. "Global U.S. Troop Deployment, 1950–2003." *Heritage Foundation*, October 27, 2004. http://www.heritage.org/defense/report/global-us-troop-deployment-1950-2003 (accessed May 22, 2017).

Kao, T. C., and Shih-Hsiang Lu. *A Baker Has a Dream: The I-Mei Story*. Taipei: Yuan-Liou Publishing, 2001.

Kaohsiung City Government, Department of Information. "Delivering Culinary Magic at Roadside Banquets: Catering Chef Tang Cin-lu." August 24, 2017. https://udn.com/news/story/6967/2623750 (accessed October 13, 2017).

Kaohsiung Museum of Fisheries Civilization. "Chronicles of Fisheries Cultural Museum." http://kcmb.kcg.gov.tw/kmfc/english/about01.htm (accessed May 25, 2017).

Kavalan Whisky. "Kavalan Celebrates World's Best Whisky Awards." July 15, 2016. http://www.prnewswire.com/news-releases/kavalan-celebrates-worlds-best-whisky-awards-300299537.html (accessed June 15, 2017).

King, Michelle. "The Julia Child of Chinese Cooking, or the Fu Pei-mei of French Food? Comparative Contexts of Female Culinary Celebrity." *Gastronomica* 18, no. 1 (February 2018).

Kuo, Grace. "Mullet Roe Brings Gold to Taiwan's Fishermen." *Taiwan Today*, February 19, 2012. http://taiwantoday.tw/news.php?unit=6,23,45,6,6&post=10789 (accessed August 22, 2017).

Kuroda, Yoshimi. "Empirical Investigation of the Rice Production Structure in Taiwan 1976–93." *The Developing Economies* 36, no. 1 (March 1998). http://www.ide-jetro.jp/English/Publish/Periodicals/De/pdf/98_01_04.pdf (accessed April 25, 2017).

Lai Shou-Cheng. "Rise and Development of Hakka Cuisine in Taiwan's Consumer Culture (1980–2004)." Hakka Affairs Council, April 14, 2008. http://www.hakka.gov.tw/Content/Content?NodeID=624&PageID=36697 (accessed October 1, 2017).

Land Snails of Taiwan. "*Achatina fulica Bowdich*, 1822." March 9, 2015. http://landsnail.biodiv.tw/node/198 (accessed June 20, 2017).

Lee, Cheng-Yi, Maa-Ling Chen, Peter Ditchfield, Li-Hung Lin, Pei-Ling Wang, A. Mark Pollard, Hsiu-Man Lin, Ching-Hua Lo, and Hsi-Kuei Tsai. "Diet and Subsistence Mode of Neolithic Yuanshan People in Taiwan: Perspective from Carbon And Nitrogen Isotope Analyses of Bone Collagen." *Archaeological Research in Asia* 7 (2016).

———. "Dietary Reconstruction of the Iron Age Population at the Fantzuyuan Site, Taiwan, Revealed by Isotopic Analysis on Human and Faunal Bone Collagen." *Archaeological Research in Asia* 9 (2017).

Lee Chung-hsien and Jake Chung. "Taichung Wine Wins Gold Medal." *Taipei Times*, March 16, 2017. http://www.taipeitimes.com/News/taiwan/archives/2017/03/16/2003666878 (accessed September 19, 2017).

Lee Hsiang-ting. "New Life in Old Vats: A Century of Vinegar Making." *Taiwan Panorama*, November 2016.

Lee Hwang-Jaw. "Overview of Food Security and Policy Directions in Taiwan." Food and Fertilizer Technology Center for the Asian and Pacific Region, February 11, 2014. http://ap.fftc.agnet.org/ap_db.php?id=202&print=1 (accessed April 19, 2017).

Lee I-chia. "Eating and Drinking Snake Still Popular Fare." *Taipei Times*, February 26, 2013. http://www.taipeitimes.com/News/taiwan/archives/2013/02/26/2003555764/1 (accessed July 15, 2017).

———. "Disposable Utensil Bans Take Effect in Taipei Next Week." *Taipei Times*, July 25, 2016. http://www.taipeitimes.com/News/taiwan/archives/2016/07/25/2003651755 (accessed September 6, 2017).

Lee Ju-chi. "Mapping the Social Contexts of Taiwan Rice Wine in Cooking: A Recipe-Narrated Investigation." Master's thesis, National Kaohsiung University of Hospitality and Tourism, 2011.

Lee Seok Hwai. "Robert Wu Turned Elite Bookshop into a Lifestyle Store." *Straits Times*, July 20, 2017. http://www.straitstimes.com/lifestyle/arts/he-turned-bookshop-into-a-lifestyle-store (accessed September 7, 2017).

Lee Te-jen. "Legacy Unearthed in Tainan Science Park." National Museum of Prehistory. http://beta.nmp.gov.tw/enews/no68/page_03.html (accessed July 31, 2017).

Lee, Vito. "Taiwan Tilapia: The Fish That Became a National Treasure." *Taiwan Panorama*, April 2006.

Li Ho-Shui and Jack E. Houston. "Factors Affecting Consumer Preferences for Major Food Markets in Taiwan." *Journal of Food Distribution Research* 98 (March 2001). http://ageconsearch.umn.edu/bitstream/26515/1/32010097.pdf (accessed July 8, 2017).

Li Kuang-ti. "First Farmers and Their Cultural Adaptation in Prehistoric Taiwan." In *A Companion to Chinese Archaeology*, ed. Anne P. Underhill. Chichester, UK: Wiley-Blackwell, 2013.

Li Kuang-ti, Cheng-Hwa Tsang, Cheng-yi Chu, and Yue-ie Hsing. "Taiwan as an Austronesian Homeland: New Evidence and an Interpretation from Shell Midden Remains." PNC 2009 Annual Conference and Joint Meetings, October 6–8, 2009. http://www.pnclink.org/pnc2009/english/PresentationMaterial/Oct08/08-Rm4-Austraonesian2/1150_08-Austronesian-ppt-Kuang-TiLi.pdf (accessed July 31, 2017).

Li Kuo-ting, *The Evolution of Policy behind Taiwan's Development Success*, second edition. Singapore: World Scientific, 1995.

Liang Hui-ming. "Red Quinoa Proved to Fight Cancer." *China Times*, February 22, 2017. http://www.chinatimes.com/realtimenews/20170222005219-260405 (accessed August 4, 2017).

Liang Yuan-ling. "Cooking with Taiwanese Memory: The Famous Tatung Electric Pot." *News Lens*, June 23, 2016. https://international.thenewslens.com/article/42647 (accessed July 24, 2017).

Liao, David S., and I. Chiu Liao. "An Economic Evaluation of Shrimp Farming Industry in Taiwan." In *Shrimp Culture: Economics, Market, and Trade*, ed. Pingsun Leung and Carole R. Engle. Hoboken, NJ: John Wiley & Sons, 2008.

Liao, George. "Reconstruction of Huannan Market Starts Nov. 6." *Taiwan News*, November 6, 2016. https://www.taiwannews.com.tw/en/news/3023259 (accessed August 30, 2017).

———. "I-Mei Foods Begins Operation of Radiation Laboratory, a First for Taiwan's Private Sector." *Taiwan News*, August 3, 2017. https://www.taiwannews.com.tw/en/news/3225078 (accessed October 10, 2017).

Liberty Times. "Eight Tea Business-People Sentenced for Smuggling Chinese Tea." March 24, 2017. http://news.ltn.com.tw/news/society/paper/1088431 (accessed July 20, 2017).

Lien Heng. *General History of Taiwan*. Taipei: Youth Cultural Enterprise, 1977.

Lin, Enru. "Behind the US Pork Protest: What's Eating Taiwan's Swine Industry." *China Post*, June 6, 2016. http://www.chinapost.com.tw/taiwan/national/national-news/2016/06/06/468437/p1/behind-the.htm (accessed June 27, 2017).

Lin, Irene. "Court Convicts Bagel Shop Owner over Poppy Seeds." *Taipei Times*, May 4, 2001. http://www.taipeitimes.com/News/front/archives/2001 /05/04/0000084299 (accessed April 4, 2017).

Lin Yi-jing. "Taipei Traditional Markets to Reproduce Classic Good Tastes." *China Times*, April 10, 2017. http://www.chinatimes.com/realtimenews/ 20170410000942-260415 (accessed August 24, 2017).

Lin Yi-zhen. "Meet Taiwan Sake in Taoyuan Brewery." *China Times*, August 27, 2010. http://www.chinatimes.com/newspapers/20140827000177-260206 (accessed June 15, 2017).

Liu Chi-Wei. "Hog Island: Agricultural Protectionism, Food Dependency, and Impact of the International Food Regime in Taiwan." PhD diss., Graduate School of State University of New York, Binghamton, 2008.

Liu, Claudia, and Elaine Hou. "21% of Married Taiwanese Aged 35 and Above Live with Parents." *Focus Taiwan*, August 31, 2016. http://focustaiwan.tw/news/ asoc/201608310018.aspx (accessed August 4, 2017).

Liu Ts'ui-jung, and Shi-yung Liu. "Disease and Mortality in the History of Taiwan." In *Asian Population History*, ed. Ts'ui-jung Liu, James Lee, David Sven Reher, Osamu Saito, and Wang Feng. Oxford: Oxford University Press, 2001.

Liu Ying-feng. "Taiwan Quinoa: An Ancient Native Variety." *Taiwan Panorama*, January 2015.

———. "Advancing Peanut Oil's Local Legacy." *Taiwan Panorama*, August 2016.

Lu Yi-Chien, Ying Chin Lin, Yen-Kuang Lin, Yi-Jui Liu, Kwang-Hwa Chang, Poon-Ung Chieng, and Wing P. Chan. "Prevalence of Osteoporosis and Low Bone Mass in Older Chinese Population Based on Bone Mineral Density at Multiple Skeletal Sites." *Science Reports* 6 (2016): 25206. https://www.ncbi.nlm.nih .gov/pmc/articles/PMC4855183/ (accessed October 7, 2017).

Luxner, Larry. "Mr. Brown Coffee: Taiwan's Local Answer to Starbucks." *Luxner News*, October 2014. http://www.luxner.com/cgi-bin/view_article.cgi? articleID=2272 (accessed June 17, 2017).

Mackay, George Leslie. *From Far Formosa: The Island, Its People and Missions.* New York: F. H. Revell, 1895.

Mao Yu-kang and Chi Schive. "Agricultural and Industrial Development in Taiwan." In *Reference Papers on Economic Development and Prospects of the Republic of China*. Taipei: Ministry of Economic Affairs, 1991. https://pdfs .semanticscholar.org/4b20/8673c618f8903b1ece46bba80ff1394239d8.pdf (accessed April 19, 2017).

MataTaiwan. "Aboriginal Food Collection." November 19, 2013. https://www .matataiwan.com/2013/11/19/amis-paiwan-snail/ (accessed June 15, 2017).

———. "Amis, the People that Eat Frogs and . . . Tadpoles!" July 10, 2014, https://en.matataiwan.com/2014/07/amis-the-people-that-eat-frogs-and-tadpoles (accessed August 2, 2017).

————. "Mr Quinoa from Tjuwabar." July 22, 2017. https://www.matataiwan
.com/2017/07/22/mr-quinoa-from-tjuwabar/ (accessed August 2, 2017).

Mehra, Gagan. "E-commerce in Taiwan: Thriving Market, Huge Mobile." *Practical Ecommerce*, May 12, 2016. http://www.practicalecommerce.com/Ecom
merce-in-Taiwan-Thriving-Market-Huge-Mobile (accessed September 6, 2017).

Miles, Philip G., and Shu-Ting Chang. *Mushrooms: Cultivation, Nutritional Value,
Medicinal Effect, and Environmental Impact*. Boca Raton, FL: CRC Press, 2004.

Ministry of Economic Affairs (Taiwan). *Annual Report of Trade and Eating-
Drinking Places Activity Surveys*. April 2017. http://www.moea.gov.tw/mns/
dos_e/content/Content.aspx?menu_id=7030 (accessed July 6, 2017).

Moskowitz, Marc L. "Drinking Modernity: Sexuality and the Sanitation of Space
in Taiwan's Coffeeshops." In *Japanese Taiwan: Colonial Rule and its Contested
Legacy*, ed. Andrew D. Morris. London: Bloomsbury Academic, 2015.

Museum of Hakka Tourism and Cuisine in New Taipei City. "Ciba." http://www
.hakka-cuisine.ntpc.gov.tw/files/15-1006-3290,c394-1.php (accessed October
14, 2017).

National Museum of History. *Early Taiwanese Coffee Culture*. Taipei: National
Museum of History, 2008.

National Museum of Natural Science. "Agriculture in Taiwan (before 1945)."
October 1, 2008. http://www.nmns.edu.tw/nmns_eng/04exhibit/permanent/
permanent/Agricultural_Ecology/taiwan-1.htm (accessed April 14, 2017).

National Museum of Taiwan History. "Fishery." http://the.nmth.gov.tw/nmth/
en-US/Location/1adc22e6-961c-4598-86cd-5a506474c383 (accessed September
4, 2017).

————. "Nom Nom Taiwan: The Story of Dietary Culture." http://en.nmth.gov.tw/
exhibition_64_356.html (accessed August 8, 2017).

National Oceanic and Atmospheric Administration (US). "Americans Added
Nearly 1 Pound of Seafood to Their Diet in 2015." October 26, 2016. http://
www.noaa.gov/media-release/americans-added-nearly-1-pound-of-seafood-to
-their-diet-in-2015 (accessed May 15, 2017).

National Palace Museum. "The Three Best Friends in Winter." https://www.npm
.gov.tw/exh91/3friends/chinese/infor.htm (accessed October 18, 2017).

National Statistics (Taiwan). Survey of Family Income and Expenditure. http://
eng.stat.gov.tw/ct.asp?xItem=3417&CtNode=1596&mp=5 (accessed February
16, 2017).

————. *2010 Agriculture, Forestry, Fishery and Animal Husbandry Census*.
https://eng.stat.gov.tw/public/Data/332910175471.pdf (accessed April 20, 2017).

National Taiwan University, Department of Agronomy. "Ethnozoology of the Tsou,
Taiwan: Fishing with Poison." http://tk.agron.ntu.edu.tw/Segawa1/fishing_
poison.htm (accessed July 25, 2017).

———. "Revival of the NTU Eikichi Iso Memorial House: History of Taiwan's Favorite Rice." 2014. http://www.ntu.edu.tw/oldenglish/highlights/2014/he140325_1.html (accessed August 11, 2017).

Nielsen Company (US). "More Than Half of Taiwan Consumers Are Willing to Buy Groceries Online." July 16, 2015. http://www.nielsen.com/tw/en/insights/reports/2015/taiwan-consumer-online-grocery-shopping-2015en.html (accessed September 6, 2017).

Overseas Community Affairs Council. "Roxburgh Sumac." http://edu.ocac.gov.tw/local/nature/e/se/se3a02.htm (accessed August 10, 2017).

Pan Chiang-tung. "Hakka Rice Food." Museum of Hakka Tourism and Cuisine in New Taipei City. http://www.hakka-cuisine.ntpc.gov.tw/files/11-1006-394.php (accessed October 11, 2017).

Pan Fuh-jiunn. *Atlas of Botanical Idioms*. Taipei: Owl Publishing House, 2002.

———. *Formosa Plant Culture: 101 Taiwan Plant Species & 27 Plant Issues*. Taipei: Yuan-Liou Publishing, 2014.

Pan Wen-Harn, Hsing-Juan Wu, Chih-Jung Yeh, Shao-Yuan Chuang, Hsing-Yi Chang, Nai-Hua Yeh, and Yao-Te Hsieh. "Diet and Health Trends in Taiwan: Comparison of Two Nutrition and Health Surveys from 1993–1996 and 2005–2008." *Asia Pacific Journal of Clinical Nutrition* 20, no. 2 (2011). http://www.apjcn.org/update%5Cpdf%5C2011%5C2%5C238-250%5C238.pdf (accessed April 20, 2017).

Pang Rice Dumplings. "What Is Commonly Used to Wrap Dumplings?" https://www.pangrice.com.tw/leafs/ (accessed October 13, 2017).

Papademetriou, M. K. "Rice Production in the Asia-Pacific Region: Issues and Perspectives." UN Food and Agriculture Organization. http://www.fao.org/3/a-x6905e/x6905e04.htm (accessed April 25, 2017).

Pei, Kurtis. "Hunting System of the Rukai Tribe in Taiwan." Institute of Wildlife Conservation, National Pingtung University of Science and Technology. http://tk.agron.ntu.edu.tw/ethnozoo/Rukai-hunting%20systsm.pdf (accessed June 18, 2017).

Peng Hsin-yi. "A Good Drink Worth the Trip: Ms. Ceng Chan Yu-cin's Millet Wine." Maritime Capital Kaohsiung, March 9, 2013. http://kcginfo.kcg.gov.tw/Publish_Content.aspx?n=A22859B204186560&sms=6A6B57F5FE966020&s=D49F29449A4C6183&chapt=7428&sort=1 (accessed October 5, 2017).

Pereira, J. A., and E. P. Guimaraes. "History of Rice in Latin America." In *Rice: Origin, Antiquity and History*. ed. S. D. Sharma. Boca Raton, FL: CRC Press, 2010.

Phillips, Carolyn. "About Me." Madame Huang's Kitchen. http://carolynjphillips.blogspot.tw/p/welcome-to-my-food-blog-heres-little.html (accessed January 10, 2018).

———. "For Double Ninth Festival, a Cake of Nine Layers." *Zester Daily*, October 19, 2012. http://zesterdaily.com/cooking/for-double-ninth-festival-a-cake-of -nine-layers/ (accessed October 4, 2017).

Pickering, William A. *Pioneering in Formosa: Recollections of Adventures among Mandarins, Wreckers, & Head-Hunting Savages.* London: Hurst & Blackett, 1898.

———. "Among the Savages of Central Formosa, 1866–1867." *The Messenger and Missionary Record of the Presbyterian Church of England*, n.s. 3.

Ping Ming Health. "Warming and Cooling Characteristics of Common Foods." September 14, 2012. http://www.pingminghealth.com/article/581/warming-and -cooling-characteristics-of-common-foods/ (accessed October 7, 2017).

Pork Checkoff. "World Per Capita Pork Consumption." July 11, 2016. http:// www.pork.org/pork-quick-facts/home/stats/u-s-pork-exports/world-per-capita -pork-consumption-2/ (accessed June 24, 2017).

The Poultry Site. "USDA International Egg and Poultry." March 11, 2015. http:// www.thepoultrysite.com/reports/?id=4977 (accessed June 27, 2017).

Prentice, David. "Taiwan's Little Burma." *The Diplomat*, March 18, 2017. http:// thediplomat.com/2017/03/taiwans-little-burma/ (accessed September 28, 2017).

Purchon, R. D. *The Biology of the Mollusca.* Amsterdam: Elsevier, 2013.

Quartly, Jules. "Taipei Coffee Culture: Rich, Robust, and Satisfying." *Taiwan Business Topics*, January 2015.

Reitaku School. "A Summary of Teng-hui Lee's Life and How He Democratized Taiwan." http://www.hs.reitaku.jp/english/ic/rpaper/2004/lee/body.htm (accessed November 5, 2017).

Roy, Denny. *Taiwan: A Political History.* Ithaca, NY: Cornell University Press, 2003.

Santa Cruz Organic Store. "Shops." http://www.santacruz.com.tw/htmlpages/shop Location.html (accessed July 10, 2017).

Sanxing District Farmers Association. *Outstanding Female Farmers Data Book.* Yilan: Sanxing District Farmers Association, 2005.

Sauer, Abe. "When Almonds Are Apricots: A Tale of Naming Woes in China." *Brandchannel.com*, March 14, 2013. http://brandchannel.com/2013/03/14/when -almonds-are-apricots-a-tale-of-naming-woes-in-china (accessed October 17, 2017).

Schirokauer, Conrad, Miranda Brown, David Lurie, and Suzanne Gay. *A Brief History of Chinese and Japanese Civilizations.* Boston: Cengage Learning, 2012.

Selya, Roger Mark. *Development and Demographic Change in Taiwan.* Singapore: World Scientific, 2004.

Seydewitz, Joe. "Kinmen Lives on Kaoliang." *Taiwan Business Topics*, January 2014.

Shapiro, Don. "Din Tai Fung: Taiwan's Culinary Icon." *Taiwan Business Topics*, January 2015.

Shepherd, John Robert. *Statecraft and Political Economy on the Taiwan Frontier 1600–1800*. Taipei: SMC Publishing, 1995.

Sheridan, Nina. "Fast-Food Chains Thrive in Taiwan." *Taiwan Business Topics*, November 2016.

Shih, Sandra. "Sorghum Liquor Helps Build Kinmen's Fortunes." *Taiwan Today*, October 18, 2007. http://taiwantoday.tw/news.php?unit=18,23,45,18&post=24148 (accessed October 5, 2017).

Shunk, Laura. "5 Reasons Why Taipei Is the Best Food City in the World." *Tasting Table*, April 25, 2017. https://www.tastingtable.com/travel/national/best-food-eats-taipei (accessed January 6, 2018).

Shurtleff, William, H. T. Huang, and Akiko Aoyagi. *History of Soybeans and Soyfoods in China and Taiwan, and in Chinese Cookbooks, Restaurants, and Chinese Work with Soyfoods Outside China (1024 BCE to 2014)*. Lafayette: Soyinfo Center, 2014.

Shurtleff, William, and Akiko Aoyagi. *Early History of Soybeans and Soyfoods Worldwide (1900–1923)*. Lafayette, CA: Soyinfo Center, 2014.

———. *History of Soybeans and Soyfoods in the Netherlands, Belgium and Luxembourg (1647–2015)*. Lafayette, CA: Soyinfo Center, 2015.

———. *History of Soybean Crushing: Soy Oil and Soybean Meal (980–2016)*. Lafayette, CA: Soyinfo Center, 2016.

Simoons, Frederick J. *Food in China: A Cultural and Historical Inquiry*. Boca Raton, FL: CRC Press, 1990.

Steere, J. B. "Formosa." *Journal of the American Geographical Society of New York* 6 (1876): 306.

Strak, John. "Taiwan's Challenging Future in Pig Farming." *Pig Progress*, October 21, 2015. http://www.pigprogress.net/Finishers/Articles/2015/10/Taiwans-challenging-future-in-pig-farming-2669362W/ (accessed April 21, 2017).

Stratfor Worldview. "Taiwan's Ruling Party Suffers after Elections." December 3, 2014. https://worldview.stratfor.com/article/taiwans-ruling-party-suffers-after-elections (accessed August 25, 2017).

Su Heng-an. "Cross-Bordered Hybrid-Creolization: Construction and Re-presentation of Gangshan Goat-Meat Eating Culture." *Journal of Dietary Culture* 9, no. 1 (2013).

Sui, Cindy. "Taiwan Transition: From City Life to the Countryside." BBC, November 26, 2014. http://www.bbc.com/news/business-30204720 (accessed April 14, 2017).

Sun Yin-rui. "History of Beef as a Food for Taiwanese." Master's thesis, National Central University, Zhongli, 2001.

Swinhoe, Robert. "Notes on the Island of Formosa." *Journal of the Royal Geographical Society of London* 34 (1864).

Taintor, Edward C. *The Aborigines of Northern Formosa: A Paper Read before the North China Branch of the Royal Asiatic Society.* Shanghai: Customs Press, 1874.

Taipei City Government, Department of Information Technology. "Demographic Overview." December 12, 2017. http://tcgwww.taipei.gov.tw/fp.asp?fpage=cp&xItem=1084529&ctNode=29491&mp=100002 (accessed January 11, 2018).

Taipei Times. "Taiwan Faces Tough WTO Fight to Slash Rice Wine Tax." August 20, 2010. http://www.taipeitimes.com/News/biz/archives/2010/08/20/2003480856 (accessed October 2, 2017).

———. "Lung Cancer Is Top Killer of Women, Study Shows." November 14, 2014. http://www.taipeitimes.com/News/taiwan/archives/2014/11/14/2003604417 (accessed July 24, 2017).

———. "Kinmen Kaoliang Liquor Wins Global Awards for Baijiu." May 8, 2016. http://www.taipeitimes.com/News/taiwan/archives/2016/05/08/2003645788 (accessed October 2, 2017).

———. "Organic Farming to Be Prioritized: COA." May 31, 2016. http://www.taipeitimes.com/News/taiwan/archives/2016/05/31/2003647558 (accessed June 20, 2017).

Taipei Water Park. "Period of Taipei Water Source Site." June 3, 2015. http://engwaterpark.water.taipei/ct.asp?xItem=99268439&ctNode=77645&mp=114022 (accessed August 7, 2017).

Taitung County Government. "*Trichodesma calycosum.*" http://fresh.ownlines.com/inside.php?oi=35 (accessed September 4, 2017).

Taiwan Historica, Entry 002385. In *Dictionary of Taiwan Folk Artifacts.* http://dict.th.gov.tw/term/view/2385 (accessed October 10, 2017).

———. Entry 002389. In *Dictionary of Taiwan Folk Artifacts.* http://dict.th.gov.tw/term/view/2389 (accessed October 13, 2017).

Taiwan Indigenous Culture Park. "Atayal Tribe." http://www.tacp.gov.tw/tacpeng/home02_3.aspx?ID=$3041&IDK=2& (accessed June 17, 2017).

Taiwan Sugar Corp. "Brief—Research & Development." http://www.taisugar.com.tw/english/CP.aspx?s=13&n=10047 (accessed June 13, 2017).

Taiwan Tea Corp. "History of Taiwanese Teas." http://www.ttch.com.tw/index.php?categoryid=99 (accessed September 1, 2017).

TaiwanTeaCrafts.com. "Going Wild for Shan Cha: Hunting Down Taiwan's Indigenous Tea Tree." July 18, 2013. https://www.taiwanteacrafts.com/2013/07/18/going-wild-for-shan-cha-hunting-down-taiwans-indigenous-tea-tree/ (accessed September 1, 2017).

Taiwan Today. "The Fruits of Foreign Trade." October 31, 2006. http://taiwantoday .tw/news.php?unit=8,29,32,45&post=12792 (accessed May 3, 2017).

———. "Study Confirms Earlier Human Activity in Taiwan." July 24, 2009. https://taiwantoday.tw/news.php?unit=10,23,45,10&post=15558 (accessed May 19, 2017).

———. "Champion Roaster Takes Taiwan Coffee to Next Level." March 10, 2016. http://taiwantoday.tw/news.php?unit=10,23,10&post=21686 (accessed June 22, 2017).

Taylor, George. "A Ramble through Southern Formosa." *China Review* 16 (1888): 137–61. http://www.reed.edu/Formosa/texts/Taylor1888.html (accessed May 22, 2017).

Teng, Cathy. "Soy Sauce: Fermenting for Four Generations." *Taiwan Panorama*, October 2016.

———. "Let's Get Sauced! Taiwan's Great Old Sauces." *Taiwan Panorama*, October 2016.

Teng, Emma Jinhua. "Taiwan in the Chinese Imagination, 17th–19th Centuries." *Asia-Pacific Journal* 5 (June 4, 2007). http://apjjf.org/-Emma-Jinhua-Teng/2450/ article.html (accessed August 10, 2017).

Ter, Dana. "Tea-sing Flavors." *Travel in Taiwan*, March–April 2016.

Thomson, John. *The Straits of Malacca, Indo-China and China or Ten Years' Travels, Adventures and Residence Abroad.* London: Sampson Low, Marston, Low, & Searle, 1875.

Tong, Elson. "Taiwan Bans the Consumption of Cat and Dog Meat." *Hong Kong Free Press*, April 11, 2017. https://www.hongkongfp.com/2017/04/11/taiwan -becomes-first-country-asia-ban-consumption-cat-dog-meat/ (accessed June 12, 2017).

Tsai, Chiung-Tzu Lucetta. "Culinary Tourism and Night Markets in Taiwan." *International Journal of Business and Information* 8, no. 2 (December 2013).

Tsai Ling-Long, Pei-Chun Wu, Mei-Yun Wang, and Chia-Ju Weng. "Analysis of Customer Channel Selection between Traditional Market and Supermarket." *Journal of Far East University* (March 2006). http://www.feu.edu.tw/adms/aao/ aao95/jfeu/23/230115.pdf (accessed July 27, 2017).

Tsai Wenting. "A Century of Rice Wine Culture." *Taiwan Panorama*, February 2003.

Tsang Cheng-Hwa. "Recent Discoveries at the Tapenkeng Culture Sites in Taiwan." In *The Peopling of East Asia: Putting Together Archaeology, Linguistics and Genetics*, ed. Roger Blench, Laurent Sagart, and Alicia Sanchez-Mazas. Abingdon, UK: Routledge, 2005.

Tsang Cheng-Hwa, Kuang-ti Li, Tze-Fu Hsu, Yuan-Ching Tsai, Po-Hsuan Fang, and Yue-Ie Caroline Hsing. "Broomcorn and Foxtail Millet Were Cultivated in Taiwan about 5,000 Years Ago." *Botanical Studies* 58, no. 1 (2017): 3.

Tsao Ming-chung. *The Humble Life of Oyster Omelet: Taiwan Food-Name Facts.* Taipei: Owl Publishing House, 2016.

Tseng Lin-Yi. "The Wu Yuan-Sheng Family and Changes in Taipei's Sha-cha (Satay) Hot Pot Businesses (1950s–1980s)." *Journal of Chinese Dietary Culture* 12, no. 1 (2016).

Tseng Pintsang. "Taiwanese Cuisine in the Japanese Era." *Dong Hwa Journal of Humanities and Social Science Online*, December 2014. http://journal.ndhu.edu .tw/e_paper/e_paper_c.php?SID=56 (accessed August 11, 2017).

Tseng Wan-lin. "The Development of Hawkers in Taiwan over 100 Years." *United Daily News*, January 16, 2017. https://reader.udn.com/reader/story/7923/2233405 (accessed September 18, 2017).

Tzeng, Emmanuelle, and Y. F. Low. "Animal Health Body to List Taiwan as FMD-Free with Vaccination." *Focus Taiwan*, May 22, 2017. http://focustaiwan.tw/ news/asoc/201705220008.aspx (accessed June 23, 2017).

Tzeng Min-Su, Mei-Ding Kao, Wen-Ting Yeh, and Wen-Harn Pan. "Food Consumption Frequency and Eating Habits among Taiwanese." *Nutritional Sciences Journal* 24, no. 1 (1999): 63.

University of Arkansas. "Per Capita Rice Consumption of Selected Countries." http://www.uark.edu/ua/ricersch/pdfs/per_capita_rice_consumption_of_selected _countries.pdf (accessed May 3, 2017).

USDA Foreign Agricultural Service. "Taiwan: Fresh Deciduous Fruit Annual." November 1, 2010. https://gain.fas.usda.gov/Recent%20GAIN%20Publications/ Fresh%20Deciduous%20Fruit%20Annual_Taipei_Taiwan_11-1-2010.pdf (accessed June 9, 2017).

———. "Taiwan Expands GE Regulations." July 15, 2015. https://gain.fas.usda .gov/Recent%20GAIN%20Publications/Agricultural%20Biotechnology%20 Annual_Taipei_Taiwan_7-15-2015.pdf (accessed September 6, 2017).

———. "Taiwan: Grain and Feed Annual." April 13, 2016. https://www.fas.usda .gov/data/taiwan-grain-and-feed-annual-0 (accessed April 3, 2017).

———. *Taiwan: 2016 Dairy and Products Annual.* October 17, 2016. https://gain .fas.usda.gov/Recent%20GAIN%20Publications/Dairy%20and%20Products %20Annual_Taipei_Taiwan_10-17-2016.pdf (accessed May 2, 2017).

Wan Tsung-Yun. *Home-Style Taiwanese Cooking.* Singapore: Marshall Cavendish International Asia, 2014.

Watanbe, Zenjiro. "The Meat-Eating Culture of Japan at the Beginning of Westernization." Kikkoman Corporation. https://www.kikkoman.co.jp/kiifc/foodculture/ pdf_09/e_002_008.pdf (accessed April 27, 2017).

Weaver, Scott. "The Blossoming of the Taiwan Whisky Market." *Taiwan Business Topics*, January 2015.

———. "Post-Monopoly Prosperity." *Taiwan Review*, April 2015.

———. "Dadaocheng: New Life in a Historic District." *Taiwan Business Topics*, July 2016.

Wehring, Olly. "San Francisco World Spirits Competition 2017, The Award Winners—Part I." Just-Drinks, May 16, 2017. https://www.just-drinks.com/news/san-francisco-world-spirits-competition-2017-the-award-winners-part-i_id123092.aspx (accessed October 2, 2017).

White, Lynn T., III. "Taiwan and Globalization." In *East Asia and Globalization*, ed. Samuel S. Kim. Lanham, MD: Rowman & Littlefield, 2000.

Wikipedia. "Mongolian Barbecue." https://en.wikipedia.org/wiki/Mongolian_barbecue (accessed September 11, 2017).

———. "Taipei." https://en.wikipedia.org/wiki/Taipei (accessed January 11, 2018).

———. "Warriors of the Rainbow: Seediq Bale." https://en.wikipedia.org/wiki/Warriors_of_the_Rainbow:_Seediq_Bale (accessed October 5, 2017).

Williams, Jack F. "Sugar: The Sweetener in Taiwan's Development." In *China's Island Frontier*, ed. Ronald G. Knapp. Taipei: SMC Publishing, 1980.

Wills, John E., Jr. "The Seventeenth-Century Transformation." In *Taiwan: A New History*, ed. Murray A. Rubinstein. Abingdon, UK: Routledge, 2015.

Woo, Elaine. "Master Chef Brought Cuisine to the Masses." *Los Angeles Times*, August 14, 2004. http://www.latimes.com/local/la-me-julia-child-20040814-story.html (accessed October 17, 2017).

World Bank. *Exporting High-Value Food Commodities: Success Stories from Developing Countries Parts 63–198*. Washington, DC: World Bank, 1993.

World Business and Investment Library. *Taiwan: Doing Business and Investing in Taiwan Guide Volume 1 Strategic and Practical Information*. New York: IBP, 2015.

Wu, Amber. "Hypermarkets Battle for Hearts and Minds of Island's Consumers." *Taiwan Today*, February 14, 2008. http://taiwantoday.tw/news.php?unit=10,23,45,10&post=14713 (accessed August 23, 2017).

Wu Che-hao and Y. F. Low. "Vietnamese Tea Found Being Passed Off as Taiwanese." *Focus Taiwan*, June 13, 2017. http://focustaiwan.tw/news/asoc/201706130017.aspx (accessed August 25, 2017).

Wu, David Y. H. "Cultural Nostalgia and Global Imagination: Japanese Cuisine in Taiwan." In *Re-orienting Cuisine: East Asian Foodways in the Twenty-First Century*, ed. Kwang Ok Kim. New York: Berghahn Books, 2015.

Wu Hsin-yun and Kuo Chung-han. "Taiwanese Barista Named 2016 World Champion." *Focus Taiwan*, June 26, 2016. http://focustaiwan.tw/news/asoc/201606260020.aspx (accessed June 22, 2017).

Wu San-Lien Foundation for Taiwan Historical Materials. "Taiwan's Early Alcohol Bottle Labels." http://www.twcenter.org.tw/thematic_series/images_series/taiwan_impression/tw_wine_label (accessed June 15, 2017).

Wufeng Farmers' Association Distillery. "About." http://www.twwfsake.com/about.php (accessed June 15, 2017).

Yan, Kuang-tao. "ROC Year 99 Taiwan Forever: State Banquets." *China Times*, January 22, 2010. http://www.cdnews.com.tw/cdnews_site/docDetail.jsp?coluid=108&docid=101043223 (accessed November 4, 2017).

Yang Chao-Chin. "Preliminary Study and Analysis of Aboriginal Dietary Culture." Seminar on Sustainable Management of Tourism Leisure and Catering Industry, April 27, 2002. http://ir.nkuht.edu.tw/retrieve/2129/02-021.pdf (accessed September 14, 2017).

Yang Min-Hsien and I. Han. "Policy Analysis of Implementation of 'Small Landlord Big Tenant' in Taiwan." Food and Fertilizer Technology Center for the Asian and Pacific Region, May 4, 2015. http://ap.fftc.agnet.org/ap_db.php?id=421 (accessed April 14, 2017).

Yang Ming-tu. "Going Back into a Future of Simplicity: Taiwan Aborigines' Sustainable Utilization of Natural Resources." In *Ecocriticism in Taiwan: Identity, Environment, and the Arts*, ed. Chia-ju Chang and Scott Slovic. Lanham, MD: Lexington Books, 2016.

Yang Ya-min. "Daughter Takes Over Bullhead Sauce." *Liberty Times*, November 14, 2007. http://news.ltn.com.tw/news/business/paper/168018 (accessed September 26, 2017).

Yang Yen-chieh. "Hakka and Hakka Food Culture." In *4th China Food Culture Symposium Proceedings (2000)*. Taipei: Foundation of Chinese Dietary Culture.

Yushan National Park. "Bunun Tribe." http://www.ysnp.gov.tw/css_en/page.aspx?path=857 (accessed June 17, 2017).

Zhou, Laura. "Taiwan Keeps Ban on Food from Japanese Radiation Zones." *South China Morning Post*, December 17, 2016. http://www.scmp.com/news/china/article/2055245/taiwan-keeps-ban-food-japanese-radiation-zones (accessed September 2, 2017).

Index

Page references for photos and maps are italicized

aborigines. *See* indigenous people and their foodways

additives. *See* food safety

adzuki beans, 44, *45*, 65, 80, 91, 92, 127

agriculture, 6, 7, 9, 10, 11, 14, 15, 17, 22, 28, 31, 52, 56, 97–118, *113*, 132, 151, 154–56, 159, 160; government policies and improvements, 21, 83, 98, 100, 109, 151, 170–71; by indigenous people, *8*, 18, 21, *105*, 117, 118, 162

alcohol: for cooking, 128, 161; for drinking, 14, 51, 82, 95, 126–27, 133, 137, 149–50, 156–63, *163*; food to accompany, 150, 170. *See also* rice wine

Americans, 12, 16, 20, 24, 43, 54, 138

animal feed, 30, 43, 54, 103, 104, 107–8, 109, 110, 112

archaeological evidence, 7–10, 17–18

Austronesian people. *See* indigenous people and their foodways; agriculture, by indigenous people

bamboo: as food, 14, 64, 89, 90, 91, 102, 119, 121, 129, 137; used in farming, gathering, eating, and preparing food, 13–14, 24, 38, 78, 82, 88, 110, 111, 120

banana, 10, 16, 65, 72, 82, 105, 106

banquets (bando), ix, 35, 46, 58, 66, 72, 74, 81, 84–94, *87*, *90*, 95, 136, 140, 149, 168

barbecuing and grilling, ix, 9, 12, 20, 41, 47, 81, 89, 111, 129, 130, 139, 172

barley, 14, 27, 65, 160, 164; tea made from, 138, 149

bars, beer-houses, and pubs, 127, 146, 150, 158, 173

basil, 16, 22, 38, 41, 64–65, 150, 171, 172

beef, 43, 49, 53–56, 73, 86, 97, 129, *136*, 139, 154, 167, 174; noodles, 35, 55, 61, 74, 173, 183; soup, 180–81. *See also* buffalo

beer and brewing, 80, 126–27, 134, 142–43, 150, 156–58. *See also* alcohol

bento. *See* lunchboxes

birds, wild, 9, 89

braising, ix, 26, 32, 35, 38, 45, 46, 48, 58, 108, 109, 111, 122, 129, 166, 170, 180–81

bread and baked goods, 25, 35, 66–69, 80–81, 100, 134, 152, 168, 173

breakfast, 15, 35, 56, 62, 129, 134, 164, 174

Buddhism, 50–51, 53, 71, 117. *See also* food offerings; religion

buffalo: draft animals, 53, 118; for meat ,16, 53–54

cabbage, 14, 35, 43, 44, 45, 54, 61, 64, 91, 102, 117, 120, 167, 174

cakes. *See* bread and baked goods

cannibalism, 57

cereals. *See* barley; corn; djulis; millet; sorghum; wheat

cheese, 42, 56, 67, 69, 192

Chen, Ivy, 172–73, 185

Cheng, Angela, 167–68, 183

Chen Shui-bian, 26, 93

Chiang, Andre, 145–47, 169, 174–77, *175*

Chiang Kai-shek. *See* Kuomintang

Chiayi, 12, 93, 109, 121

chicken: eggs, 12, 19, 22, 25, 35, 37, 38, 41, 42, 45, 48, 54, 61, 66, 67, 68, 73, 77, 78, 86, 89, 91, 95, 103, 108, 110–11, 143, 144, 159, 169, 174; meat, 10, 21, 31, 33, 34, 54, 62, 64, 69, 73, 83, 88, 90–91, 95, 105, 109–10, 114, 121, 137, 138, 140–41, 150, 159, 167, 170, *171*, 172, 173, 174, 189–90; stock, 16, 42, 86, 90, 91

chili, 16, 32, 35, 44, 63, 89, 91, 101, 142, 173

Chinese Nationalists. *See* Kuomintang

Chinese New Year. *See* Lunar New Year

Chiu, Mingchin, 169–70, 181, 187

chopsticks. *See* utensils

climate, x, 42, 98, 101, 105, 115, 160

coffee: canned, 152–53, 159, 162; fresh, 26, 50, 56, 62, 93, 151–53, 159, 162

convenience stores, 26, 46, 111, 119, 120, 133–34, 140, 150, 188

cookbooks, ix, 24, 166, 167–69

corn, 45, 49, 54–55, 90–91, 97, 109, 110, 146

Council of Agriculture (COA), 98, 100, 102, 110, 116, 117, 122, 155, 170–71

crabs, ix, 10, 15, 41, 42, 58, 73, 120, 129, 141, 161

culinary education, 165–68, 172–74, 175–77

curries, 16, 49–50, 59, 62, 133–34, 145, 168

Dadaocheng, 5, 68, 92, 125–26, 130, 152, 154

daikon (radish), 43, 46, 48, 49, 50, 64, 75, 76, 77, 78, 83, 86, 102, 141, 170

desserts and puddings, 44, 65, 66, 73, 92, 93, 107, 135, 144

dieting and weight loss, 118, 134

djulis, *8*, 9, 78, 118, 127, 162

dogs, 15; used as food, 10, 57, 73

DPP (Democratic Progressive Party), 61, 93, 94

duck: eggs, 83, 110; meat and blood, 45, 73, 83, 90, 109, 110, 121, 139

dumplings, 24, 29, 32, 55, 59–60, 61, 77–78, 108, 121, 131, 139, 141, 167, 173

Dutch, 4, 9, 10, 14, 19, 26, 98, 101, 103, 104, 105, 161

exported foods, 53, 101, 103, 104, 106, 107, 111, 114, 120, 151, 153

Facebook. *See* social media

farming. *See* agriculture

fast food, 38, 59, 69, 152, 164, 176

female: chefs and cooks, 21, 85, 131, 165–73, 177; entrepreneurs, 44, 51, 121, 127–28, 138, 162

fermented foods, 12, 26–30, *27*, 32, 34, 44, 55, 64, 169–70, 174

festivals and festival foods, 60, 64, 65, 71–82, 85, 121, 122, 144, 161

fish, 11, 12, 18, 19–20, 21, 24, 25, 26, 32, 33, 35, 37, 45, 47, 48, 49, 72–73, 80, 81, 82, 88, 89, 91, 93, 95, 120, *136*, 138, 144, 146, 167, 169–70, 173, 179–80; fishing/fisheries, 7, 9, 10, 13, 40–41, 98, 111–13; roe, 19, 86, *112*, 170. *See also* seafood

food in local media/books, ix, 25, 26, 35, 38, 59, 62, 80, 86, 93, 127, 130, 143, 145, 165, 167, 169. *See also* social media

food offerings, 33, 65, 71–74, 75, 76–77, 78, 79–80, 82, 95, 184

food safety, 31, 54, 69, 86, 94, 115, 131–33, 158, 169

food security, 97–98

food waste, 73, 108, 117, 127

foraged foods, 7, 8, 9, 11, 15–16, 17–19, 20, 75, 99, 107, 151, 171

frogs, 16–17, 64

fruits, 10, 14, 63, 66, 67, 68, 72, 79, 81, 100, 104–7, 117, 120–21, 146, 156, 158; juices, 25, 90, 131, 164, 170, 172. *See also* banana; pineapple; mango

Fu Pei-mei, 165–66, 167, 168, 183

Fujian, 4, 5, 10, 16, 17, 19, 58, 62, 71, 75, 98, 99, 103, 138, 151

garlic, 9, 12, 14, 16, 32, 38, 41, 43, 50, 51, 64, 65, 78, 86, 89, 91, 92, 94, 102, 108, 110, 121, 129, 140, 142, 150
gathering. *See* foraged foods
ginger, 12, 14, 16, 19, 21, 32, 33, 35, 44, 45, 50, 74, 77, 78, 83, 89, 95, 102, 108, 118, 121, 140, 154, 170, 172
GM foods, 28, 98
goat: meat, 9, 11, 56; milk, 56
goose: eggs, 111; meat, 88, 103, 109
grilling. *See* barbecuing and grilling
guabao, 58, 81–82, 138, 172, 173, 185–86
Guangdong, 5, 62, 71, 103, 141, 166

Hakka people and their foodways, 5, 16, 17, 62–65, 72, 73, 74–76, 78, 93, 103, 118, 121, 143–44
halal food, 55, 62, 145
healthy eating, 19, 25, 34, 40, 83, 107, 117, 138, 164, 167, 169, 171. *See also* dieting and weight loss
honey/honeycomb, 13, 44, 67, 82, 102, 107, 137, 164
hot pot, 26–27, 56, 76, 83, 86, 91, 114, 141–43, 181–83
Hsinchu, 48, 63, 64, 116, 128, 169
Hsu, Sean A., 139–40, 180
Hualien, 18
hunting and trapping, 9, 10, 11–14, 15, 17, 99

idioms, food-related, 14, 20, 35, 81, 103, 165
imported foods and ingredients, 21, 28, 31, 43, 52, 55, 56, 67, 72, 80, 97–98, 99, 100, 102, 109, 116, 117, 118, 119, 122, 127, 133, 146, 149, 152, 154, 155, 156, 158, 159
indigenous people and their foodways, 4, 5, *8*, 9–10, 11–14, 15, 16, 17–18, 19–22, 24, 63, 82, 93, 103, 151, 154, 161–62; restaurants, 21, 137, 171–72. *See also* agriculture, by indigenous people
irrigation, 8, 20, 98, 99

Jaian, Zoe, 189
Japanese: colonial period and policy, ix, 1, 5, 13, 45, 56, 71, 74, 84, 92, 99, 100, 101, 104, 109, 136, 151, 152, 156, 162; cuisine and restaurants, 45, 46–50, 133–34, 135, 138, 139, 146; foods exported or introduced to Taiwan, 15, 22, 26, 27, 43, 53–54, 56, 66, 67, 69, 103, 105, 133; sake, 158–59

Kaohsiung, 19, 85, *105*, 121, 127, 158
Keelung, 4, 23, 79, 128–29
kitchens/kitchen equipment, 23–26, 48, 76, 164
Kuomintang (KMT), 5–6, 47, 54, 55, 56, 61, 66, 68, 92, 93, 104, 132, 160
konnyaku, 65, 144, *145*

lamb and mutton, 33, 83, 86, 129, *136*, 139
lard, 30, 31, 80, 92, 132, 182, 184
Lee Teng-hui, 6, 66, 92
leftovers, 25, 65, 82, 86, 91, 107, 109, 138. *See also* food waste
Liao, Morgan, 193
Lin Ming-tsan, 85–92, *90*, 168, 179, 181–82, 184
liquor. *See* alcohol, for drinking
Lunar New Year, 24, 33, 64, 76–77, 106
lunchboxes (bento boxes), 23, 38, 44, 48, 133, 134

mainland Chinese foods, 6, 24, 33, 48, 55, 60–61, 124, 130–31, 138, 140–42, 166
mango, 20, 104, 106, 156
maqaw, 20–21, 137, *171*, 172, 179
marketing of food and restaurants, 38–40, 49, 59, 62, 64, 67, 101, 116, 118, 126–27, 129, 139–40, 143
markets, 26, 40, 60, 61, 103, 109, 116–17, 119–23, 124–25. *See also* night markets; supermarkets
medicinal foods and drinks, 19, 21, 42, 45, 57, 66, 83, 89, 95, 127, 154, 162
Miaoli, 63
military dependents' villages. *See* mainland Chinese foods
milk and dairy products, 26, 51, 52, 54, 56, 65, 66, 67, 69, 74, 102, 144, 153, 154, 160, 162, 164. *See also* cheese

millet, ix, 7–8, 9, 10, 12, 13, 14, 37, 82,
    137, 161–62, 172
mochi, 76, 80, 82, 93
monosodium glutamate (MSG), 34–35, 94,
    111, 167
mushrooms and edible fungus, 14, 19, 32,
    35, 43, 45, 52, 64, 74, 75, 77, 81, 82, 89,
    91, 95, 98, 102, *113*, 113–15, 121, 126,
    128, 137, 144, 150, 159, 164, 167, 169

Nantou, 22, 115, 121, 144, 159
night markets, 40, *41*, 42, 46, *49*, 58, 102,
    107, 110, 111, 128–31, 133, 146, 168,
    173. *See also* snacks; street food
noodles, 32, 35, *39*, 42, 45, 46, 47, 59, 60,
    77, 89, 129, 131, 134, *136*, 139; rice, 61,
    64, 75, 81, 102, 126, 128, 144. *See also*
    beef, noodles
nuts, seeds, and drupes, 10, 17–18, *18*, 30,
    52, 63, 65, 72, 75, 78, 80, 83, 86, 91, 95,
    101, 107, 126, 127, 128, 142, 154, 166.
    See also peanuts; sesame

offal, 12, 41, 45, 64, 86, 95, 98
oils for cooking, 14, 23, 24, 30–32, 35, 43,
    44, 60, 62, 83, 84, 90, 95, 110, 126, 132,
    140, 150, 167, 170, 172
organic foods/farming, 28, 52, 115–18, 164,
    170

Pan, Penny, 168
peanuts, 44, 58, 65, 66, 75, 76, 77, 78, 95,
    142, 144, 150, 154; oil, 30–31
pickling and pickles, 12, 14, 18, *18*, 21,
    29, 44, 48, 58, 63, 64, 88, 102, 110,
    118, 121, 129, 174, 189. *See also*
    preservatives and preservation
    methods
pineapple, 30, 63, 64, 66, 67, 72, 79, 80,
    90, 105, 106, 121, 150, 156, 192
ponlai. *See* rice
pork and pig products, 12, 14, 15, 18, 19,
    25, 29, 35, 38, 41, 42, 44, 46, 49, 54,
    58, 59, 61, 63, 65, 73, 77, 78, 81, 88,
    89, 91, 95, 102, 107–10, 121, 122, 128,
    129, 132, 133, 134, 138, 141, 143, 166,
    174, 182
postpartum foods, 94–95, 167
potato, 34, 49, 90, 102, 146, 176

preservatives and preservation methods,
    11–12, 66, 69, 73, 110, 164. *See also*
    pickling and pickles; refrigeration and
    freezing; salt
Puli. *See* Nantou

"Q," 74, 76, 78, 144, 189
Qing Dynasty, 4–5, 11, 17, 37, 53, 57, 65,
    99
quinoa. *See* djulis

rabbit meat, 15, 57
radish. *See* daikon
raw foods, 12, 14, 15, 22, 32, 161
ready-cooked food and ready meals, 121,
    122, 133–34
recipes, 40, 49–50, 60–61, 91, 92, 167, 168,
    179–94
refrigeration and freezing, 21, 26, 88, 119,
    122, 133–34, 138, 158, 172
religion, 33, 51, 52–53, 56, 71, 76, 82, 85,
    128. *See also* Buddhism; food offerings
restaurants: famous, 46, 59, 137, 140–41,
    145–47; historic, 136, 141; indigenous,
    15, 21, 82, 137, 161, 171–72, *171*
rice, 8, 10, 12, 24, 25, 29, 60, 61, 63, 73–76,
    98–100, 104, 106, 114, 124, 128, 129,
    139, 141, 146, 160, 161; foods served
    with, 15, 21, 30, 35, 37, 38, 41, 46, 48,
    49, 93, 95, 108, 109, 133, *136*, 174;
    glutinous, 13, 32, 45, 64, 74, 75, 76, 77,
    78, 81, 82, 89, 93, 95, 100, 137, 159,
    162; indica, 64, 74, 75, 100–101, 121;
    ponlai (japonica), 34, 74, 76, 78, 100,
    101, 126, 156, 159
rice wine, 12, 14, 16, 30, 33–34, 55, 58, 65,
    76, 80, 83, 90, 95, 108, 110, 114, 150,
    159, 160, 162
rodents, 9, 12, 13–14, 15, 137

salads, 14, 35, 54, 102, 134, 144
salt, 9, 11, 14, 15, 19, 23, 24, 27, 32, 34,
    35, 43, 44, 46–47, 55, 60, 62–63, 64, 74,
    77, 82, 84, 89, 90, 94, 111, 137, 138,
    140, 143, 150, 156, 167, 171; substitutes,
    10, 169, 172. *See also* preservatives and
    preservation methods
Sanxia, 22, 151

sauces and pastes, 12, 13, 21, 26, 29, 31–32, 35, 42, 43, 44, *45*, 52, 55–56, 63, 64, 67, 75, 76, 80, 81, 90, 92, 105, 108, 126, 128, 134, 141–42, 159, 161, 167, 169, 172. *See also* soy sauce

seafood, x, 21, 29, 37, 40–42, 86–88, 89, 93, 111, *112*, 120, 122, 123–24, *123*, 129. *See also* crabs; fish; shellfish

sesame: oils, 14, 16, 31, 32, 44, 83, 95, 110, 150, 170, 172; sauces and pastes, 43, 76, 77, 134; seeds, 72, 75, 83, 130, 142

shark's fin, 35, 58, 86, 91, 93, 113

shellfish, 7, 9, 19, 20, 24, 26, 34, 35, 41, 42, 44, 64, 73, 75, 78, 86, 90, 91, 95, 111, 113, 128, 129, 138, 142, 150, 167. *See also* crabs

Slow Food Foundation for Biodiversity, 19, 21, 103

smuggling: of animals and food, 98, 107, 112, 155; of pesticides, 132; of tea, 155

snacks, 5, 44, 45, 74–76, 80, 82, 93, 107, 118, 125, 128, 131, 134, 141, 146, 152, 168. *See also* street food

snails, 15–16, 21, 35, 100, 171

snakes, 15, 75, 109, 161

social media, 51, 126, 143, 164

sorghum, 160

soups, x, 12, 15, 17, 19, 21, 22, 25, 32, 33, 34, 35, 37, 41, 42, 43, 44, 46, 54–55, 58, 59, 65, 83, 85, 86, 91, 92, 93, 95, 102, 108, 110, 128, 135, *136*, 137, 139, 144, 159, 172, 180–81

Southeast Asia, immigrants from, 49, 61–62, 131

soybeans and soyfoods, 6, 27, 28, 29–30, 35, 43–45, 50, 52, 55–56, 63, 97, 108, 110, 174. *See also* soy milk; soy sauce; tofu

soy milk, 43–44, 66, 91, 164

soy sauce: alternatives and substitutes, 26, 172; for cooking, 16, 24, 26, 32, 45, 47, 50, 55, 58, 78, 89, 108, 110, 111, 140, 142, 150; for flavoring and dipping, 14, 26, 43, 45, 63, 139, 170; making of, 27–29, 126, 132

Spanish, 4, 98

spicy condiments and foods, 21, 32, 35, 42, 44, 55, 131, 139, 140, 150, 156

starches, 29, 35, 38, 42, 61, 66, 74, 91, 121, 132, 138, 140

steaming, x, 12, 18, 24, 25–26, 30, 35, 37, 41, 43, 48, 58, 59, 61, 64, 75, 76, 78, 81, 88, 89, 90, 92, 102, 121, 126, 137, 139, 146, 170, 179–80

street food, 45, 89, 108, 129–31, 132–33, *136*. *See also* night markets; snack foods

sugar, 10, 11, 14, 24, 30, 32, 35, 43, 44, 58, 66, 67, 68, 75, 76, 77, 78, 81, 89, 90, 91, 92, 101, 102, 108, 110, 111, 130, 140, 142, 154, 164, 170, 172

sugarcane: for cooking, 101, 110, 118, 120–21; for juice, 164

supermarkets, 18, 28, 31, 42, 47, 69, 109, 116, 119–20, 122, 126, 127–28, 154

sustainability, 38, 93, 100, 102, 106, 108, 109, 110, 115–18, 127, 147

sweet potato, ix, 9, 13, 15, 34, 35, 37, 64, 74, 77, 81, 91, 93, 100, 103–4, 110, 128, 129, 138, 160, 170, *171*, 172; leaves, 43, 104, 109

taboos, 9, 11, 53, 57–58, 72, 73, 94

Taichung, 25, *39*, 61, 100, 102, 104, 114, 149, 158, 159

Tainan, 4, 5, 7, 9, 10, 13, 19, 26, 32, 81, 93, 98, 101, 103, 105, 129, 151

Taiwan Tobacco & Liquor Corporation (TTL), 34, 156, 158, 159, 160

Tamsui, 4, 52, 98, 111, 151, 173

tana, 21–22, *171*, 172

Taoyuan, 40, 61, 63, 104, 144, 159

tapioca, 44, 64, 65, 138, 144, 154

taro, 9, 10, 12, 13, 17, 34, 42, 64, 65, 74, 76, 80, 81, 84, 90, 91, 92, 93, 100, 102, 144, 170

tea, 5, 21, 24, 62, 63, 74, 77, 80, 81, 93, 98, 99, 111, 126, *136*, 137, 138, 149, 150–51, 153–56, 164; bottled, 155; in recipes, 31, 154

three-cup recipes, 16, 17, 31, 33, 114, 137, 150, 174

tofu, 22, 29–30, 32, 38, 42, 43, 44–45, 48, 61, 65, 66, 77, 78, 83, 91, 133, 141, 166, 167, 170. *See also* soybeans and soyfoods

TTL. *See* Taiwan Tobacco & Liquor Corporation

Tu, Calvin, 173–74, 192
turkey, 46, 93, 109
turtle, ix, 9, 14

United States, 5, 168; aid from, 6, 55, 61, 104, 114; food exports to Taiwan, 28, 30, 43, 55, 65, 67, 109. *See also* Americans
utensils, 12, 13, 14, 24, 37, 38, 86, 130, 135

veganism, 51–53, 144
vegetables, 14, 18–19, 33, 37, 38, 51, 52, 102–4, 115–18, 120–22, 131–32
vegetarianism, 42, 44, 50–53, 75, 102, 117, 137, 144. *See also* veganism
vinegars, 9, 14, 24, 32, 43, 44, 89, 129, 140, 170
VOC. *See* Dutch

Wanhua, 5, 60, 120, 128, 130, 173. *See also* Taipei

waste. *See* food waste
wellness. *See* healthy eating
Western foods and influences, 42, 67, 146, 149, 152, 174
wheat, 6, 27, 34, 52, 61, 97, 100, 110, 131, 159, 160. *See also* noodles
whisky. *See* alcohol, for drinking
wine. *See* alcohol, for drinking
wonton. *See* dumplings
WTO, 33, 98, 116, 158, 170
Wulai, 82, 137, *163*

Ximending, 55, 142

Yabung Tally, 171–72
yam, 10, 12, 44, 172
Yilan, 80, 94, 102, 110, 138, 146, 158, 162, 172
Yunlin, 94, 104, 151

About the Authors

Steven Crook, an Englishman who has made Taiwan his home for the past twenty-seven years, has been writing about travel, culture, business, and environmental issues as well as food since 1996. He is the author of three previous books, including *Taiwan: The Bradt Travel Guide* (the third edition of which will appear in early 2019).

Katy Hui-wen Hung is a Taipei native and an avid collector of recipes and culinary stories. She has assisted a number of US-based food writers assigned to report on the city's culinary landscape.

Lightning Source UK Ltd.
Milton Keynes UK
UKHW040827250619

344992UK00006B/141/P